NATIONAL DEFENSE RESEARCH INSTITUTE

T0131049

# The Emerging Risk of Virtual Societal Warfare

Social Manipulation in a Changing Information Environment

Michael J. Mazarr, Ryan Michael Bauer, Abigail Casey, Sarah Anita Heintz, Luke J. Matthews

Prepared for the Office of the Secretary of Defense

Approved for public release; distribution unlimited

For more information on this publication, visit www.rand.org/t/RR2714

**Library of Congress Cataloging-in-Publication Data** is available for this publication.
ISBN: 978-1-9774-0272-1

Published by the RAND Corporation, Santa Monica, Calif.
© Copyright 2019 RAND Corporation
**RAND**® is a registered trademark.

### Support RAND
Make a tax-deductible charitable contribution at
www.rand.org/giving/contribute

www.rand.org

# Preface

This analysis is part of a larger study on techniques of social manipulation and was motivated by recent Russian efforts to manipulate Western information environments. This study focuses on the future of social manipulation efforts and involved a survey of multiple, overlapping information-related technologies and their potential for manipulation. It describes the emerging phenomenon of *virtual societal warfare* and suggests avenues for Western democracies to respond.

The research was sponsored by the Office of Net Assessment, Office of the Secretary of Defense, and conducted within the International Security and Defense Policy Center of the RAND National Defense Research Institute, a federally funded research and development center sponsored by the Office of the Secretary of Defense, the Joint Staff, the Unified Combatant Commands, the Navy, the Marine Corps, the defense agencies, and the defense Intelligence Community.

For more information on the RAND International Security and Defense Policy Center, see https://www.rand.org/nsrd/ndri/centers/isdp.html or contact the director (contact information is provided on the webpage).

# Contents

# Table

# Summary

The year 2016 and beyond saw an explosion of interest in issues of disinformation, propaganda, information manipulation and fakery, "fake news," "Truth Decay," and related trends—a broad phenomenon that can be termed *hostile social manipulation*. In this study, we define this concept as *the purposeful, systematic generation and dissemination of information to produce harmful social, political, and economic outcomes in a target country by affecting beliefs, attitudes, and behavior.* Examples of this rising challenge include Russian efforts to influence elections and sow discord in the West through propaganda and disinformation; the role of social media platforms such as Facebook in spreading such misinformation; and burgeoning Chinese programs to shape regional narratives and gain political leverage in specific countries. U.S. intelligence services have concluded that Russia employed such techniques to influence the 2016 election, and Moscow continues to employ them—sometimes brazenly despite U.S. warnings—in the United States and Europe.

As significant as these developments have been, they may only represent the beginning of what an aggressive nation can accomplish with techniques and technologies designed to disrupt and shape the information environment of a target country. This report's primary conclusion is that, as significant as social manipulation efforts have already been, the United States and other democracies have only glimpsed the tip of the iceberg of what these approaches may someday be able to achieve.

The intersection of multiple emerging technologies, from artificial intelligence to virtual reality and personalized messaging, is creating the potential for aggressors to change people's fundamental social reality. Two well-known information-related threats are classic cyberattacks on major infrastructure sites and internet-enabled disinformation, but this report calls attention to the burgeoning landscape in between—areas of the emerging information-based foundation of society that are vulnerable to persistent disruption and manipulation. Especially with the rise of the "Internet of Things" (IoT) and algorithmic and big-data–driven decisionmaking, advanced societies are becoming perilously dependent on networks of information and data gathering, exchange, communication, analysis, and decisionmaking. These risks are especially significant today because of the changing nature of the *infosphere* (the information environment governing postmodern democracies), which is characterized, among other trends, by the fragmentation of authority, the rise of silos of belief, and a persistent "trolling" ethic of cynical and aggressive harassment in the name of an amorphous social dissent.

As much as it feels to citizens of advanced economies that we already live in an information society, we have in fact seen only the first hints of this transformation. And that transition will open unprecedented opportunities for hostile rivals—state or nonstate—to reach into those societies and cause disruption, delay, inefficiency, and active harm. It will open the door to a form of virtual societal aggression that will make countries more persistently vulnerable than they have been for generations. Such virtual aggression will force a rethinking of the character of national security and steps taken to protect it.

Traditional forms of information-based social manipulation have focused on disseminating narratives—through, for example, propaganda, public diplomacy, and social media posts—to affect beliefs. Classic hostile cyberattacks have often used information networks as a highway to attack physical targets, such as banks, power stations, or centrifuges. The evolution of advanced information environments is rapidly creating a third category of possible aggression: efforts to manipulate or disrupt the information foundations of the effective functioning of economic and social systems. Aggressors will increasingly have the opportunity, not merely to spread disinformation or favorable narratives or damage physical infrastructure, but to skew and damage the functioning of the massive databases, algorithms, and networks of computerized, computer-enhanced, or computer-dependent things on which modern societies will utterly depend.

What we are calling *virtual societal warfare* can involve any combination of a broad range of techniques, including the following:

- deploying classic propaganda, influence, and disinformation operations through multiple channels, including social media
- generating massive amounts of highly plausible fabricated video and audio material to reduce confidence in shared reality
- discrediting key mediating institutions that are capable of distinguishing between true and false information
- corrupting or manipulating the databases on which major components of the economy increasingly rely
- manipulating or degrading systems of algorithmic decisionmaking, both to impair day-to-day government and corporate operations and to intensify loss of faith in institutions, as well as increase social grievances and polarization
- using the vulnerabilities inherent in the connections among the exploding IoT to create disruption and damage
- hijacking virtual and augmented reality systems to create disruption or mental anguish or to strengthen certain narratives
- inserting commands into chatbot-style interactive systems to generate inefficiencies and in some cases personal frustration and anxiety.

In many cases, the primary goal of such aggression may not be physical harm so much as confusion and an accelerating loss of confidence in the operation of major social institutions. And the emergence of information-dependent societies will broaden and deepen the array of social manipulation techniques available to attackers, allowing them to seek highly tailored combinations of physical damage and changes in attitudes. The role of trust is a consistent theme in this analysis: Attacks on the effective operation of information systems strike directly at levels of social trust, creating the sense that the institutions and processes of advanced societies cannot be trusted and generating a sense of persistent insecurity and anxiety.

To shed light on how these techniques might evolve, RAND researchers built on a first-phase analysis from this project that focused on Russian and Chinese efforts at hostile social manipulation. This project was not yet aimed at solutions, but rather understanding—i.e., comprehending the character of the emerging challenge. It was designed to set the stage for more-detailed discussion of potential responses to the threat. But one lesson of this phase of research is that many of these trends, technologies, and capabilities remain poorly understood, and some possible responses have potentially dramatic implications for the operation of the information environment, the character of free speech, and other issues. It would be dangerous to begin promulgating possible solutions without rigorous analysis of their likely consequences. This report is designed to set the stage for such work by first analyzing the scope and nature of the problem.

To understand the risk of virtual societal warfare, we surveyed evidence in a range of categories to sketch out some initial contours of how these techniques might evolve in the future. We grounded the assessment in (1) detailed research on trends in the changing character of the information environment in the United States and other advanced democracies; (2) the insights of social science research on attitudes and beliefs; and (3) developments in relevant emerging technologies that bear on the practices of hostile social manipulation and its more elaborate and dangerous cousin, virtual societal warfare (terms which are defined further in Chapter One). In all three cases, we gathered data on established research findings and existing trends.

Chapter Two offers our analysis of the characteristics of the infosphere—the context in which such hostile techniques will be employed. Chapter Three derives insights from social science, surveying what research into beliefs and attitudes suggests about the forms of social manipulation likely to be most effective. Chapter Four examines current developments in several technologies, from artificial intelligence to virtual reality and the IoT, that could play a role in future manipulation campaigns.

A second primary approach taken in this analysis was to employ a scenario planning methodology to describe the possible shape of social manipulation futures. In Chapters Five through Seven, we sketch out—based on the findings of the research on trends and realities, the insights of the previous study on Russian and Chinese social manipulation strategies, and other research—three scenarios for how social manipulation could affect advanced societies over the next decade. The three are not mutually exclusive; each one emphasizes a different theme, but elements of all three are likely to combine to characterize an actual future. In each case we cite extensive research to support different assumptions of the scenarios, and in each case we describe ways in which aggressive social manipulators could use the aspects of that scenario to gain advantage.

The analysis suggests that virtual societal warfare is likely to have many essential characteristics, which together reflect the essential nature and character of this new form of warfare. A full understanding of these characteristics will only emerge over time, but this analysis points to an initial set of characteristics that can help define this emerging challenge. They include the following:

- *National security will increasingly rely on a resilient infosphere and, even more fundamentally, a strong "social topography."* The elements of a resilient infosphere are not well understood, but they likely include classic forms of information security as well as strong mediating institutions and a population continuously inoculated against the techniques of social manipulation.
- *The barrier between public and private endeavors and responsibilities is blurring; national security will rely on the cooperation of private actors as much as public investments.* The technologies and techniques of this form of conflict are increasingly available to a wide range of actors. Private power in this realm matches and, in some cases, exceeds public power.
- *Conflict will increasingly be waged between and among networks.* We see this pattern already in, for example, the complex, international network of hackers, activists, and informal propagandists being employed by Russia as part of its information campaigns,

and in China's use of Chinese citizens and ethnic Chinese abroad to further its control over key narratives. State actors are likely to develop such networks to avoid attribution and strengthen their virtual societal warfare capabilities against retaliation. It will be much more difficult to understand, maintain an accurate portrait of, and hit back against a shadowy global network.

These are only three initial suggestions of the sorts of principles that will govern conflict in the virtual societal realm. More research is urgently required to understand this realm more fully and to begin to understand the sorts of responses that will protect democratic societies against its worst effects. Chapter Eight concludes by pointing to several initial avenues of response to enhance democratic resilience in the face of this growing risk. These include the following:

- *Invest in research and understanding.* A consistent theme in many of our conversations and analyses for this study has been the limits of our awareness: the true character of the evolving infosphere and its likely directions, key causal dynamics in that evolution, how populations react to various forms of social manipulation, and what the most effective answers might be. What are the main hallmarks of a resilient infosphere and a robust social topography? What metrics can we use to assess whether we are attaining those goals?
- *Begin building forms of inoculation and resilience against the worst forms of information-based social manipulation.* Campaigns should not limit themselves to countering outside claims after they occur, but rather take steps in advance to create resilience against such claims and campaigns. Forewarning may be more effective than post hoc treatment of established narratives.
- *Take seriously the leading role played by social media today and the precedent-setting character of many of the information control debates playing out in that realm.* Governments should increasingly look to actions that can incentivize social media platforms to solve the problems themselves to the greatest degree possible. In the process, governments should identify four to five things that

the platforms can do over the next two to three years to make a dent in the problem.

- *Make investments designed to erect new, broadly trusted informational mediating institutions that can help Americans make sense of events.* Governments (as well as private foundations and activists) can also prompt trial-and-error work among information companies, such as internet browsers (especially those willing to take the lead in new approaches), to experiment with revised algorithms, new browser extensions, and rating and ranking different sites and sources to see what works. The goal would be to send signals that would contribute to the overall inoculation effect being sought by government policy. A major source of the challenges today is the decline of any respected, trusted intermediary sources that the public can rely on to get a sense of whether what they are seeing is accurate. Apart from basic fact-checking organizations, experimenting with different varieties of such revised intermediary institutions could help mitigate the effect of virtual societal aggression.

- *Begin working toward international norms constraining the use of virtual societal aggression.* The biggest risk of virtual societal warfare may be that it represents an insidious, gradual degradation of the territorial integrity norm that has largely prevailed since 1945 and helped to keep the peace among countries. To the extent that nations begin attacking one another in virtual but highly damaging ways, the prevailing consensus on territorial nonaggression could collapse, leading eventually to large-scale armed adventurism. As with other forms of aggression, deterrence can contribute strongly to defense, but so can international norms that help tie the status and prestige of countries to their respect for fundamental principles.

- *Better understand the workings and vulnerabilities of emerging technologies, especially artificial intelligence–driven information channels, virtual and augmented reality, and algorithmic decisionmaking.* If the United States and other democracies are not careful, advances in the private application of these technologies will race ahead of policy and even understanding, creating intense vulnerabilities for democratic societies. The dangers of virtual societal warfare and the specific emerging dependence of democratic societies and advanced economies on such information applications point to the need for research on their potential implications and steps democracies can take to protect themselves.

These categories represent only a broad sketch of the sort of response likely to be required for democracies to armor themselves against the potential threat of virtual societal warfare. These emerging forms of aggression represent a significant danger to advanced democracies, a form of national security threat that has not been seen before. Especially in the nuclear age, and in an era when a general global consensus has prevailed against outright territorial aggression, large-scale invasions have become mostly a thing of the past. But while armies can be deterred, gradual, low-level hostile manipulation of the infosphere and larger social topography of nations may be the new frontier of aggression. The *potential* for virtual societal warfare is certainly emerging. The only question today is whether democracies band together to control and defend themselves against this threat.

# Acknowledgments

The authors would like to thank the Office of Net Assessment for its support and guidance of the project. We extend our sincere thanks to the management of the RAND International Security and Defense Policy Center—Seth Jones (for the beginning of the project), Christine Wormuth (for its latter phases), Mike McNerney, and Rich Girven—for their help in managing the project and developing the reports. We would like to thank formal peer reviewers Miriam Matthews of RAND and Adam Segal of the Council on Foreign Relations for their very helpful reviews. The authors also received informal comments on earlier drafts from Tim Hwang and Philip Smith, and we are very grateful for their assistance.

# Abbreviations

AI          artificial intelligence
AR          augmented reality
CGI         computer-generated imagery
EVM         Eulerian Video Magnification
GAN         generative adversarial network
GPS         Global Positioning System
HD          high definition
IIWAM       information/influence warfare and manipulation
IoT         Internet of Things
NATO        North Atlantic Treaty Organization
PFR         pervasive facial recognition
POPE        principle of passive election
PTSD        posttraumatic stress disorder
RFID        radio-frequency identification
VR          virtual reality

# CHAPTER ONE

# A New Form of Conflict

The year 2016 and beyond saw an explosion of interest in a phenomenon that can be termed *hostile social manipulation*. Examples of this rising challenge include Russian efforts to influence elections and sow discord in the West through propaganda and disinformation; the role of social media platforms such as Facebook in spreading such misinformation; and burgeoning Chinese programs to shape regional narratives and gain political leverage in specific countries.[1] Experts in the field, as well as members of Congress and senior U.S. officials, have increasingly warned of the pernicious effects of such tactics on U.S. democracy and the stability of European societies.

As part of this project, we defined the challenge of hostile social manipulation and specifically traced the activities of Russia and China in this sphere. We define the concept as *the purposeful, systematic generation and dissemination of information to produce harmful social, political, and economic outcomes in a target country by affecting beliefs, attitudes, and behavior.* With this report, we turn the focus of study to the future. We examine potential future scenarios for the technologies and techniques behind social manipulation and offer some initial thoughts about their possible implications for democracy.

Our research suggests that, as significant as social manipulation efforts have already been, the United States and other democracies have only glimpsed the tip of the iceberg of what these approaches may someday be able to achieve. The intersection of multiple emerging

---

[1]  Nicholas Thompson and Fred Vogelstein, "Facebook's Two Years of Hell," *Wired*, March 2018.

technologies—targeted marketing based on vast databases of information on specific individuals, virtual and augmented reality, manufactured video and audio, and several others—is increasingly creating the potential for aggressors to change peoples' fundamental social reality. These risks are especially significant today because of the changing nature of the *infosphere*, or information environment governing postmodern democracies. The infosphere is characterized by, among other trends, the fragmentation of authority, the rise of silos of belief, and a persistent "trolling" ethic of cynical and aggressive harassment in the name of an amorphous social dissent.

It would be wrong to project in a linear sense all the trends that are under way today, and this analysis has not done so. There is reason to believe that a reaction to these trends—in the form of, to take just two examples, increasingly prominent fact-checking organizations and a demand for social media platforms to emphasize reliability measures when posting information—is already under way. But as this report will make clear, many of the leading trends in the infosphere are worrying, and the potential effects of emerging technologies are very dangerous. In ways not yet fully understood, advanced societies are becoming perilously dependent on vulnerable networks of information and data gathering, exchange, communication, analysis, and decisionmaking.

Advanced algorithms are increasingly assessing data on issues from shopping patterns and human health to personality factors and hiring, making forecasts and decisions with critical ramifications for people's lives. The emerging Internet of Things (IoT) will have over a trillion connected devices within a decade—smart homes, cars, factories, wearable sensors, and many other forms of data-gathering that communicate with one another and guide much of the day-to-day operation of advanced societies. Many people will come to interact with the world—in video games, entertainment choices, work, and social media—through virtual reality (VR) or augmented reality (AR) devices that allow them to tweak the character of the world they "want" to see.

Artificial intelligence (AI) capabilities will be integrated into all of these applications, allowing nonhuman systems to increasingly process—and understand—large data sets and recommend or make key decisions. AI-driven "players" have already defeated top-ranked human players in checkers, chess, Go, and poker. It is only a matter of time before AI decisionmakers take over significant components of the diagnosis of disease, or the hiring of staff at large companies.

For decades, social scientists have argued that advanced democracies have been shifting from an industrial era to an *information economy*, grounded more in the production and exchange of information than physical goods.[2] Recent shifts in the infosphere and trends in emerging technologies make clear that this larger transition has in fact only begun, and we have only begun to glimpse its implications. The emergence of much more information-centric societies—where fundamental day-to-day choices about health, economic equality, hiring, consumer behavior, and much else are shaped and, in some cases, determined by systems of automated information processing—will turbocharge the results of this transition and its impact on people's lives.

As much as it feels to citizens of advanced economies that we already live in an information society, we have in fact seen only the first stages of this transformation. And that transition will open unprecedented opportunities for hostile rivals—state or nonstate—to reach into those societies and cause disruption, delay, inefficiency, and active harm. It risks opening the door to virtual societal aggression that will make countries more persistently vulnerable than they have been for generations. In the process, such virtual aggression may force a rethinking of the character of national security and steps taken to protect it.

The information security expert Bruce Schneier has issued some of the most urgent warnings about the vulnerabilities of the emerging infosphere, and in particular the marriage of software vulnerability, an emerging IoT in which billions of devices are linked into complex networks, and advanced algorithms that increasingly make complex decisions on behalf of society. Risks, he argues, "are becoming catastrophic" as billions upon billions of things come to have computer

---

[2]   One of the classic accounts is Manuel Castells, *The Rise of the Network Society*, New York: Wiley-Blackwell, 2009.

brains—including refrigerators, cars, homes, prisoner sentencing systems, and medical diagnosis processes.[3]

This report joins a range of other RAND work in investigating the larger context for a phenomenon known as Truth Decay, the subject of a centerpiece RAND analysis. That report defined *Truth Decay* as the declining role of facts and analysis in American life, characterized by the following four components:

- increasing disagreement about facts and analytical interpretations of facts and data
- a blurring of the line between opinion and fact
- the increasing relative volume, and resulting influence, of opinion and personal experience over fact
- declining trust in formerly respected sources of factual information.[4]

From the standpoint of this study, Truth Decay as defined in that work constitutes one of the leading trends in the larger infosphere—trends that are rendering postmodern democracies vulnerable to hostile social manipulation. This vulnerability highlights a critical relationship: Aggressive techniques of social manipulation build on and take advantage of—but usually cannot *create*—social and informational trends in democracies. Truth Decay and associated trends in the infosphere, as well as parallel social trends such as rising inequality and declining faith in elites, are the essential problem. Hostile social manipulation is a technique employed by state or nonstate actors to harm democracies and plays upon the changing character of society and information.

In pursuing social manipulation, aggressors could have a range of objectives. They could seek to change attitudes within target countries—though, as the review of literature on social science find-

---

3    Bruce Schneier, *Click Here to Kill Everybody: Security and Survival in a Hyper-Connected World*, New York: W. W. Norton, 2018, p. 78.

4    Jennifer Kavanagh and Michael D. Rich, *Truth Decay: An Initial Exploration of the Diminishing Role of Facts and Analysis in American Public Life*, Santa Monica, Calif.: RAND Corporation, RR-2314-RC, 2018, pp. x–xi.

ings will suggest, forced attitude change is among the most demanding goals of any such strategy. They could seek to take existing attitudes and push them toward more extreme ends of the spectrum, or they could seek to normalize and support groups with extreme views. They could try to catalyze existing impulses into action, as when social media posts have managed to generate actual protests or rallies that would not have occurred otherwise. They could seek to disrupt the activities and effectiveness of an information-based economy, imposing economic costs in the process.

To be sure, the causal link between social manipulation and outcomes—beliefs or behavior—is not always straight or linear. A society's foundation of attitudes, beliefs, and behavior patterns is not subject to easy, direct manipulation. Changing attitudes is hard, and research suggests that the link between attitudes and behavior can be weak.[5] Our other research suggests that while manipulation campaigns can sometimes produce significant measurable *outputs*, such as numbers of tweets or posts, the actual *outcomes*, such as changes in attitudes or behaviors, are much tougher to find. There is no simple relationship between social manipulation programs and results in the target country.

## Definitions and Concepts

In this study, we use the term *infosphere* to refer to the ongoing social process of information production, dissemination, and perception in a society.[6] A society's infosphere is, most simply, its information envi-

---

[5]   See, for example, Joshua J. Guyer and Leandre R. Fabrigar, "Attitudes and Behavior," in James Wright, ed., *International Encyclopedia of the Social & Behavioral Sciences*, Vol. II, 2nd ed., New York: Elsevier, 2015.

[6]   For a similar definition, see John Arquilla and David Ronfeldt, *The Emergence of Noopolitik: Toward an American Information Strategy,* Santa Monica, Calif.: RAND Corporation, MR-1033-OSD, 1999, pp. 11–12, 16–17. For a U.S. Department of Defense definition of the "information environment," see U.S. Department of Defense, *Joint Publication 1-02: Department of Defense Dictionary of Military and Associated Terms,* Washington, D.C., November 2010.

ronment. The concept encompasses broadcast and print media; social media; government messaging and propaganda; the internet and all networks of communication and broadcasting that it carries; all the channels of information production that feed those outlets; and the ways in which individuals interact with information. It is the terrain in which campaigns of hostile social manipulation unfold.

Recent dialogues on the problem of information shaping and manipulation have employed a blizzard of terms to describe what is going on: misinformation, disinformation, Truth Decay, propaganda, and others. For this study, we chose a term designed to refer to the specific idea of intentional efforts by hostile actors to use information channels to do harm to the United States or other democracies. We therefore initially employed the term *hostile social manipulation*, which we define as the purposeful, systematic generation and dissemination of information to produce harmful social, political, and economic outcomes in a target country by affecting beliefs, attitudes, and behavior. (This term, and other closely related ones, are defined in the box on p. 7.)

One critical distinguishing factor is that hostile social manipulation targets beliefs and attitudes, not physical assets or military forces. Nonetheless, the intent of such manipulation is aggressive: The user of hostile social manipulation seeks to do damage to the target state or use the information campaign to allow it to undertake aggressive, hostile actions.

One distinction to be drawn is between hostile social manipulation and what are generally understood as classic cyberattacks. In fact, there is a significant overlap between the two, with much of hostile social manipulation made possible by cyber techniques.[7] When an

---

[7]  This approach is very close in spirit to the concept of *information/influence warfare and manipulation* (IIWAM) offered by Herbert Lin and Jackie Kerr. They define IIWAM as "the deliberate use of information by one party on an adversary to confuse, mislead, and ultimately to influence the choices and decisions that the adversary makes." It is thus a "hostile non-kinetic activity" whose targets are "the adversary's perceptions." Their concept of IIWAM is therefore distinct from classic cyberaggression because attacks in the IIWAM realm focus on "damaging knowledge, truth, and confidence, rather than physical or digital artifacts. . . . IIWAM seeks to inject fear, anxiety, uncertainty, and doubt into the adversary's decision making processes." Yet they still recognize that many IIWAM attacks will be made

## Key Terms

- **Infosphere.** The ongoing process of producing, disseminating, and perceiving information in a society, including media, data-based algorithmic processes, and information exchange in networks.
- **Hostile social manipulation.** The purposeful, systematic generation and dissemination of information to produce harmful social, political, and economic outcomes in a target country by affecting beliefs, attitudes, and behavior. Tends to focus on manipulating beliefs, perceptions, and facts.
- **Virtual societal warfare.** The most elaborate or extreme form of hostile social manipulation that encompasses that term or concept but implies a more broad-based effort to disrupt and manipulate the information networks of a society. Can include mechanisms to degrade or manipulate outcomes from electronic networks, algorithmic decisionmaking, and virtual and augmented reality. The concept refers to a gradual, persistent approach to such goals.
- **Cyber infrastructure attack.** Efforts to use malware or other forms of cyberaggression to cause catastrophic damage to major economic or social infrastructure to create significant physical damage, harm to individuals, or social disruption and chaos.

aggressor breaks into government databases to steal information that becomes the basis of a harassment campaign or propaganda effort, it has employed cyber means to fuel what is essentially an effort at social manipulation. The use of automated bots to spread disruptive tweets or to post fabricated information on Facebook also employs information manipulation tools for such ends. The primary distinction between the two categories, then, is not in the means but the ends: When an aggressor is using cyber means to achieve physical damage to such things as energy or water infrastructure, the attack will have effects on attitudes, but those effects are not its main purpose. Such classic cyberattacks would be outside the bounds of what we are terming hostile social manipulation.[8]

---

possible by cyber intrusions of one sort or another, and so they also use the term "cyber-enabled IIWAM." See Herbert Lin and Jackie Kerr, *On Cyber-Enabled Information/Influence Warfare and Manipulation*, working paper, Stanford, Calif.: Stanford Center for International Security and Cooperation, August 13, 2017, pp. 5–7.

[8]   Attacks on information security can be used for a wide range of purposes, but a major national security focus has been on the use of cyber tools to infiltrate, disrupt, and potentially cause severe damage to critical infrastructure in a society. For one treatment of these risks, see Richard A. Clarke, *Cyber War: The Next Threat to National Security and What to Do About It*, New York: Ecco, 2010.

Yet drawing these boundaries is becoming even more difficult as emerging technologies work to further blur them. This difficulty stems from the infosphere increasingly serving as the foundation of most economic and social activity, including decisionmaking, in advanced democracies. Algorithms are increasingly employed to make key judgments and choices—for example, about the risk of disease, the right treatment for illnesses, optimal financial investments, and even appropriate sentences for crimes. The IoT is increasingly linking "smart" cars, appliances, watches, and much else into an interacting network that shares data and anticipates needs.

A primary finding of this research is that, as a result of such trends, the very meaning of manipulating a society's infosphere is changing. Traditional forms of information-based social manipulation have focused on disseminating narratives through propaganda, public diplomacy, social media posts, and so forth, to affect beliefs. Classic hostile cyberattacks have often used information networks as a highway to attack physical targets, such as banks, power stations, or centrifuges. The evolution of advanced infospheres is rapidly creating a third category of possible aggression: Efforts to manipulate or disrupt the information foundations of social functioning. Aggressors will increasingly have the opportunity not merely to spread disinformation or favorable narratives or damage physical infrastructure, but to skew and damage the functioning of the massive databases, algorithms, and networks on which modern societies will utterly depend. These actions outline the related concept or category of virtual societal warfare defined above, and it is the primary focus of this study—a form of information-based aggression that includes but goes well beyond what has been understood as social manipulation.

These trends increasingly erase the distinction between various forms of information aggression. If an aggressor can tweak the algorithm being used to diagnose cancer in thousands of hospitals, it could disrupt treatment and reduce faith in the medical institutions in a country (as well as perhaps contributing to the early death of some patients). If it can subtly change the information being broadcast to food stores by smart refrigerators, it could create frustration on the part of customers and perhaps wasted food, and thus economic inefficiency.

These examples still involve the use of information channels to disrupt ultimately physical activities, and thus are perhaps closer to what we have understood as cyberattacks rather than disinformation. But in many cases an aggressor's primary goal might not be physical harm so much as confusion and an accelerating loss of confidence in the operation of major social institutions. Ultimately, as in all warfare, the target is the adversary's *will*; attacks on physical targets are merely a means to that end. And the emergence of information-dependent societies will broaden and deepen the spectrum of social manipulation techniques available to attackers, allowing them to seek highly tailored combinations of physical damage and changes in attitudes. For the most part, we find the priority will be on attitudinal effects, because direct and devastating physical attacks (the cyber infrastructure category defined above) are more likely to prompt retaliation and because the enemy's beliefs are the grand prize.

Neal Pollard, Adam Segal, and Matthew Devost have written on the same distinction and emphasized a theme critical to the intent of hostile social manipulation: trust. Classic worries about cyberattacks have focused on what they term "the 'bytes and blood' scenario" of efforts to cause extreme physical damage. While that risk remains serious, they write, "so far, cyber conflict has taken a different path," generally seeking "to subvert the integrity of political, social and economic systems," aiming to "undermine trust in institutions through manipulation, distortion, and disruption." Such attacks "have a much lower threshold, are harder to detect and deter, and can cascade through interconnected systems."[9]

This notion of a gradual, persistent form of aggression is central to the concept of virtual societal aggression. Using such techniques, attackers can conceal and scale an attack to make it unclear that something intentional is going on. To the victim, it will look like natural flaws and inefficiencies in highly complex systems. But the effect will be to both degrade the effectiveness (and perhaps economic performance) of the target state and further reduce faith in major institu-

---

[9]   Neal A. Pollard, Adam Segal, and Matthew G. Devost, "Trust War: Dangerous Trends in Cyber Conflict," *War on the Rocks*, January 16, 2018.

tions. Indeed, the role of trust is a consistent theme in this analysis. As sociologist Anthony Giddens and other scholars have argued, massive, highly complex, technology-dependent societies already have a trust problem: They demand that their citizens place trust for their security and prosperity into technological networks whose operation they do not understand and cannot control.[10] Attacks on the effective operation of information systems strike directly at this vulnerability, creating the sense that their workings cannot be trusted and generating an underlying sense of persistent insecurity and anxiety.

This report, then, broadens the focus of analysis beyond propaganda, disinformation, targeted marketing, social media campaigns, and other more direct and discrete efforts to shape beliefs and narratives. We include efforts to disrupt and skew the operation of information processes on which advanced democracies will depend to affect public attitudes about their government, their society, and themselves. And the concept includes the notion that such efforts represent broad-based campaigns across multiple informational tools, which together amount to a coordinated and systematic, rather than ad hoc and issue-specific, effort.

Many different actors could employ such techniques, not only states. Given the declining cost, scalability, and replicability of many information manipulation techniques, as well as the growing potential for AI-driven programs to produce malware, bots, or other armies of manipulation tools in seconds, this threat clearly includes nonstate actors. This analysis primarily focused on the changing vulnerabilities rather than the authors of the techniques, but it is important to keep in mind that such tools will be widely available.

## Approach and Methodology

The future of phenomena as complex as hostile social manipulation and virtual societal warfare is impossible to forecast with any accuracy.

---

10   See, for example, Anthony Giddens, *The Consequences of Modernity*, Cambridge, United Kingdom: Polity, 1990.

To shed light on how these techniques might evolve, this analysis took two primary approaches. First, we grounded the assessment in detailed research on three foundational issues: (1) trends in the changing character of the infosphere in the United States and other advanced democracies; (2) the insights of social science research on attitudes and beliefs; and (3) developments in relevant emerging technologies that bear on the practice of social manipulation. In all three cases, we gathered data on established research findings and existing trends. We also asked how they were likely to play out over the next five to ten years.

Chapter Two offers our analysis of the characteristics of the emerging infosphere, that is, the nature of the information environment in which social manipulation will play out, and its implications for the future of such techniques. Chapter Three derives insights from social science, surveying what research into beliefs and attitudes suggests about the forms of social manipulation likely to be most effective. Chapter Four examines current developments in several technologies, from AI to VR and the IoT, that could play a role in future manipulation campaigns.

The second primary approach taken in this analysis was to employ a scenario planning methodology to describe the possible shape of social manipulation futures. In Chapters Five through Seven, we sketch out three scenarios for how social manipulation could affect advanced societies over the next decade, based on the findings of the research on trends and realities, the insights of the parallel study on Russian and Chinese social manipulation strategies, and other research. The three are not mutually exclusive; each one emphasizes a different theme, but elements of all three are likely to combine to characterize an actual future. In each case, we cite extensive research to support different assumptions of the scenarios, and we describe ways in which aggressive social manipulators could use the aspects of that scenario to gain advantage.

Finally, Chapter Eight offers overall findings and lessons from the analysis.

# CHAPTER TWO

# The Evolving Infosphere

Techniques of social manipulation are not evolving in a vacuum. They are emerging within a rapidly changing ecosystem of information in developed democracies. This context for information generation, sharing, and consumption is unprecedented in its diversity, extent, fragmentation, and reach. The problem that the United States is trying to deal with may be as much about this changing ecosystem as it is about purposeful manipulation.[1] In this section, we briefly survey several aspects of the changing ecosystem.

As the RAND study on Truth Decay has cataloged, previous eras of U.S. history have seen astonishing levels of "yellow journalism," fabricated stories, viral disinformation, and other "information pollution" that would appear to have affected at least as big a proportion of the population as is affected today.[2] But the current infosphere may be very different from its equivalent in those earlier periods, largely as a result of some of the major trends related to the information environment. The sections below outline a few of the major trends that emerged in our research. Together they create an infosphere with both significant new vulnerabilities and a much greater potential to shape public beliefs and understanding—for good or ill.

---

[1] This argument is made in Stephan Lewandowsky, Ullrich K. H. Ecker, and John Cook, "Beyond Misinformation: Understanding and Coping with the 'Post-Truth' Era," *Journal of Applied Research in Memory and Cognition*, Vol. 6, No. 4, December 2017.

[2] Kavanagh and Rich, 2018, pp. 41–78.

## Broader Social Trends

We first briefly surveyed several trends in areas beyond the infosphere that help set the context for it. The characteristics of the emerging infosphere described below interact with, and are in many ways exacerbated by, several broader trends in the society and politics of the United States and most of the West. These trends are critical to informational development because campaigns of social manipulation generally rely on the broader social context for their effectiveness. Social manipulation can rarely create broad-based perceptions in a society on its own. It can, however, piggyback on emerging social and attitudinal trends to its advantage.

The most comprehensive and important trend is the *emergence of social institutions of massive scale and reach that challenge citizens' ability to understand or control their operation and which pose an inherent problem of trust.* Giddens has examined the role of "expert systems" in postmodern societies, in situations already characterized by a fragmentation of authority, an increased pace of change, and a diffusing of the sense of territorial identity. Large, technological societies have a need for "systems of technical accomplishment or professional expertise that organize large areas of the material and social environments in which we live today." They are abstract systems that people must rely on for their daily lives, but over which they have little control and about which they have little knowledge.[3] Such institutions can include everything from massive corporations for which people work or with which they interact, to global information networks and platforms, to enormous government bureaucracies. These institutions are the beyond–human-scale organizational constructs that have become the basis of advanced societies. The very nature of postmodern, highly technology-dependent society creates sources of anxiety that can be played upon by social manipulation campaigns.

---

3    Giddens, 1990, pp. 27, 83–100.

This form of alienation attacks people's *sense of agency*, their perception of control over their actions and the consequences.[4] As Michael Specter has argued in his study of "denialism," there is a rising sense that "we are ceding control of our lives to technology, particularly to highly sophisticated technology we can barely understand, and that we are doing so at a speed that seems to accelerate every year."[5] Many of the other developments listed below are a function of this overarching trend: the tendency of massive, complex, impersonal social institutions to shake people's trust in social authority.

As many scholars have argued, this trend represents a threat to what Giddens and others have termed *ontological security*. This refers to a fundamental feeling of confidence in one's identity, as reflected in the stability of events and patterns in one's life. It is critically dependent on interpersonal relations and a sense that events are congruent with one's sense of self. Some have argued that states depend on the ontological security of their citizens for their stability.[6] Information-based aggression is in part an effort to attack this rising vulnerability and further undermine people's trust in social institutions, their interpersonal exchanges, and the stability and reliability of the facts and narratives surrounding them.

A related trend is the *decline of faith in institutions that played a role in sustaining generally agreed social truths*.[7] This is demonstrated, in one critical example, in terms of Americans' faith in the media itself: A 2016 Gallup poll found that Americans' trust in mass media had sunk to an unprecedented low.[8] But it is also demonstrated more broadly,

---

[4]   James W. Moore, "What Is the Sense of Agency and Why Does It Matter?" *Frontiers in Psychology*, Vol. 7, Article 1272, August 2016.

[5]   Michael Specter, *Denialism: How Irrational Thinking Hinders Scientific Progress, Harms the Planet, and Threatens Our Lives*, New York: Penguin Press, 2009, p. 33.

[6]   Jennifer Mitzen, "Ontological Security in World Politics: State Identity and the Security Dilemma," European Journal of International Relations, Vol. 12, No. 3, 2006.

[7]   Nathaniel Persily, "Can Democracy Survive the Internet?" *Journal of Democracy*, Vol. 28, No. 2, April 2017, p. 64.

[8]   Art Swift, "Americans' Trust in Mass Media Sinks to New Low," *Gallup*, September 14, 2016. See Kavanagh and Rich, 2018, pp. 33–35, 108–109.

with the number of Americans expressing a "great deal" or "quite a lot" of confidence in institutions such as Congress, big business, the presidency, organized labor, and the medical establishment sinking well below 20 percent.[9]

Changes in the sources of news and other information have something to do with these trends. Through much of U.S. history, the leading sources of news and content had a financial interest in being credible and conveying accurate information. With news aggregators today, whether Facebook, Twitter, or HuffPost, that is no longer the case: At least until recently, they have explicitly rejected the idea that they are responsible for the content on their platforms. They are connection aggregators, not content providers—a distinction enshrined in Section 230 of the Communications Decency Act of 1996, which absolved aggregator platforms of legal responsibility for the content that appears on their site.[10] (Several social media platforms are now modifying this stance, taking more focused efforts to combat disinformation and extreme views, but none appear to be ready to surrender the fundamental legal status of Section 230.)[11] That distinction changes the financial incentives and leaves less motivation for the platforms to take steps on their own. The scholar Cass Sunstein phrases this trend as the decline of "general-interest intermediaries": the wide-scope, generally shared news broadcasts and newspapers that span many topics and perspectives.[12]

The declining faith in important social institutions is part of a third social trend, the even broader *weakening in measures of social capital in the United States*.[13] Authors such as Robert Putnam, Amitai Etzioni, and William Galston have cataloged the decline of civic par-

---

[9]   For one series of data, see Gallup, *In Depth: Topics A to Z: Confidence in Institutions*, 2018.

[10]   United States Code, Title 47, Section 230, Protection for Private Blocking and Screening of Offensive Material, January 3, 2012.

[11]   Jonathan Vanian, "Facebook, Twitter Take New Steps to Combat Fake News and Manipulation," *Fortune*, January 20, 2018.

[12]   Cass R. Sunstein, *#Republic: Divided Democracy in the Age of Social Media*, Princeton, N.J.: Princeton University Press, 2017, p. 20.

[13]   Lewandowsky, Ecker, and Cook, 2017, p. 357.

ticipation and other measures of public social capital.[14] Measures of social trust have been falling for some time, as have public levels of commitment to shared well-being goals, such as environmental health and social safety net guarantees. This trend is closely linked to the parallel fragmentation of a shared infosphere and the rise of mutually suspicious echo chambers.

A fourth trend is *the rise in partisan polarization* in the United States (and indeed throughout much of the Western world). Such partisan bias strongly shapes the way people see information, for all the reasons that social science would predict. The effect of information-based aggression on social divisions is greater in a polarized context than it would be in a more nonpartisan one.[15] This trend is now well documented, but its relation to social media—and indeed the broader information context—remains somewhat unclear. As Levi Boxell, Matthew Gentzkow, and Jesse Shapiro have documented, polarization is just as great, and often greater, among older Americans less likely to be heavily engaged in social media. Polarization, they point out, was already on the rise before the emergence of social media.[16] Alternative factors such as partisan cable news and economic status may be more closely correlated with its growth than social media campaigns.[17] Once established, however, such polarization provides fertile ground for social manipulation.

Fifth and partly as a product of the other trends, the West has witnessed *the rise of populist movements* that reflect deep dissatisfaction with the economic and cultural conditions of many developed

---

[14] Robert Putnam, *Bowling Alone: The Collapse and Revival of American Community*, New York: Simon and Schuster, 2001.

[15] Amanda Taub, "The Real Story About Fake News Is Partisanship," *New York Times*, January 11, 2017.

[16] Levi Boxell, Matthew Gentzkow, and Jesse M. Shapiro, "Greater Internet Use Is Not Associated with Faster Growth in Political Polarization Among U.S. Demographic Groups," *Proceedings of the National Academy of Sciences*, Vol. 114, No. 40, October 2017a.

[17] Gregory J. Martin and Ali Yurukoglu, "Bias in Cable News: Persuasion and Polarization," *American Economic Review*, Vol. 107, No. 9, 2017. See also Levi Boxell, Matthew Gentzkow, and Jesse M. Shapiro, "Is Media Driving Americans Apart?" *New York Times*, December 6, 2017b.

societies.[18] This widespread phenomenon has fueled the rise of both right- and left-wing extremist parties throughout Europe and seems set to continue for some time. It has exacerbated the polarization of U.S. and European politics, underwritten new bouts of protectionism and xenophobia, and called into question the credibility of Western political institutions.

Campaigns of social manipulation and virtual societal aggression are taking place, therefore, within a turbulent political and socioeconomic context. Virtual aggression against societies has a significant effect to the degree that it can play on existing vulnerabilities in societies. Our colleague Rand Waltzman has proposed the idea of "cognitive vulnerability," and the current context generates a significant degree of such vulnerability.[19] The changing character of the infospheres of advanced democracies can therefore serve to exacerbate (or mitigate) these more fundamental social trends.

## Trends in the Infosphere: Knowledge and Awareness

Even as these general social trends create avenues for information-based aggression, such aggression can also take advantage of emerging realities in the character of the infosphere itself. The sections that follow examine eight such realities, including

- networked dynamics and the role of viral spread of information
- broad-based sensationalism in news and other media

---

18   The literature on the populist wave in the West is vast, including numerous books and reports and hundreds of news accounts. For broad assessments, see John B. Judis, *The Populist Explosion*, New York: Columbia Global Reports, 2016; and Jan-Werner Müller, *What Is Populism?* Philadelphia, Pa.: University of Pennsylvania Press, 2016. For an examination of the economic versus cultural arguments for the populist wave, see Ronald Inglehart and Pippa Norris, *Trump, Brexit, and the Rise of Populism: Economic Have-Nots and Cultural Backlash*, faculty research working paper, Cambridge, Mass.: Harvard Kennedy School, RWP16-026, August 2016.

19   Rand Waltzman, "The Weaponization of Information: The Need for Cognitive Security," testimony presented before the Senate Armed Forces Committee, Subcommittee on Cybersecurity, Santa Monica, Calif.: RAND Corporation, CT-473, April 27, 2017, p. 3.

- fragmentation of the infosphere
- concentration of information platforms
- the effect of self-reinforcing echo chambers
- the role of influencers
- the emergence of a "trolling ethic" on the internet
- the explosive growth of data collection on individuals and groups.

In some cases, the current status of the infosphere is not demonstrably different from the past. But developments in several of these areas—notably fragmentation, echo chambers, and the trolling ethic—have characteristics that sharply distinguish the current and emerging information context from previous ones.

One question goes to the essential information baseline for these trends: the issue of whether the public is any more misinformed than in previous eras.[20] "Misperceptions appear to be widespread, on issues ranging from the economy to foreign policy."[21] Several studies have offered stark criticisms of U.S. college graduates for not gaining sufficient critical thinking or baseline knowledge.[22] Some research on the content of major newspapers between the late 1970s and the late 1990s, for example, found a growing emphasis on entertainment, opinion, and sensationalism and a reduced focus on pure fact. Newspaper subscriptions are giving way to cable news viewership, and many shows on such networks emphasize argument, dispute, and, in some cases, partisan spin over facts.[23]

But the real question is whether misinformation is worse than before, and most of the available evidence suggests it is not. Instead,

---

[20] On the general issue of ignorance, see Jason Brennan, "Trump Won Because Voters Are Ignorant, Literally," *Foreign Policy*, November 10, 2016; Jared Meyer, "The Ignorant Voter," *Forbes*, June 27, 2016; and Andrew Romano, "How Ignorant Are Americans?" *Newsweek*, March 20, 2011.

[21] D. J. Flynn, Brendan Nyhan, and Jason Reifler, "The Nature and Origins of Misperceptions: Understanding False and Unsupported Beliefs About Politics," *Political Psychology*, Vol. 38, Supp. 1, 2017, p. 129. They also cite other literature on this point.

[22] Tom Nichols, "Our Graduates Are Rubes," *Chronicle of Higher Education*, January 15, 2017a.

[23] Kavanagh and Rich, 2018, pp. 106–107.

the evidence suggests a general public in a democracy typically sustains many misimpressions about many phenomena. One Pew Research Center study, for example, suggested that between 1989 and 2007 the overall degree of public awareness of issues—such as trade policy, the names of top political leaders, and the party balance in Congress— had changed little. Some issues showed a slight decline, others a slight increase.[24] The study found persistent patterns in information distribution, such as the existence of a "most knowledgeable third" of the public who seek out information more than others and end up better informed. Education remained the "single best predictor of knowledge."

Respect for factual accuracy has not disappeared; people still value seriousness and expertise. One United Kingdom poll found that 85 percent of respondents want their news sources to consult experts. Nearly 90 percent of Americans believe that it is important to get the facts right.[25] Even studies that show a significant effect of "motivated reasoning"—the tendency of people to seek out and credit information that agrees with their established views—is counteracted to some degree by an "accuracy motivation."[26]

In the process, these trends can affect people's perceptions and ultimately behavior at several distinct levels. The term *attitudes* is widely used but refers to a specific sort of construct: people's evaluations of things, such as ideas, issues, events, and other people. But the changing character of the infosphere can affect other levels of perception and understanding as well, including the type of knowledge they hold and the behaviors they view as appropriate. It is indeed one of the

---

[24]  Pew Research Center, *Public Knowledge of Current Affairs Little Changed by News and Information Revolutions*, Washington, D.C., April 15, 2007, p. 1.

[25]  Bruce Wharton, "Remarks on 'Public Diplomacy in a Post-Truth Society,'" in Shawn Powers and Markos Kounalakis, eds., *Can Public Diplomacy Survive the Internet?* Washington, D.C.: U.S. Advisory Commission on Public Diplomacy, 2017, p. 8.

[26]  A classic treatment is Ziva Kunda, "The Case for Motivated Reasoning," *Psychological Bulletin*, Vol. 108, No. 3, November 1990. See also Nicholas Epley and Thomas Gilovich, "The Mechanics of Motivated Reasoning," *Journal of Economic Perspectives*, Vol. 30, No. 3, 2016; and David P. Redlawsk, "Hot Cognition or Cool Consideration? Testing the Effects of Motivated Reasoning on Political Decision Making," *Journal of Politics*, Vol. 64, No. 4, 2002.

both exciting and perilous aspects of a comprehensive, deeply embedded infosphere that it can affect so many psychological domains at the same time, and that its manipulation can shape knowledge, attitudes, and behavior.

But the basic level of information held by democratic publics is only part of the equation shaping the character of any infosphere. The sections below outline several leading characteristics of the information environment that appears to be emerging.

## Networked Dynamics and the Viral Spread of Information

A central component of the infosphere is its increasingly networked, interdependent character: an essential property of "interrelatedness" that creates both opportunities and significant vulnerabilities.[27] This networked quality includes exchanges of information, with claims and narratives being spread rapidly through dense networks on social media and other channels, as well as the increasing interconnectedness of databases and networks. These exchanges range from the emerging IoT to databases of information on consumers collected by various apps and companies owned by the same larger technology firm.

One implication of this interlinkage is the potential for viral spread of ideas, information, or narratives. The problem of "virality"—understanding which reports go viral and which do not—remains poorly understood.[28] A few suggestive research findings point to several characteristics that help information "go viral," but there is not yet any comprehensive theory that can anticipate such outcomes in all circumstances. Research has suggested, for example, that identifiable influential people in a network will play a disproportionate role in the spread of information, and some research has begun to identify the

---

[27] This is the central thesis of Albert-László Barabási, *Linked: How Everything Is Connected to Everything Else and What It Means for Business, Science, and Everyday Life*, New York: Basic Books, 2014, p. 5.

[28] Sunstein, 2017, pp. 102–103, cites cases to suggest that the reasons for informational cascades remain unclear, and the actual shared information (such as songs) that goes viral is fairly random.

spread patterns and characteristics of viral news.[29] Beyond that, however, it is not well understood what makes a given story go viral. Only a tiny proportion of stories will do so, and it appears that the list will be arbitrary, involving a significant level of chance.[30]

Recent research does point to one other characteristic of stories that tend to go viral: They tend to be novel and fascinating. Fabricated or exaggerated news items can play to this factor to increase their spread. "Falsehood diffused significantly farther, faster, deeper and more broadly than the truth in all categories of information in the study," the authors of one study concluded. In some cases, it took truthful stories six times as long as false ones to reach 1,500 people; falsehoods were 70 percent more likely to be retweeted than truthful stories.[31] Yet the study also had an interesting implication: These qualities of virality apply to human reactions, not automatic ones. Botnets tended to diffuse truth and falsehood in equal amounts, perhaps because they were not reacting to novelty elements in the stories.

These factors point to one undeniable aspect of this phenomenon: Viral spread or cascading of information is a phenomenon of

---

[29]  See, for example, Justin Cheng, Lada Adamic, P. Alex Dow, Jon Michael Kleinberg, and Jure Leskovec, "Can Cascades Be Predicted?" *Twenty-Third International World Wide Web Conference, Conference Proceedings*, Seoul: Association for Computing Machinery, 2014. For a broader treatment, see Lee Daniel Kravetz, *Strange Contagion*, New York: Harper-Collins, 2017, who emphasizes the role of social connections in sparking viral spread. The marketing professor Jonah Berger has studied the issue and proposed six essential characteristics of virality: social currency (facts that people want to share because they look cool and in-the-know); triggering stimuli; the use of emotional appeals; popular attention; facts that have practical value to people; and facts that are embedded in narratives or stories; Jonah Berger, *Contagious: Why Things Catch On*, New York: Simon and Schuster, 2013.

[30]  One massive study of viral patterns on Twitter, for example, found that although more-influential users were more associated with the viral spread of stories or hashtags, in fact virality remained a relatively unpredictable phenomenon, meaning that the only effective strategy to spread information was simply to target as many influencers as possible and hope for the best. See Eytan Bakshy, Jake M. Hofman, Winter A. Mason, and Duncan J. Watts, "Everyone's an Influencer: Quantifying Influence on Twitter," *Fourth ACM International Conference on Web Search and Data Mining, Conference Proceedings*, Hong Kong: Association for Computing Machinery, 2011.

[31]  Soroush Vosoughi, Deb Roy, and Sinan Aral, "The Spread of True and False News Online," *Science*, Vol. 359, No. 6380, 2018, p. 1146.

social influence. People are following what other people are saying, doing, and "liking." The specific reasons why one story, meme, gif, or song goes viral as opposed to another may be mysterious, but the basic mechanism is not: It is a form of social proof effect. One implication is that such cascades can be triggered by early and significant endorsements, especially from socially influential actors. Either way, cascades can either start or run aground very quickly, pointing again to a critical first-mover advantage in the social manipulation space.[32]

Information is not the only thing that can spread through digitized networks. A 2012 Facebook study of almost 700,000 users found that "moods are contagious." By changing the balance of positive and negative stories going into people's news feeds, Facebook was able to shift their moods in measurable ways, and produce resulting behaviors, such as higher numbers of negative posts, from those people. "Emotional states," the study concludes, "can be transferred to others."[33]

## Sensationalism

A major trend in the news media and the infosphere more broadly in the last three decades has been a measurable increase in the degree of sensationalism in the content and style of reporting. The general problem of sensationalism is not new—today's trend mirrors earlier periods, such as the infamous age of yellow journalism at the end of the 19th century.[34] Moreover, while there is a strong anecdotal sense of the rise of sensationalism, few studies have tried to measure its growth over the last decade. Nonetheless, evidence from a range of sources suggests that mainstream and niche information sources are increasingly relying on sensational accounts to attract attention.

Part of the engine of growing sensationalism is that many websites are purpose-built to generate sensationalistic content in order to

---

[32] Sunstein, 2017, pp. 111–114.

[33] Cathy O'Neil, *Weapons of Math Destruction: How Big Data Increases Inequality and Threatens Democracy*, New York: Broadway Books, 2016, p. 184.

[34] Kavanagh and Rich, 2018, pp. 42–50.

draw the greatest number of viewers, which is the essential business model of the sites. Gawker is a leading example: the political activist Eli Pariser describes the "Big Board" of site traffic that hovers over the room of content creators. The essential requirement for Gawker writers is to generate traffic and make the Big Board; content is secondary, if not irrelevant.[35] Even traditional news media, in order to retain readers and viewers in an era of extreme content, have become more sensationalist in the form and content of their stories.[36]

Other research suggests the extremist bias even of sites that do not produce their own content, such as YouTube. Its playlist algorithm was found to disproportionately "lead users to channels that feature conspiracy theories, partisan viewpoints and misleading videos."[37] This bias appears to be a result of an algorithm that prioritizes keeping users watching, and will thus search for videos to recommend that have high interest, which can be a product of sensationalism.

The YouTube results reflect a larger trend related to connectedness, in the sense that virality now plays a major role in determining what content gets recommended.[38] The primary goal of media outlets is to sustain viewership. That means pushing articles that others have viewed, shared, or recommended the most, and those are often the most sensational, attention-grabbing articles. The result is a self-reinforcing process that pushes media outlets in the direction of more-

---

35  Eli Pariser, *The Filter Bubble: What the Internet Is Hiding from You*, New York: Penguin Press, 2011, p. 69.

36  See, for example, P. H. Vettehen and M. Kleemans, "Proving the Obvious? What Sensationalism Contributes to the Time Spent on News Video," *Electronic News*, Vol. 12, No. 2, 2018; and D. K. Thussu, *News as Entertainment: The Rise of Global Infotainment,* London: SAGE Publications, 2007.

37  Jack Nicas, "How YouTube Drives People to the Internet's Darkest Corners," *Wall Street Journal*, February 7, 2018.

38  Bharat N. Anand, "The U.S. Media's Problems Are Much Bigger than Fake News and Filter Bubbles," *Harvard Business Review*, January 5, 2017.

sensationalist, often extreme content.[39] These effects may be especially notable on social media.[40]

One implication of the trend toward sensational coverage is what has been termed the "pessimism syndrome."[41] Partly fueled by media coverage that is overwhelmingly negative—coverage that is now exacerbated by the one-sided messages of many echo chambers—many people have come to believe that the condition and trends of important social indicators (on such topics as unemployment, immigration, and crime) are far worse than is the case. This coverage constitutes a generalized form of misinformation, one biased toward a negative view of major trends and social realities. Some analysis suggests that the negative bias in political news reporting remains very significant and contributes to the decline of faith in major institutions.[42] The results, once again, are levels of grievance and frustration that could be employed by social manipulation strategies.

## Fragmentation of Information Sources

In his history of the broadcast and information industries, *The Attention Merchants*, writer and professor Tim Wu stresses a fundamental trend of fragmentation in the sources of information reaching Americans.[43] This fragmentation reflects a notable change from the era of peak attention between the 1950s and 1970s, when a few television networks (and within them, specific shows) dominated the infosphere. As Wu documents, the most dominant shows (such as *I Love Lucy*)

---

[39] Anand, 2017.

[40] Robert Kozinets, "How Social Media Fires People's Passions—and Builds Extremist Divisions," *The Conversation*, November 13, 2017.

[41] Michael J. Mazarr, "The Pessimism Syndrome," *Washington Quarterly*, Vol. 21, No. 3, 1998.

[42] See Tom Stafford, "Psychology: Why Bad News Dominates the Headlines," *BBC*, July 29, 2014.

[43] Tim Wu, *The Attention Merchants: The Epic Scramble to Get Inside Our Heads*, New York: Vintage Books, 2016.

grabbed over 70 percent of the watching public, and some unusual events (like Elvis Presley's appearance on *The Ed Sullivan Show*) garnered more than an 80 percent share. In both entertainment and news, most Americans watched many of the same things. Beginning with the emphasis on "clusters" of variation among the population in the late 1970s, especially in the famous PRIZM marketing model that created forty specific "sub-nations" within the United States, the fragmentation of the audience began in ways accelerated by the internet, leading to today's incredibly diverse broadcasting environment of dozens of channels and millions of blogs, websites, and social media feeds, and the accompanying microtargeting of tiny niche segments.

The resulting fragmentation is arguably the single most important structural change reflected in the current infosphere. Americans (and citizens of all advanced, open societies) today have essentially unlimited options for getting news, information, and awareness, from dozens of cable channels and radio stations; a wide selection of print sources with online presences; and hundreds of websites, blogs, and podcasts. The resulting confusion arguably makes it far more difficult for any society to sustain common narratives or public understandings. It also empowers the sort of echo chambers that will be discussed in the next section, allowing people an unprecedented ability to tailor their incoming information to reinforce their established beliefs.

The challenge is more fundamental than merely making sense of competing news stories: It relates to the evolving nature of advanced societies. Giddens has argued that "The condition of post-modernity is distinguished by an evaporating of the 'grand narrative'—an overarching 'story line' by means of which we are placed in history as beings having a definitive past and a predictable future."[44] In a fragmented media space, there is no grand narrative to bring coherence to daily events.

Two-thirds of Americans now report in surveys that they get at least some of their news from social media—including older Americans, where some of the most significant recent gains have been measured. They continue to get news and information from multiple other

---

[44] Giddens, 1990, p. 2.

sources: local television, cable television stations, network news, radio, and (least of all) print newspapers.[45] Online news consumption in general, distributed among dozens or hundreds of sites, is catching up to television news viewing: In an August 2017 poll, 43 percent of Americans said they "often" got news online, compared with 50 percent from television. The gap had closed from almost 20 percent just a year earlier and looks likely to continue narrowing. Those online sources include some significant degree of social media viewing: In the same survey, two-thirds of Americans reported getting "some" news from social media.[46] A 2018 survey found that 20 percent of Americans "often" get news from social media and 27 percent "sometimes" do.[47] The result is a complex web of information sources that lacks the uniformity of earlier eras.

Some research suggests that the confusion of conflicting messages does have one advantage: It may offer a safeguard against social manipulation.[48] When people are exposed to a lone source of information, meaningful influence on beliefs is possible. But in an atmosphere of contested truths, it becomes much more difficult. Few Americans *trust* news they get from online sources—just 5 percent have "a lot of" trust in information—and this lack of trust, in theory, ought to provide some filter against the easy effect of such information on attitudes.[49]

Obviously, however, there is a dilemma here: Fragmentation may make it harder for a manipulator to create a single alternative reality, but it also undermines the shared social institutions of information and

---

[45] Elisa Shearer and Jeffrey Gottfried, "News Use Across Social Media Platforms 2017," *Pew Research Center*, September 7, 2017.

[46] Kristen Bialik and Katerina Eva Matsa, "Key Trends in Social and Digital News Media," *Pew Research Center*, October 4, 2017.

[47] Katarina Eva Matsa and Elisa Shearer, "News Use Across Social Media Platforms 2018," *Pew Research Center*, September 10, 2018.

[48] Research has found that while "single-source" or single-issue information or massively tilted information environments can have significant effects on attitudes and behavior, these effects drop off quickly once the ground is meaningfully contested or blurred among many different issues; Anthony R. Pratkanis and Elliot Aronson, *Age of Propaganda: The Everyday Use and Abuse of Persuasion*, New York: Henry Holt and Company, 2001, pp. 29–30, 83–84.

[49] Bialik and Matsa, 2017.

awareness that once provided the leading bulwark against disinformation and social manipulation. The challenge for the future is to build a complex mosaic of smaller information intermediaries within an environment that will remain largely fragmented.

## Concentration of Information Platforms

As people have access to dozens of new channels of information and data, the basic social media platforms over which so much information is now exchanged—as well as associated systems and platforms for data management and information processing—are now concentrated in five enormous corporations: Apple, Google (or Alphabet, as the parent company is known), Amazon, Facebook, and Microsoft. Each of these firms owns many related companies: Google, for example, owns YouTube, the navigation app Waze, and the smart home product company Nest; Facebook owns dozens of companies, including the virtual reality firm Oculus. They have such immense capital reserves that they can typically buy up start-up competitors and preserve their market position. As of November 2017, the market value of these five companies alone made up over 40 percent of the Nasdaq stock index.[50]

*The New York Times*' Farhad Manjoo has dubbed this set of technology companies the "frightful five," a reference to their immense social power.[51] Because of the way they dominate specific platform services—online retaining, for example, or social networking—they offer services that are basically unavoidable. And, in some cases, their business models generate network effects, suggesting that the more people who use the platforms, the more indispensable they become to others, drawing in even more users.

These same firms are developing the AI-driven, voice-activated concierges (such as Siri and Alexa) that will become increasingly ubiq-

---

50  Conor Sen, "The 'Big Five' Could Destroy the Tech Ecosystem," *Bloomberg*, November 15, 2017.

51  Farhad Manjoo, "Tech's 'Frightful 5' Will Dominate Digital Life for Foreseeable Future," *New York Times*, January 20, 2016.

uitous means of interacting with technology. They are already collecting significant data on users—sometimes, apparently, without the users' awareness. The responses they provide to questions, especially when posed as requests for advice, should not be expected to be objective: They will reflect the best advantage of the business model of the platform developing them.

This emerging reality is affecting end users in a number of ways. Perhaps the most significant effect is that a handful of big firms are developing massive, interconnected databases of information on Americans (and others). This information accumulation allows these platforms to study and forecast behavior and attitudes in unprecedented ways and helps advertisers target consumers with pinpoint accuracy. These databases are also vulnerable to theft and manipulation as part of large-scale information manipulation campaigns.

The broad reach of these platforms also provides them with significant influence over attitudes.[52] This degree of influence is partly a product of the platforms' ability to segment their user base and appeal to highly individualized elements, sometimes even specific individuals, based on the information they possess about them. To the extent that these platforms and their multiple interfaces play a dominant role in shaping public perceptions, they will attain an unprecedented degree of influence.

## The Role of Echo Chambers

Related to the trend of a fragmented infosphere is the rise of echo chambers: self-defined silos of information and belief that constrain people's awareness and information search, allowing only information that supports their existing beliefs to get through. Settings within social media platforms or on search engines allow users to tailor and filter the information they see in ways not available to earlier generations, and the algorithms of some of those platforms have the same effect, using the

---

52  National Public Radio, "How 5 Tech Giants Have Become More Like Governments Than Companies," *Fresh Air*, October 26, 2017.

"if you liked that, you are likely to enjoy this" rule of providing content that fits established patterns. The result would be to reinforce those beliefs and perhaps spur them to greater degrees of extremism.

Research on this trend is mixed, suggesting that, at least so far, the measurable effect of echo chambers may not be as great as some reports have suggested. Nonetheless, there is sufficient evidence that the trend has the potential to constrain people's information searches and openness to contrary views that it should be taken seriously.

Several recent studies have found evidence that exposure to the chaotic, often ideologically segmented menu of options online increases affinity for existing ideological views and in effect allows people to wall themselves off from contrary views.[53] Other work shows, not surprisingly, that political bloggers tend to link to ideologically similar blogs.[54] Sunstein has marshaled extensive research to claim that echo chambers are an urgent threat to democracy.[55] Another study points to the risk of "stratamentation," a situation in which the politically active few are locked in silos resistant to contrary information, whereas the majority of the population consume very little political news.[56] One study examined efforts to create specially skewed search engines that favored one political party in their search results, much as an echo chamber would; they found voting preferences affected by as much as 20 percent.[57]

Pariser has written of the ultimate form of an echo chamber: An entirely personalized information bubble for each person online, built from the immense data about their preferences that are now available.

53   One study that demonstrated ideological convergence online is Diana C. Mutz and Paul S. Martin, "Facilitating Communication Across Lines of Political Difference: The Role of Mass Media," *American Political Science Review*, Vol. 95, No. 1, 2001.

54   Lada Adamic and Natalie Glance, "The Political Blogosphere and the 2004 U.S. Election: Divided They Blog," paper presented at the Second Annual Workshop on the Weblogging Ecosystem, Chiba, Japan: Association for Computing Machinery, 2005.

55   Sunstein, 2017.

56   W. Lance Bennett and Shanto Iyengar, "A New Era of Minimal Effects? The Changing Foundations of Political Communication," *Journal of Communication*, Vol. 58, No. 4, 2008.

57   O'Neil, 2016, p. 184.

"Your identity shapes your media" in such a situation, he argues, "and your media then shapes what you believe and what you care about." Clicking, searching and shopping generate more data that can be used to sharpen the tailoring of information, in effect hardening the walls of the information bubble. "You become trapped in a you loop, and if your identity is misrepresented, strange patterns begin to emerge, like reverb from an amplifier." And as he explains, the combination of big data and AI is creating a potential to generate such singular bubbles at lightning speed: "The faster the system learns from you, the more likely it is that you can get trapped in a kind of identity cascade . . . in which a small initial action" brands you as a particular sort of person, and intensifies the resulting echo chamber.[58]

The internet is not alone in having these effects and may not even be the most important cause of them. Partisan television networks have had this effect: Viewers of Fox News and MSNBC have become more ideologically polarized over time. Using social identity theory, one set of researchers showed that dislike between political poles had increased significantly in the United States, partly because of highly negative advertising.[59] Another study found that people are more interested in a headline if it is associated with an ideologically aligned network. Research suggests that Twitter users more commonly interact with those of similar views, that people are drawn to headlines with stories that support their views, and that Facebook users are much more likely to click on or "like" information that confirms their views.[60]

Sunstein also points to a worrying line of social science research that indicates the possible result of echo chambers: work on a phenomenon that has become known as *group polarization*. It was long believed that putting people into groups to discuss issues would temper opinions. However, multiple studies have found that groups tend to produce *more*-extreme attitudes than the individuals held beforehand, compared with attitudes expressed by individuals before group dia-

---

[58] Pariser, 2011, pp. 125–127.

[59] Shanto Iyengar, Guarav Sood, and Yphtach Lelkes, "Affect, Not Ideology: A Social Identity Perspective on Polarization," *Public Opinion Quarterly*, Vol. 76, No. 3, 2012.

[60] Sunstein, 2017, pp. 61, 64–65, 81, 114–115, 119–126.

logues.[61] This finding is true even of groups that are not ideologically consistent, but echo chambers of such people could be expected to have an even greater effect in this regard. Indeed, Sunstein quotes research indicating that group polarization effects are materializing online.

One important study confirms these effects. Researchers attempted to examine how the existence of a fragmented information context offering the possibility of extreme and polarized views would affect information search and resulting "affective polarization": the degree to which members of opposing political groups are viewed in a harshly negative light. They found that, indeed, "discretionary information search"—the ability to seek out polarized, confirming evidence in a highly fragmented information environment—has the effect of increasing such affective polarization by as much as 15 percentage points.[62] A related study found that access to broadband internet, and thus a wider array of potential information sources (including highly polarized ones), increases affective polarization.[63] Another study found that Facebook friends tend to highlight news stories and other information that reinforce existing beliefs of self-selected groups.[64]

Yet even with such evidence, the findings of research on echo chambers remain highly conflicted. Much research, as Sunstein indicates, suggests that many people "dislike echo chambers. . . . [M]any members of the public are keenly interested in seeing perspectives that diverge from their own."[65] One extensive study, by economists Gentz-

---

61　Sunstein, 2017, pp. 68–69, 77–78. For one review of the literature, see Daniel J. Isenberg, "Group Polarization: A Critical Review and Meta-Analysis," *Journal of Personality and Social Psychology*, Vol. 50, No. 6, 1986.

62　Richard R. Lau, David J. Andersen, Tessa M. Ditonto, Mona S. Kleinberg, and David P. Redlawsk, "Effect of Media Environment Diversity and Advertising Tone on Information Search, Selective Exposure, and Affective Polarization," *Political Behavior*, Vol. 39, No. 1, 2017.

63　Yphtach Lelkes, Guarav Sood, and Shanto Iyengar, "The Hostile Audience: The Effect of Access to Broadband Internet on Partisan Affect," *American Journal of Political Science*, Vol. 61, No. 1, 2017.

64　Eytan Bakshy, Solomon Messing, and Lada Adamic, "Exposure to Ideologically Diverse News and Opinion on Facebook," *Science*, Vol. 348, No. 6329, 2015.

65　Sunstein, 2017, p. 5.

kow and Shapiro, aimed to measure the degree to which people only visit websites they agree with, or their "isolation index." (Conservatives who spent all their time at Fox News would have an isolation index of 100.) Their surveys found that self-identified conservatives have an average isolation index online of 60.6 percent and self-identified liberals of 53.1 percent.[66] Another study found people's online news consumption displaying "a remarkable degree of balance."[67] A major study of the browsing habits of 50,000 individuals found that patterns did reflect ideological gaps, but that these gaps were mostly a product of habitual visits to established mainstream media sites. In fact, general browsing brought them into contact with more rather than fewer differing views than offline news consumption.[68]

Recent polling by the Pew Research Center offers several perspectives on the issue of echo chambers. One survey indicates that people use multiple social media sites for their news, suggesting that they may not be trapped in silos.[69] Another poll found that only 9 percent of social media users said they "often discuss, comment or post about politics of government," indicating that online environments are mostly nonpolitical in nature and thus might have mild effects on political views. The same survey found that most people report their social media friend groups contain people of differing viewpoints.[70]

An important 2013 study found little evidence of "defensive avoidance" online—that is, the pattern of avoiding sites with content that disagrees with the person's political beliefs. People who visited ideologically identified sites were more likely to visit mainstream sites

---

[66] Matthew Gentzkow and Jesse M. Shapiro, "Ideological Segregation Online and Offline," *Quarterly Journal of Economics*, Vol. 126, No. 4, 2011.

[67] Andrew M. Guess, *Media Choice and Moderation: Evidence from Online Tracking Data*, job market paper, New York: New York University, September 6, 2016.

[68] Seth Flaxman, Sharad Goel, and Justin M. Rao, "Filter Bubbles, Echo Chambers, and Online News Consumption," *Public Opinion Quarterly*, Volume 80, No. S1, 2016.

[69] Elizabeth Grieco, "More Americans Are Turning to Multiple Social Media Sites for News," *Pew Research Center*, November 2, 2017.

[70] Maeve Duggan and Aaron Smith, "The Political Environment on Social Media," *Pew Research Center*, October 25, 2016, p. 7.

and even "ideologically discrepant" ones.[71] Some research suggests that while people do tend to look for information that agrees with their beliefs, there is little evidence that people actively avoid information contrary to their views.[72] Other studies find that people who go online looking for political information tend to be more ideologically extreme than those who rely mostly on broadcast and mainstream media.[73] This makes sense—politically active people would be in the market for information and take more steps to gather it—but it also means that findings showing a greater polarization of online users may be showing a symptom, not the cause. Two scholars who have done extensive work on the issue conclude that "the best evidence so far, based on actual reader behavior, suggests that ideological segregation on the Internet is limited." Moreover, they stress that the risk of segregation on the internet is a relatively recent threat, and there could be many policy responses that would attenuate it over time.[74]

Yet the sum of this evidence does point to the very real danger of increasingly isolated polarized groups gathering self-confirming evidence from a fragmented information environment. As three scholars have summarized the rising infosphere: "We are now facing a situation in which a large share of the populace is living in an epistemic space that has abandoned conventional criteria of evidence, internal consistency, and fact-seeking." They continue:

---

71  R. Kelly Garrett, Dustin Carnahan, and Emily K. Lynch, "A Turn Toward Avoidance? Selective Exposure to Online Political Information, 2004–2008," *Political Behavior*, Vol. 35, No. 1, 2013, pp. 113–134.

72  R. Kelly Garrett, "Echo Chambers Online?: Politically Motivated Selective Exposure Among Internet News Users," *Journal of Computer-Mediated Communication*, Vol. 14, No. 2, 2009a. See also R. Kelly Garrett, "Politically Motivated Reinforcement Seeking: Reframing the Selective Exposure Debate," *Journal of Communication*, Vol. 59, No. 4, 2009b.

73  Norman H. Nie, Darwin W. Miller III, Saar Golde, Daniel M. Butler, and Kenneth Winneg, "The World Wide Web and the U.S. Political News Market," *American Journal of Political Science*, Vol. 54, No. 2, 2010.

74  R. Kelly Garrett and Paul Resnick, "Resisting Political Fragmentation on the Internet," *Daedalus*, Vol. 140, No. 4, Fall 2011.

An obvious hallmark of a post-truth world is that it empowers people to choose their own reality, where facts and objective evidence are trumped by existing beliefs and prejudices. This can be amplified by leaders who model deception and delusion as adequate means to garner support. In this world, lying is not only accepted, it is rewarded. Falsifying reality is no longer about changing people's beliefs, it is about asserting power.[75]

The resulting pattern of self-segregated groups able to arm themselves with information that supports their views, and those groups becoming increasingly extreme and polarized in their views, is one of the leading dangers of the emerging information context. As we will see, it is also the foundation on which hostile social manipulation efforts have strongly relied to date.

## The Role of Influencers

Related to the idea of silos is the broader concept of *influencers*: people or small groups that function as key nodes in information networks and exercise disproportionate influence over information flows and what is believed and circulated. Research suggests that a small proportion of people in any social media or other informational network will account for a significant component of information sharing.

The critical question is how patterns of interactions emerge—what influences the clustering or grouping that occurs in large networked patterns. Those clusters in social networks often take place around influential individuals or groups or sources of information that are often termed influencers. Albert-László Barabási has termed the resulting actors *connectors* and *hubs*. Connectors—which he defines as "nodes with an anomalously large number of links"—in networks serve to "create trends and fashions, make important deals, spread fads, or help launch a restaurant." Especially influential doctors, for example, are responsible for a disproportionate degree of thinking in their field. Within the online world, research suggests that a relatively small

---

75 Lewandowsky, Ecker, and Cook, 2017, pp. 360–361.

number of hubs, such as Amazon and Yahoo, play the same function. Pages linked to only a few other places for all purposes "do not exist"; only through massive sharing over hubs does news spread virally.[76]

One possible result of a number of these intersecting trends is that social media, where information flows are more dependent on self-selected echo chambers and shaped by influencers, reflects a far higher dosage of disinformation than general news consumption. One 2018 study of European news consumption, for example, found that news sites built around fabricated or exaggerated claims garnered only a tiny proportion of the attention of "real" news sites. No false news site had a monthly reach of over 3.5 percent of the population, and most were far lower, compared with between 22 percent and 51 percent reach for major newspaper sites. Yet on Facebook, the total interaction measures "generated by a small number of false news outlets matched or exceeded that produced by the most popular news brands."[77]

## The Trolling Ethic

Another characteristic of the infosphere is the prevalence of what can be called a *trolling ethic* on the part of hundreds of thousands or even millions of internet users. This term describes the effort to use exaggerated or invented stories, satirical memes, and sometimes vicious attacks to disrupt the conventional dialogue online, create mischief, and intensify argumentation. It is an ironic and insolent mindset determined to use the sensationalism of the media environment for humorous, disruptive, and aggressive purposes. In some ways, trolls represent the apotheosis of related trends on the modern internet, such as sensationalism and

---

76   Barabási, 2014, pp. 56–58; the reference to doctor hubs of influence is on p. 129.

77   Richard Fletcher, Alessio Cornia, Lucas Graves, and Rasmus Kleis Neilsen, *Measuring the Reach of "Fake News" and Online Disinformation in Europe*, Oxford, United Kingdom: Reuters Institute for the Study of Journalism, University of Oxford, February 2018.

echo chambers. They are, as the scholar Whitney Phillips has put it, "the grimacing poster children for the socially networked world."[78]

The defining web collective for the trolling ethic is the site 4chan, and in particular its infamous "/b/" board, ground zero for a roiling series of ironic, hostile, and parodic commentary on issues, websites, and individuals. Between 2008 and 2010, 4chan became a massive web presence, receiving over 8 million daily page views, 200 million visitors a month, and 400,000 daily posts.[79]

Trolls have now engaged in a series of famous campaigns and attacks. In more purely ironic and humorous ways, they have staged ongoing campaigns of harassment against what they perceive to be silly and pointless web humor sites. The hacker collective "Anonymous" has roots in the troll movement in particular in the 4chan community, but eventually split off to become a more active presence in the "real world," organizing formal protests as well as continuing a series of disruptive hacks and trolling campaigns. They have attacked such targets as random online forums and corporations.

In more sinister terms, trolls have banded together to launch the most heinous forms of cyberbullying against individuals they perceive "not to get it" and to oppose trolling ethics. In one of the more sinister examples of the process, internet trolls began a practice of "RIP trolling" in which they posted brutal and often obscene comments to memorial sites on Facebook or other locations, even attacking the families of children who had died in tragic ways.

Such attacks would seem incomprehensible, but as Whitney Phillips has pointed out, one of the most important aspects of the trolling movement is its "emotional dissociation." Many trolls undertake hostile attacks online precisely because they make a sharp distinction between virtual and real selves. Many, Phillips reports from her research, are in real life quiet, thoughtful, and respectful individuals who insist they would never engage in face-to-face attacks in the way they do online.

---

[78] Whitney Phillips, *This Is Why We Can't Have Nice Things: Mapping the Relationship Between Online Trolling and Mainstream Culture*, Cambridge, Mass.: MIT Press, 2015, p. 8; cf. also pp. 5–6.

[79] Phillips, 2015, pp. 55–56.

They "insist that their troll selves and their offline ('real') selves are subject to totally different sets of rules."[80]

The distinction may be morally objectionable, but it allows trolls to justify dramatically different behavior online. And such practices are in fact closely related to a wider online practice of dissociation and playing with sensational content to garner attention. The idea of "click-bait" is just a step away from "trollbait"; the idea in both cases is to generate content that attracts attention rather than offering any meaningful substance. In both cases, the pattern is in part alienated individuals or groups attacking what they perceive to be the "conventional" ethics and institutions of the system.

Such trolling and harassment have gone global and have been used by many international actors, both state and nonstate, for coercive purposes. Haroon Ullah catalogs ways in which extremists have created fake videos to undermine the credibility of political leaders, as well as promotional videos for the radical lifestyle. He depicts the modern battle with extremism as dominated by information channels, many of which employ trolling tactics to harass and discredit those opposed to the extremist message.[81]

## The Rule of Data

Finally, the infosphere is increasingly characterized by the accumulation and manipulation of massive databases used to drive everything from marketing algorithms, to health care decisions, to educational choices. These databases are becoming the basis for AI and the increasingly algorithmic decisionmaking in many fields.

Many companies are assembling vast troves of data on individual Americans. Facebook boasts that it can target more than 1,300 unique categories. Amazon's Alexa collects information on purchases but also, because it is active in people's homes, "when you wake up,

---

[80]  Phillips, 2015, pp. 33–35.

[81]  Haroon K. Ullah, *Digital World War: Islamists, Extremists, and the Fight for Cyber Supremacy*, New Haven, Conn.: Yale University Press, 2017, pp. ix–xv.

what you watch, read, listen to, ask for, and eat." Based on data collected from personal phones, advertisers know "what times of day you usually browse, watch videos, answer e-mail, travel to the office—and what travel routes you take." They know what sorts of hotels people stay in on travel and what parts of the world they're interested in visiting. Such data can fuel AI-driven marketing: Armed with such precise preference information, "[m]achines will craft ads, just as machines will drive cars."[82]

"With little notice or fanfare," Pariser has argued, "the digital world is fundamentally changing. What was once an anonymous medium where anyone could be anyone . . . is now a tool for soliciting and analyzing our personal data."[83] Every time someone makes a travel reservation, looks up a word in an online dictionary, searches for anything, makes a social media post, buys something online, or conducts any activity whatsoever, companies are vacuuming up thousands of pieces of information and assembling portraits of individuals. This information gathering is the defining business model of most leading internet companies, and specialist firms such as Acxiom and Cambridge Analytica are compiling thousands of discrete pieces of information about every American. This information can include names of family and friends, loan history and purchase history, credit card balances, pet ownership, and just about every other measurable characteristic of individuals. Using such databases, private companies will be able to monitor and predict life patterns, from our daily routine to our purchasing preferences.[84]

Stolen data can become an important element of the toolkit of social manipulators. A leading example is the theft of information from the Office of Personnel Management, which could be used to blackmail Americans. The alleged Chinese intrusion netted personnel files, digital fingerprints, Social Security numbers, and much else. In a traditional cyberattack, an aggressor could use the information to "lock out

---

[82] Ken Auletta, "How the Math Men Overthrew the Mad Men," *New Yorker*, May 21, 2018.

[83] Pariser, 2011, p. 6.

[84] Stacey Higginbotham, "IBM Is Bringing in Watson to Conquer the Internet of Things," *Fortune*, December 15, 2015.

medical records, wipe away financial information, manipulate social media, and spread lies and half-truths about personal misconduct." The attacker could harass friends and relatives and even send death threats via Twitter.[85] But in a more gradual form of social manipulation, an attacker could do hundreds of these things a month to create just enough confusion, frustration, and anxiety to add more sand into the gears of a rival society, without ever reaching the degree of manipulation that would count as a large-scale cyberattack.

## Summary: A Changing Information Environment for Advanced Democracies

These trends point to several ways in which the emerging infosphere could be vulnerable to advanced social manipulation campaigns. The trends depict an emerging information environment that is

- fragmented and decentralized, subject to a significant degree of the echo chamber effect and lacking grand narratives that unify social perceptions and give people a sense of grounding and belonging in a political community
- increasingly networked and interlinked and dependent on the platforms provided by a handful of major technology firms sitting on vast troves of data about individual Americans, which together create an increasing degree of systemic risk
- characterized by significant degrees of sensational news and hostile trolling and harassment of participants in social media.

The result could be an infosphere that is increasingly disaggregated in ways that undermine social coherence, interconnected in ways that create networked vulnerabilities, and extreme and sensational in ways that persistently skew public perceptions and depress ontological security, trust in the future, and social institutions. Even before

---

85   Ian Brown, "Imagining a Cyber Surprise: How Might China Use Stolen OPM Records to Target Trust?" *War on the Rocks*, May 22, 2018.

we consider active, hostile measures taken from outside to manipulate a country's infosphere, the evidence suggests that baseline trends are already generating an information environment likely to have corrosive effects on democratic institutions and social stability. The problem, in other words, is one of the changing infosphere first and foremost, and only secondarily measures of social manipulation.

# CHAPTER THREE

# Insights from Social Science

To this point, we have reviewed the character of the emerging information environment and the potential implications for the weaponization of this evolving infosphere. To get a better understanding of the basis for and effects of social manipulation, we also surveyed several fields of research that bear on the issue. An obvious case in point is cognitive and social psychology. What does it have to say about the effectiveness of social manipulation, and what can be done to counter social manipulation's effectiveness?

The analysis in this chapter builds on a prior RAND study on Russian disinformation techniques by Christopher Paul and Miriam Matthews. That study reviewed major findings of social science literature on attitudes, persuasion, and belief systems to lay the groundwork for assessing the approaches used by Russian propagandists.[1] The goal of this chapter is the same, with a somewhat broader focus: to understand what established findings in social science might imply about the future of social manipulation.

The key lesson of this field is a basic aspect of epistemology: Knowledge and understanding are *interpretive* acts. Human beings are constantly making sense of the facts they encounter. The most important aspect of those facts is not their "objective" validity, but what people make of them. This constant process is in turn a product of the larger phenomenon of *cognitive miserism*. People are bombarded with

---

[1] Christopher Paul and Miriam Matthews, "The Russian 'Firehose of Falsehood' Propaganda Model: Why It Might Work and Options to Counter It," Santa Monica, Calif.: RAND Corporation, PE-198-OSD, 2016.

far more information than they can process. They are constantly in the market for shortcuts: ways to make sense of the incoming flood, especially by judging the validity of specific facts. People use various such techniques, including fitting incoming information into established worldviews, accepting information from sources they believe to be reliable, and "going with the crowd." These shortcuts limit the potential effectiveness of social manipulation campaigns: Efforts to break people away from preestablished beliefs they are seeking to bolster can be very difficult.

Indeed, *motivated reasoning*—using information to support conclusions we have already reached rather than objectively evaluating it—is fundamental to human ways of thinking.[2] Research suggests that there is an accuracy motivation—people want to be in possession of "true" information—but that motivation is constantly at war with a countervailing impulse to sustain and reinforce existing viewpoints, which is in many circumstances the stronger motivation.[3] The result is an ongoing habit of "bounded rationality" and misperception that can sometimes be intentionally manipulated.

This foundational nature of human cognition produces arguably the most important entry point for social manipulation: Belief and expectation create the lens through which people perceive events and facts. Belief is, in many ways and on most occasions, more powerful than facts.[4] This provides a potential social manipulator with raw material, in the form of the belief systems of subgroups within a population, to shape with all the tools and techniques described above. There is, as we will see, a certain degree of accuracy motivation on the part of many people much of the time. But it is highly contingent, and in some groups at some times it can entirely give way to preconceptions

---

2   A fundamental resource on motivated reasoning is Kunda, 1990. For a connection to misinformation, see John Cook, Ullrich K. H. Ecker, and Stephan Lewandowsky, "Neutralizing Misinformation Through Inoculation: Exposing Misleading Argumentation Techniques Reduces Their Influence," *PLOS One*, Vol. 12, No. 5, 2017, p. 2.

3   Flynn, Nyhan, and Reifler, 2017, pp. 131–135.

4   Elizabeth Kolbert, "Why Facts Don't Change Our Minds," *New Yorker*, February 27, 2017; Troy Campbell and Justin Friesen, "Why People 'Fly from Facts,'" *Scientific American*, March 3, 2015.

and biases, cognitive faults that skilled social manipulators can employ to achieve their goals.

## Attitudes and Attitude Change

An attitude is an individual's association between a given object, topic, or person and his or her "summary evaluation" of that thing.[5] The most important aspect of an attitude is the evaluative judgment, i.e., whether a person generally feels positively or negatively toward the subject. There are related bodies of literature on attitude change in social psychology, political science, and advertising, all of which draw heavily from cognitive psychology.[6]

Deeply held personal attitudes, especially about political ideology and similar issues, are "remarkably" resistant to change.[7] Once a person internalizes information and forms a belief, it is difficult to change his

---

[5]  Gregory R. Maio and Geoffrey Haddock, *The Psychology of Attitudes and Attitude Change*, Thousand Oaks, Calif.: SAGE Publications, 2009, p. 4. For more on the "attitude" concept in social psychology, see Richard E. Petty, Russell H. Fazio, and Pablo Briñol, eds., *Attitudes: Insights from the New Implicit Measures*, New York: Psychology Press, 2008.

[6]  Much of social psychology of the early to mid–20th century was focused on the study of attitudes and, more specifically, defining and measuring them; Herbert C. Kelman, "Attitudes Are Alive and Well and Gainfully Employed in the Sphere of Action," *American Psychologist*, Vol. 29, No. 5, 1974. One of the first studies of attitudes was Gordon Allport's 1935 work in which he defined *attitude* as "a mental and neural state of readiness organized through experience, and exerting a directive influence upon the individual's response to all objects and situations which it is related"; Gordon Allport, "Attitudes," in Carl Murchison, ed., *A Handbook of Social Psychology*, Worcester, Mass.: Clark University Press, 1935, p. 798; referenced in Garth S. Jowett and Victoria O'Donnell, *Propaganda and Persuasion*, 3rd ed., Thousand Oaks, Calif.: SAGE Publications, 1999, pp. 166–167.

[7]  This consensus emerged after a series of studies in the 1970s demonstrated the resiliency of fixed attitudes to change even after subjects were presented with new information. Researchers concluded that "once formed, impressions are remarkably resilient"; Lee D. Ross, Mark R. Lepper, Fritz Strack, and Julia Steinmetz, "Social Explanation and Social Expectation: Effects of Real and Hypothetical Explanations on Subjective Likelihood," *Journal of Personality and Social Psychology*, Vol. 35, No. 11, 1977; Charles G. Lord, Lee D. Ross, and Mark R. Lepper, "Biased Assimilation and Attitude Polarization: The Effects of Prior Theories on Subsequently Considered Evidence," *Journal of Personality and Social Psychology*, Vol. 37, No. 11, 1979. See also Pratkanis and Aronson, 2001, pp. 40–47.

or her mind, even if the information creating the belief is erroneous and is later corrected.[8] This is sometimes termed *belief perseverance*, and it is especially pronounced when the attitude is important to an individual's identity or social position.[9] Numerous studies have found that the introduction of factual information can sometimes change an individual's policy preferences, but the effectiveness of providing new information on attitude change is not consistent.[10] In general, information that challenges an individual's beliefs is unwelcome and can prompt compensatory responses, such as actively suppressing that unwanted information, especially when those beliefs are strongly held.

Research on persuasion also suggests that, to be successful, persuaders must (1) reach the intended audience; (2) craft the message in such a way that it is understandable to the intended audience; and (3) ensure that the message will not be distorted en route. These are all potential pitfalls of social manipulation before the message even reaches the individual, where it will be distorted through that individual's internal prisms.

Research suggests that even fixed attitudes, perhaps fostered by motivated reasoning, can be changed by some degree of contrary information. One study found that motivated reasoners can correct actively held mistaken views. But the amount of information required is significant, and the risk of the backfire effect remains. The study found that initial efforts to correct mistaken views indeed produced a backfire

---

8    Brendan Nyhan and Jason Reifler, *Misinformation and Fact-Checking: Research Findings from Social Science*, Washington, D.C.: New America, February 2012, p. 3; Rohini Ahluwalia, "Examination of Psychological Processes Underlying Resistance to Persuasion," *Journal of Consumer Research*, Vol. 27, No. 2, 2000.

9    See Jonathan Haidt, "Moral Psychology for the Twenty-First Century," *Journal of Moral Education*, Vol. 42, No. 3, 2013; Hugo Mercier and Dan Sperber, *The Enigma of Reason*, Cambridge, Mass.: Harvard University Press, 2017; and Steven Sloman and Philip Fernbach, *The Knowledge Illusion: Why We Never Think Alone*, New York: Riverhead Books, 2017.

10    Nyhan and Reifler (2012, pp. 8–10) provide an overview of several studies from the 1990s to 2012 that measure whether the introduction of new information can change an individual's opinion on a certain policy. Important variables include the importance of the policy position to a person's worldview, how strongly they believe in that position or policy, and the source providing the new information. This will be further discussed in the next section.

effect of strengthening those views, which persisted until nearly 15 percent of the total information received ran counter to the reasoner's beliefs. But the effect at that point only leveled off: Motivated reasoners did not begin to actively question their commitments until nearly 30 percent of available information ran in the opposite direction.[11]

Yet hostile social manipulation need not always run up against well-established attitudes. If the receiving population does not have fixed attitudes about a given issue—whether the North Atlantic Treaty Organization (NATO) should defend the Baltics, for example—new information may be able to shape emergent beliefs in ways it could not with fixed attitudes. This is especially true if the social manipulators employ framing techniques to shape the context in which people see the issue. This distinction helps to clarify a possible difference between persuasion aimed at advertising consumer products and that aimed at political attitudes: Attitudes governing devotion to a specific product may be far less intensely held than political attitudes. On the other hand, some political attitudes are more strongly held than others, suggesting some room for influence.

Moreover, there is indeed some tantalizing evidence that information acquired through social media can have an actual effect of changing attitudes. In one recent Pew Research Center poll, some 20 percent of Americans claimed they have changed their mind about a political issue, and 17 percent changed their mind about a political candidate,

---

[11]  David P. Redlawsk, Andrew J. W. Civettini, and Karen M. Emmerson, "The Affective Tipping Point: Do Motivated Reasoners Ever 'Get It'?" *Political Psychology*, Vol. 31, No. 4, 2010, p. 583. This effect shows up even in online forums devoted to helping people critically assess their own views. A recent study that analyzed thousands of discussion threads on ChangeMyView, an online forum on Reddit of more than 200,000 members that allows users to present their opinions and invite others to try to change their minds, found that using the ChangeMyView platform provided researchers the opportunity to observe real-life attempts to change others' fixed (and likely strongly held) attitudes on contentious political and social issues. The researchers found that even though this community was composed of people who were relatively open-minded (demonstrated by their choosing to participate in this forum), in the majority of cases (70 percent) originally held opinions did not change; Chenhao Tan, Vlad Niculae, Cristian Danescu-Niculescu-Mizil, and Lilian Lee, "Winning Arguments: Interaction Dynamics and Persuasion Strategies in Good-Faith Online Discussions," *25th International World Wide Web Conference, Conference Proceedings*, Montreal, Canada: International World Wide Web Conferences Steering Committee, April 2016.

because of something they saw on social media. "Still," a report on the poll concluded,

> it is important to note that the majority of social media users are not swayed by what they see in their networks. Some 82 percent of social media users say they never modified their views on a particular candidate—and 79 percent say they have never changed their views on a social or political issue—because of something they saw on social media.[12]

Causing a change in even 10 percent of citizens could have dramatic political effects. If the numbers are accurate, they may suggest more potential for influence than many other studies have proposed.

## When Attitudes Change: Criteria for Attitude Shift

Although fixed attitudes are resistant to change, research has shown that new information can have a greater impact on an individual's attitudes under several conditions, outlined below. These factors provide the basis for much of modern persuasion theory.[13] These are, in effect, criteria for susceptibility, i.e., times when listeners will be most susceptible to the messages they are receiving.

When attitudes do change, that change can either be temporary or permanent, depending on the issue, the context, and the basis for the attitude change. Existing research suggests that information is more likely to affect attitudes and then, in some cases, behavior in several specific circumstances, outlined in the following sections.

---

[12]  Duggan and Smith, 2016, pp. 18–19.

[13]  As Pratkanis and Aronson, 2001, p. 51, summarize the basic rules, persuasion works by establishing the ground in advance ("pre-persuasion"), using credible sources, developing a compelling narrative or message, and targeting emotions as much as or instead of reasoning. See also Jowett and O'Donnell, 1999, pp. 164–168.

### When the Information Is Repeated

Human beings have a tendency to believe information is true after repeated exposure to it (often known as the *illusory truth effect* or the *frequency-validity relationship*), after it has become so familiar as to be easily available.[14] Messages that are familiar will generally be subjected to less scrutiny than unfamiliar messages.[15] One study even found that hearing the same opinion multiple times from the same person can result in the erroneous impression that it is a widely held opinion, which makes people more receptive to it.[16]

### When the Information Comes from Multiple Sources

Information, facts, or claims appear stronger when restated by multiple sources. Social science research suggests that "[p]eople assume that information from multiple sources is likely to be based on different perspectives and is thus worth greater consideration."[17] It stands to reason that the engagement of multiple sources would convey the common-sense reaction on the part of the receiver that the information must be accurate. This reaction can be true even within echo chambers, with multiple sources of the same partisan or ideological persuasion working together to reinforce the apparent validity of a message.

---

[14]  Nyhan and Reifler, 2012, p. 16. Ian Skurnik, Carolyn Yoon, Denise C. Park, and Norbert Schwarz, "How Warnings About False Claims Become Recommendations," *Journal of Consumer Research*, Vol. 31, No. 4, 2005. The impact of the illusory truth effect has been documented in both political and consumer behavior. While it was initially believed that the effect only occurred when individuals were highly uncertain about a subject or statement, the same study demonstrated that repetition of a statement makes it easier to cognitively process, which makes it seem more plausible, even when people are knowledgeable about a subject; Lisa K. Fazio, Nadia M. Brashier, B. Keith Payne, and Elizabeth J. Marsh, "Knowledge Does Not Protect Against Illusory Truth," *Journal of Experimental Psychology*, Vol. 144, No. 5, 2015.

[15]  Matt Chessen, "Understanding the Psychology Behind Computational Propaganda," in Shawn Powers and Markos Kounalakis, eds., *Can Public Diplomacy Survive the Internet?* Washington, D.C.: U.S. Advisory Commission on Public Diplomacy, 2017a, p. 21.

[16]  Kimberlee Weaver, Stephen M. Garcia, Norbert Schwarz, and Dale T. Miller, "Inferring the Popularity of an Opinion from Its Familiarity: A Repetitive Voice Can Sound Like a Chorus," *Journal of Personality and Social Psychology*, Vol. 92, No. 5, 2007.

[17]  Paul and Matthews, 2016, p. 3.

## When Other Members of an Individual's Social Group[18] Demonstrate Receptiveness

People assess that it is appropriate to believe or act in a certain way when they perceive that people comparable to them are also believing or acting in the same way.[19] A 2012 study of how online political mobilization messaging influences behavior found that messages including social "cues" from a person's Facebook network were more effective than messages that only included information.[20] Other research has found that urban legends were transmitted more readily when they contained socially meaningful information even than when they contained information bearing on survival.[21]

More broadly, one of the most prominent related effects in social science research is the *social proof effect*: the idea that people are more highly influenced by peer groups. This effect is grounded in the fact that it is often more economical to learn social cues from observing others' behavior than to re-create them through individual experience. The result is a powerful effect of group influence, conformism, and social cueing. One implication of this phenomenon is that people tend to become more extreme in their views through exposure to groups holding similar beliefs. A constant diet of reinforcing opinion tends to move people further along the spectrum of belief to more polarized and extreme positions. Research on viral spread demonstrates that such social proof effects are a dominant explanatory variable. One study of "get out the vote" messages on Facebook found that the effectiveness

---

[18] *Social group* can include one's virtual network and physical social group; social group can also be expanded to mean one's political party. On this point of the importance of "social proof," see, for example, Flynn, Nyhan, and Reifler, 2017, p. 136.

[19]   Robert Cialdini, *Pre-Suasion: A Revolutionary Way to Influence and Persuade*, New York: Simon and Schuster, 2016, pp. 192–208.

[20]   Robert M. Bond, Christopher J. Fariss, Jason J. Jones, Adam D. I. Kramer, Cameron Marlow, Jaime E. Settle, and James H. Fowler, "A 61-Million-Person Experiment in Social Influence and Political Mobilization," *Nature*, Vol. 489, 2012.

[21]   Joseph M. Stubbersfield, Jamshid J. Tehrani, and Emma G. Flynn, "Serial Killers, Spiders and Cybersex: Social and Survival Information Bias in the Transmission of Urban Legends," *British Journal of Psychology*, Vol. 106, No. 2, 2015.

rose significantly when paired with images of friends who had already voted.[22]

## When the Incoming Information Fits in with an Individual's Preexisting Beliefs and Worldview

According to the closely related psychological theories of confirmation bias and motivated reasoning, people's evaluations of new information are shaped by their beliefs, hopes, and fears. People tend to seek out or favor information and arguments that confirm their existing views, and criticize those that do not.[23] When incoming information aligns with what people *want* to believe, they are more likely to believe it.[24] People interpret scientific evidence, for example, as more persuasive when it is consistent with their preexisting opinions.[25] Some

---

[22]  These dynamics are described in Alex Pentland, *Social Physics: How Good Ideas Spread—The Lessons from a New Science*, New York: Penguin Press, 2014, pp. 50–61, 64–65.

[23]  Lord, Ross, and Lepper, 1979; Kari Edwards and Edward E. Smith, "A Disconfirmation Bias in the Evaluation of Arguments," *Journal of Personality and Social Psychology*, Vol. 71, No. 1, 1996; Charles S. Taber and Milton Lodge, "Motivated Skepticism in the Evaluation of Political Beliefs," *American Journal of Political Science*, Vol. 50, No. 3, 2006; Stephan Lewandowsky, Ullrich K. H. Ecker, Colleen M. Seifert, Norbert Schwarz, and John Cook, "Misinformation and Its Correction: Continued Influence and Successful Debiasing," *Psychological Science in the Public Interest*, Vol. 13, No. 3, 2012, p. 112; Brendan Nyhan and Jason Reifler, "The Roles of Information Deficits and Identity Threat in the Prevalence of Misperceptions," *Journal of Elections, Public Opinion and Parties*, 2018. A series of studies in 2005 and 2006 found that when misinformed people were presented with corrections in news stories that contradicted their political predispositions, they rarely changed their minds. In fact, they often became even more strongly set in their beliefs (Nyhan and Reifler, 2012, p. 10). A similar 2007 study examined whether providing misled people with correct information about the proportion of immigrants in the U.S. population would affect their views on immigration. It did not. See John Sides and Jack Citrin, *How Large the Huddled Masses? The Causes and Consequences of Public Misperceptions About Immigrant Populations*, paper presented at the 65th Annual National Conference of the Midwest Political Science Association, Chicago, 2007.

[24]  Nyhan and Reifler, 2012.

[25]  Geoffrey D. Munro and Peter H. Ditto, "Biased Assimilation, Attitude Polarization, and Affect in Reactions to Stereotype-Relevant Scientific Information," *Personality and Social Psychology Bulletin*, Vol. 23, No. 6, 1997. As Paul Lazarsfeld and his colleagues found in their assessment of U.S. voters, people often seek out opinion leaders who reinforce their preexisting ideas when forming opinions. In the authors' words, "exposure is always selective;

studies suggest that confirmation bias has a physiological component: People experience a rush of dopamine when processing information that supports their beliefs,[26] and one study suggests that specific neural mechanisms are involved in rejecting information contrary to established beliefs.[27] Interestingly, this effect is not reliably counteracted by being well informed: Some studies have shown that it is in fact the *best-informed* people about a particular issue that hold most tightly to their established beliefs.[28] There is evidence that, at some point, even people engaged in motivated reasoning confront enough contrary information that they must revise their attitude toward a specific issue, but that threshold can be very high.[29]

### When the Information Is Embedded in an Existing, Wider Narrative that Lends Coherence and Persuasiveness to the Specific Story[30]

People search for frameworks to make sense of events, and general narratives that connect a number of developments with a causal logic provide one way of meeting that need. When individual facts are presented outside the scope of such narratives, they have less sticking

---

... a positive relationship exists between the people's opinions and what they chose to listen to or read;" Paul Lazarsfeld, Bernard Berelson, and Hazel Gaudet, *The People's Choice: How the Voter Makes Up His Mind in a Presidential Campaign*, New York: Duell, Sloan, and Pearce, 1948; referenced in Jowett and O'Donnell, 1999, p. 172. Frank Biocca, "Viewers' Mental Models of Political Messages: Toward a Theory of the Semantic Processing of Television," in Frank Biocca, ed., *Television and Political Advertising*, Vol. I: *Psychological Processes*, Hillsdale, N.J.: Lawrence Erlbaum Associates, 1991, p. 29; referenced in George C. Edwards III, *On Deaf Ears: The Limits of the Bully Pulpit*, New Haven, Conn.: Yale University Press, 2006, p. 208.

[26] Jack Gorman and Sara Gorman, *Denying to the Grave: Why We Ignore the Facts That Will Save Us*, New York: Oxford University Press, 2016.

[27] Jonas T. Kaplan, Sarah I. Gimbel, and Sam Harris, "Neural Correlates of Maintaining One's Political Beliefs in the Face of Counterevidence," *Scientific Reports*, Vol. 6, Article 39589, 2016.

[28] John M. Carey, Brendan Nyhan, Benjamin Valentino, and Mingnan Liu, "An Inflated View of the Facts? How Preferences and Predispositions Shape Conspiracy Beliefs About the Deflategate Scandal," *Research and Politics*, Vol. 3, No. 3, July-September 2016.

[29] Redlawsk, Civettini, and Emmerson, 2010.

[30] Lewandowsky et al., 2012, pp. 112–113.

power. Using such narratives as scaffolding for specific misinformation can be highly effective, however, especially when such narratives line up with people's preexisting beliefs.

### When an Individual Is Feeling Secure, in Control, and Not Threatened

The more threatened or vulnerable people feel, the less open they are to new information.[31] *Threat* can refer to a perceived threat to one's identity (abstract) or a perceived threat to one's well-being (tangible— for example, perceiving a threat posed by refugees). According to one study, the greater the perceived threat to an individual's identity posed by a challenge to a certain attitude, the more likely that individual is to double down on his or her position and even "proselytize" the belief being challenged.[32] The less threatened or attacked people feel, the more receptive they will be to new information. Yet other research shows that when people feel a lack of control over a situation, they may "compensate with strategies that lead to greater acceptance of misperceptions," which could include being more open to information that feeds into their fear and provides an explanation for it, even if that explanation is outlandish.[33] Indeed, there is strong research that fear is an especially potent catalyst of attitude change.[34]

---

[31]  Nyhan and Reifler, 2018.

[32]  David Gal and Derek D. Rucker, "When in Doubt, Shout! Paradoxical Influences of Doubt on Proselytizing," *Psychological Science*, Vol. 21, No. 11, 2010, pp. 1701–1707. See also Nyhan and Reifler, 2012, p. 11.

[33]  Nyhan and Reifler, 2012, p. 17. In a paper published in *Science* in 2008, two management professors found that inducing a lack of control in participants increased their tendency to see patterns where there were none, including perceiving the presence of conspiracy theories; Jennifer Whitson and Adam Galinsky, "Lacking Control Increases Illusory Pattern Perception," *Science*, Vol. 322, No. 5898, 2008.

[34]  Research conducted by Witte (1992) identified certain conditions under which fear appeals were most persuasive. She found that for fear appeals to be persuasive, they needed to both communicate the threatening information to the audience and suggest a means by which to reduce or eliminate the threat; Kim Witte, "Putting the Fear Back into Fear Appeals: The Extended Parallel Process Model," *Communication Monographs*, Vol. 59, No. 4, 1992, referenced in Jowett and O'Donnell, 1999, p. 174. In her later work with Mike Allen, Witte found that "strong fear appeals and high-efficacy messages produce the greatest

### When an Individual Trusts the Source Providing the Information and Perceives It to Be Credible

Source credibility is an important factor in determining receptivity to new information.[35] Rather than evaluating a story directly, people often use trust as a shortcut and look to see if someone credible believes it. They rely on that person's judgment to fill in the gaps in their knowledge.[36] In a related sense, when the information is coming from someone people perceive as similar to themselves, they are more likely to believe it (this argument draws on the psychological concept of *implicit egotism*, which asserts that people have an unconscious preference for things we associate with ourselves).[37]

### When Negative Information and Language Is Employed

Interestingly, multiple studies seem to indicate that negative information and language is more persuasive and has more staying power than positive information and language. There is evidence indicating

---

behavior change, whereas strong fear appeals with low-efficacy messages produce the greatest levels of defensive-responses." See Kim Witte and Mike Allen, "A Meta-Analysis of Fear Appeals: Implications for Effective Public Health Campaigns," *Health Education and Behavior,* Vol. 27, No. 5, 2000, p. 591.

35   Pratkanis and Aronson, 2001, pp. 121–153.

36   James Druckman, "On the Limits of Framing Effects: Who Can Frame?" *Journal of Politics,* Vol. 63, No. 4, 2001; Lewandowsky et al., 2012, p. 113. In a study examining the impact of message origin on the likelihood that a consumer will believe an advertisement's claim, the credibility of a source correlated with its ability to persuade; Shailendra Pratap Jain and Steven S. Posavac, "Prepurchase Attribute Verifiability, Source Credibility, and Persuasion," *Journal of Consumer Psychology,* Vol. 11, No. 3, 2001. Consumers were more likely to believe claims if the source was viewed as trustworthy or had experience with the product. Surveys show that an alarming number of Americans still believe that vaccines are dangerous, even though this theory was discredited years ago (Nyhan and Reifler, 2012, p. 7).

37   Chessen, 2017a. There is even research to support that someone is more likely to believe information coming from someone with an easily pronounceable name (according to the individual consuming the information); Eryn J. Newman, Mevagh Sanson, Emily K. Miller, Adele Quigley-McBride, Jeffrey L. Foster, Daniel M. Bernstein, and Maryanne Garry, "People with Easier to Pronounce Names Promote Truthiness of Claims," *PLOS One,* Vol. 9, No. 2, 2014; and that people are more likely to be persuaded to adopt a position by someone they find physically attractive; Alice H. Eagly and Shelly Chaiken, "An Attribution Analysis of the Effect of Communicator Characteristics on Opinion Change: The Case of Communicator Attractiveness," *Journal of Personality and Social Psychology,* Vol. 32, No. 1, 1975.

that belief perseverance and belief echoes are stronger with negative information.[38] One possible interpretation of some of these findings is that a critical dynamic in misinformation campaigns is the *relationship between forewarning and the first mover advantage*. If the defender can inoculate enough people with the right preventive techniques and information, it can deprive the information aggressor of the ability to implant a narrative that becomes very difficult to dislodge. A central finding is that social connections matter: People will trust information *from trusted sources*, rather than placing their trust in some abstract conception of accuracy or "truth." One Nielsen survey, for example, found that 83 percent of online users trust recommendations from family and friends, compared with other studies that show collapsing levels of trust in formal media institutions.[39]

This research would suggest a few basic conclusions for the utility of hostile social manipulation. Such campaigns will be more effective by working within established beliefs rather than trying to change them—to spark extreme actions by people of strong views, for example. They will be more effective if they can employ social proof as the basis of credibility. They will be successful if they use easy-to-grasp, graphically based presentations of information.[40] And they will have greater success the more they can repeat their message or restate the claimed facts, achieving a presumed credibility through repetition.

## Correcting Disinformation: Beyond the Backfire Effect

What we know from the social science analysis of attitudes and attitude change suggests that efforts to affect large-scale attitudes will be

---

[38]  Michael D. Cobb, Brendan Nyhan, and Jason Reifler, "Beliefs Don't Always Persevere: How Political Figures Are Punished When Positive Information About Them Is Discredited," *Political Psychology*, Vol. 34, No. 3, June 2013; Emily Thorson, "Belief Echoes: The Persistent Effects of Corrected Misinformation," *Political Communication*, Vol. 33, No. 3, 2016.

[39]  Todd C. Helmus and Elizabeth Bodine-Baron, "Empowering ISIS Opponents on Twitter," Santa Monica, Calif.: RAND Corporation, PE-227-RC, 2017, p. 2.

[40]  Lewandowsky, Ecker, and Cook, 2017, pp. 355–356.

less effective than more-targeted interventions that operate within specific echo chambers and attempt to use existing beliefs and seemingly credible sources of information to exacerbate social divisions. The difficulty in changing attitudes can also apply on the other side of the policy ledger, through efforts to correct misinformation or disinformation once it has been absorbed in a population.

Correcting such invalid beliefs can be extraordinarily difficult. Some studies, consistent with the general social science finding that people cling to existing beliefs, suggest that efforts to correct misimpressions simply do not work.[41] Corrections and attempts to change someone's mind can, in some cases, be counterproductive and reinforce confidence in the original attitude.[42] In some cases, the restatement of

---

[41] Lewandowsky et al., 2012, pp. 113–116; Brendan Nyhan and Jason Reifler, "Does Correcting Myths About the Flu Vaccine Work? An Experimental Evaluation of the Effects of Corrective Information," *Vaccine*, Vol. 33, No. 3, 2015b; Nyhan and Reifler survey some of the relevant literature in "Displacing Misinformation About Events: An Experimental Test of Causal Connections," *Journal of Experimental Political Science*, Vol. 2, No. 1, 2015a, p. 81; see also Flynn, Nyhan, and Reifler, 2017, pp. 130–131.

[42] There is a significant body of research to support this phenomenon: Lakoff (2014) posits that when we negate a frame, we evoke the frame, further embedding the undesirable association in an individual's mind; George Lakoff, "Mapping the Brain's Metaphor Circuitry: Metaphorical Thought in Everyday Reason," *Frontiers in Human Neuroscience*, Vol. 8, Article 958, 2014. Tormala and Petty (2002, 2004) demonstrated that when people resist persuasive attacks, they can become more certain of their initial attitudes; Zakary L. Tormala and Richard E. Petty, "What Doesn't Kill Me Makes Me Stronger: The Effects of Resisting Persuasion on Attitude Certainty," *Journal of Personal and Social Psychology*, Vol. 83, No. 6, 2002; Zakary L. Tormala and Richard E. Petty, "Source Credibility and Attitude Certainty: A Metacognitive Analysis of Resistance to Persuasion," *Journal of Consumer Psychology*, Vol. 14, No. 4, 2004. Nyhan and Reifler (2012) argue that corrections can fail due to such factors as motivated reasoning and limitations of memory and cognition, as well as identity factors, such as race and ethnicity. One study found that when "confronted with information compellingly debunking a preexisting belief, only a minute proportion of people—2% of participants in one study—explicitly acknowledged their beliefs were mistaken." Most instead "displayed some form of motivated reasoning by counterarguing against the refutation." See John Cook, Ullrich K. H. Ecker, and Stephan Lewandowsky, "Misinformation and How to Correct It," in Robert Scott and Stephan Kosslyn, eds., *Emerging Trends in the Social and Behavioral Sciences*, New York: John Wiley and Sons, 2015, p. 22. See also Tan et al., 2016. Belief perseverance appears to be more pronounced when negative information is corrected than when positive information is corrected; Cobb, Nyhan, and Reifler, 2013.

the incorrect information necessary to counteract it has turned out to be more influential than the subsequent correction.[43]

The strength of this *backfire effect*, however, has come under significant scrutiny. Some researchers have been unable to replicate the findings of the original studies, and some of those involved in the first backfire effect work have in effect recanted the generalizability of that effect. It turns out that trying to correct a misimpression does *not* always strengthen the original belief. Such efforts might have that effect in narrow circumstances, but it is possible to correct invalid information when done in the right way.[44] The broader truth about motivated reasoning remains strongly validated: People tend to adhere to preexisting beliefs even in the face of contrary evidence. It is just that trying to correct those beliefs does not necessarily *deepen* their commitment.

More recent evidence, therefore, suggests that this backfire effect may be specific to certain circumstances, and that fact-checking and debunking can have meaningful positive effects in combating misinformation if properly designed. (One study found that a critical criterion for the success of debunking efforts is the detail of the

---

Research shows that once a piece of information is encoded, which happens quickly, it has lingering effects on subsequent attitudes and reasoning even if the person receives new information and changes his or her mind (Nyhan and Reifler, 2012, pp. 12–14). People tend to continue to rely on outdated information even when it has been successfully retracted or corrected. Dr. Emily Thorson calls this phenomenon *belief echoes*, and has conducted several studies that demonstrate how exposure to a piece of negative information can influence attitudes, even if a correction is provided immediately, an individual fully accepts that correction, *and* that individual's political leanings predispose him or her to want to believe that correction. Thorson's research challenges the implicit assumption of well-intentioned fact-checkers that "correction will eliminate the misinformation's effect on attitudes," and suggests that even completely baseless accusations or criticism of an individual may result in "substantial reputational damage" (Thorson, 2016, p. 476). On the effects of beliefs on presidential elections, see also Edwards, 2006.

[43] Brendan Nyhan and Jason Reifler, "When Corrections Fail: The Persistence of Political Misperceptions," *Political Behavior*, Vol. 32, No. 2, 2010; Lewandowsky et al., 2012, pp. 119–120.

[44] A superb summary of the debate over the backfire effect is Daniel Engber, "LOL Something Matters," *Slate*, January 3, 2018.

countermessage.[45]) But it does appear that "the process of correcting misinformation is complex and remains incompletely understood."[46]

This flip side of many of the criteria governing the role of efforts to achieve attitude change suggests several parallel criteria for successfully displacing incorrect information, as follows:

- *Corrections should be preceded by warnings and inoculations (early warnings to target populations that they are being deceived).*[47] Studies seem consistent that groups of people who have been forewarned about the potential for misinformation are more on guard for it and do not allow it to become as embedded as when they are not warned.
- *The effort needs a counternarrative: A causal explanation that sets the corrective information in the context of a persuasive explanation for events.*[48] Efforts to counter misinformation cannot merely deny individual facts. These contests of fact and interpretation pose one narrative against another. The response must contest individual claims from the context of a more comprehensive story.
- *Retractions must be repeated.*[49] In line with the importance of repetition of facts, denials of misinformation have to be consistent and repeated.
- *Reputational effects or other social costs should be brought to bear.* There is some evidence that when political leaders were confronted by the potential that clinging to misinformation would

---

[45]  Man-pui Sally Chan, Christopher R. Jones, Kathleen Hall Jamieson, and Dolores Albarracín, "Debunking: A Meta-Analysis of the Psychological Efficacy of Messages Countering Misinformation," *Psychological Science*, Vol. 28, No. 11, 2017.

[46]  Chan et al., 2017.

[47]  Cook, Ecker, and Lewandowsky, 2015, p. 6; Pratkanis and Aronson, 2001, pp. 332–334; Lewandowsky et al., 2012, p. 116; Cook, Ecker, and Lewandowsky, 2017.

[48]  Nyhan and Reifler, 2015a, pp. 83, 90; Lewandowsky et al., 2012, pp. 117–118.

[49]  Cook, Ecker, and Lewandowsky, 2015, p. 6; Lewandowsky et al., 2012, pp. 116–117.

generate public opposition or "naming and shaming," they moderated their behavior.[50]

One proposed route to countering disinformation points to the potential value of media literacy programs.[51] These have been employed with some success in several countries. The optimal design and empirical effects of such programs needs more research, but the limited impact of the backfire effect and the beginnings of some success in these programs does indicate that enhancing public awareness of disinformation can be one part of an effective response.

## Factors Influencing Social Trust

As noted in the introduction to this chapter, the theme of trust is fundamental to an understanding of the implications of information societies and the risk of social manipulation. Campaigns of hostile manipulation are often targeted at trust in ways designed to undermine citizens' ontological security, faith in their social institutions, and the perceived reliability of facts. Social science research has examined the factors that tend to support or undermine social trust.

The literature is careful to distinguish different forms of trust, each of which could be the target of hostile social manipulation. A commonly discussed form is trust in social institutions, measured by recurrent public surveys. Another form is sometimes referred to as *generalized interpersonal trust*, which goes beyond faith in institutions to a residual degree of trust in the interpersonal interactions people conduct in society. Trust in political institutions and processes is sometimes

---

[50]  Brendan Nyhan and Jason Reifler, "The Effect of Fact-Checking on Elites: A Field Experiment on U.S. State Legislators," *American Journal of Political Science*, Vol. 59, No. 3, 2015c.

[51]  There is a growing literature on this issue. See, for example, Monica Bulger and Patrick Davison, *The Promises, Challenges, and Futures of Media Literacy*, New York: Data and Society Research Institute, February 2018; and Jennifer Fleming, "Media Literacy, News Literacy, or News Appreciation? A Case Study of the News Literacy Program at Stony Brook University," *Journalism and Mass Communication Educator*, Vol. 69, No. 2, 2014.

measured separately. In this brief section, we are interested in factors that influence levels of trust across these various types, though some factors are more relevant to one or more of the categories than others.[52]

One variable that seems associated with social trust across nations is fairness, in terms of procedural rules, application of rules and laws, and perceived fairness in outcomes. Radically unfair income distribution would violate this criterion.[53]

Other research suggests that the closely related issues of equality of opportunity and equality of economic outcomes are also associated with elevated levels of social trust.[54] High levels of corruption that impede equality of opportunity would constitute a direct assault on these avenues to social trust, as would, again, significant and rising levels of economic inequality. Research suggests a possible catch-22 in responding to such situations, from the standpoint of trust: Once trust has begun to collapse, a society becomes fragmented in ways that obstruct the exact sort of universalistic remedies to shore up perceived fairness that would be required to restore trust.

Somewhat related to the issue of fairness, there is some evidence that people's degree of confidence in the performance of social institutions affects their levels of institutional and broader social trust.[55] When the institutions of governance are perceived to be ineffective,

---

[52] Though the evidence is mixed, there is some research support for the idea that these various versions of trust are linked—i.e., that low generalized social trust is associated with low trust in institutions. See Sonja Zmerli and Ken Newton, "Social Trust and Attitudes Toward Democracy," *Public Opinion Quarterly*, Vol. 72, No. 4, 2008. See also Chan S. Suh, Paul Y. Chang, and Yisook Lim, "Spill-Up and Spill-Over of Trust: An Extended Test of Cultural and Institutional Theories of Trust in South Korea," *Sociological Forum*, Vol. 27, No. 2, 2012.

[53] Jong-sung You, "Social Trust: Fairness Matters More Than Homogeneity," *Political Psychology*, Vol. 33, No. 5, 2012.

[54] Bo Rothstein and Eric M. Uslaner, "All for All: Equality, Corruption, and Social Trust," *World Politics*, Vol. 58, No. 1, 2005.

[55] Natalia Letki, "Investigating the Roots of Civic Morality: Trust, Social Capital, and Institutional Performance," *Political Behavior*, Vol. 28, No. 4, 2006; Blaine G. Robbins, "Institutional Quality and Generalized Trust: A Nonrecursive Causal Model," *Social Indicators Research*, Vol. 107, No. 2, 2012.

this may affect not only people's faith in those institutions, but also their degree of social trust more broadly.

The nature of social ties and networks appears to affect levels of trust. Some research suggests that the quality of people's informal social contacts influences their degree of generalized social trust.[56] When people have well-developed informal networks that provide a sense of reliable social contacts, they gain greater faith in their ability to trust more broadly.

Comparative and cross-cultural research reveals that strong differences in levels of trust emerge between societies. In some Scandinavian countries, well over half of people respond in surveys that other people can generally be trusted, whereas in some low-trust countries (such as Brazil and Turkey) the figure hovers near the single digits.[57] Other research suggest that these differing levels of trust may even persist across generations, among the children and grandchildren of immigrants from these various regions.[58] Some research has therefore suggested that there is a cultural or ethnic component to social trust.

From an individual perspective, a person's life experiences have a significant effect on their degree of social trust.[59] People *learn* to trust (or not to trust) in part through the accumulation of their experiences, including both experience with out-groups and educational and parenting lessons.[60]

Social science research also points to strong evidence for the importance of social trust, and thus the significant dangers that could

---

[56] Jennifer L. Glanville, Matthew A. Andersson, and Pamela Paxton, "Do Social Connections Create Trust? An Examination Using New Longitudinal Data," *Social Forces*, Vol. 92, No. 2, 2013.

[57] Rothstein and Uslaner, 2005, p. 42.

[58] Eric M. Uslaner, "Where You Stand Depends upon Where Your Grandparents Sat: The Inheritability of Generalized Trust," *Public Opinion Quarterly*, Vol. 72, No. 4, 2008.

[59] Jian Huang, Henriëtte Maassen van den Brink, and Wim Groot, "College Education and Social Trust: An Evidence-Based Study on the Causal Mechanisms," *Social Indicators Research*, Vol. 104, No. 2, 2011.

[60] Jennifer L. Glanville and Pamela Paxton, "How Do We Learn to Trust? A Confirmatory Tetrad Analysis of the Sources of Generalized Trust," *Social Psychology Quarterly*, Vol. 70, No. 3, 2007.

arise if hostile social manipulation succeeds in undermining it. High levels of interpersonal and institutional trust appear to be an essential fuel for effectiveness of social institutions, contributing to such outcomes as effective governance, civic engagement, social cooperation on issues of shared concern, efficient economic transactions, higher economic growth, and much more.[61] In lower-trust situations, many more details of transactions must be spelled out, both economically and politically.[62] A reduction in trust could thus fuel intensified bureaucratization, regulatory overreach, and political ossification.

One risk for societies is that social manipulation strategies would be designed to build on natural trends in the infosphere to replace *generalized* trust, essential to greasing the operations of a society as a whole, with *particularized* trust, that is, trusting only one's in-group. An emphasis on particularized trust over generalized trust may be a cardinal risk of an era of social segmentation combined with informational echo chambers. Many of the recent Russian efforts to foment class, racial, and other divisions in the United States, for example, by stepping in to aid *both* sides in a dispute, have exactly this effect of elevating the particular over the general. The long-term consequences for advanced societies, if such a trend were to accelerate, could be severe.

## The Nature of Attitudes and the Shifting Infosphere

This summary of social science research on the role of information attitudes, attitude change, and persuasion suggests several overarching themes. Broadly speaking, core attitudes and beliefs are difficult to change, especially when they deal with foundational political or ideological issues. Influences from people's social networks and other trusted sources tend to have more effect than those from random or

---

[61]   Francis Fukuyama, *Trust: The Social Virtues and the Creation of Prosperity*, New York: Free Press, 1995. See also Stephen Knack and Philip Keefer, "Does Social Capital Have an Economic Payoff? A Cross-Country Investigation," *Quarterly Journal of Economics*, Vol. 112, No. 4, 1997.

[62]   Christian Bjørnskov and Stefan Voigt, "Constitutional Verbosity and Social Trust," *Public Choice*, Vol. 161, No. 1/2, 2014.

unknown sources. Information that is consistently repeated in large volume from multiple sources has more effect than claims by single sources. Once information has been accepted and internalized, it becomes difficult to displace.

Placing these themes alongside the trends in the infosphere discussed in Chapter Two produces several potential lessons. The role of echo chambers, or silos of belief, looms especially large: When people are operating in self-selected groups of perceived ideological fellows, they are more likely to accept what they hear uncritically. This fragmentation points to a potential risk of a spiral of echo chamber beliefs, with people becoming more entrenched in their silos over time. In a more fragmented, subjective information environment, credibility—essential to the acceptance of messages in some cases—becomes more difficult to establish. At the same time, the technologies of automated information dissemination now make it easier for individuals or small groups to achieve the "firehose" of claims from seemingly multiple sources that can enhance the acceptance of their claims.

This brief survey also places special emphasis on the role of social trust as well as the potential impact of hostile social manipulation and the more elaborate and dangerous practice of virtual societal aggression in undermining it. Many characteristics of a corrupted infosphere directly attack the foundations of social trust, such as faith in mediating institutions in society. Some take advantage of areas within personal networks, in which trust is likely to be strongest, to spread disinformation.

We now turn to a survey of technologies that will help to shape the future of information-based aggression. The report then compares all three foundations for understanding that future—the characteristics of the evolving infosphere, the relationship of information to attitudes and beliefs, and emerging technologies—to draw general lessons in the form of three scenarios depicting the ways in which these trends could unfold.

# CHAPTER FOUR

# Emerging Technologies

To understand the ways in which information-based aggression, including the current approaches to hostile social manipulation and the more elaborate potential for virtual societal warfare, could evolve in coming years, it is important to understand trends in key areas of technology related to this tool of statecraft. So far, social manipulation largely has reflected the marriage of simple cyberintrusions (to steal compromising information or gain access to key networks) with updated versions of propaganda and disinformation, such as social media advertising and the use of bots to spread viral messages. Increasingly, however, developments in the data-driven foundations of advanced societies and in cutting-edge AI and VR technologies could dramatically broaden the scope of available social manipulation techniques. The full range of these tools could pose an unprecedented danger of remote disruption of the workings of open societies.

Table 4.1 summarizes the technologies discussed in this chapter. In particular, these technologies open up the third realm of cyber-enabled information aggression mentioned in Chapter One. Much of the concern about cyberattacks has focused on interventions that cause physical damage (to critical infrastructure, for example). Most social manipulation to date has focused on updated versions of propaganda combined with some degree of political warfare—i.e., direct intervention to shape political outcomes. Increasingly, hostile social manipulation will be able to target the information foundations of digitized societies: the databases, algorithms, networked devices, and artificial

**Table 4.1**
**Emerging Technologies of Social Manipulation and Virtual Societal Aggression**

| Technology | Description |
|---|---|
| Precision targeting of influence | Techniques of targeting messages, often but not always through social media platforms, to very specific subgroups or, increasingly, even individuals |
| AI | Computer-based simulation of human thinking and behavior—for the purpose of this study, with the goal of gathering, evaluating, or manipulating information |
| Algorithmic decisionmaking | The use of algorithms to process data and produce automated recommendations or decisions |
| VR and AR | Systems that provide partial or complete artificial environments for users |
| IoT | Interlinked network of devices providing mutual awareness and sharing data |
| Voice-enabled interfaces | Systems that allow users to request information or direct actions through voice commands |
| Blockchain and distributed finance systems | Ledger-based, grassroots systems for exchanging money or information |
| Video and audio fakery | Programs capable of generating highly realistic fabricated video and audio |
| Surveillance systems | Technologies, such as facial recognition, allowing moment-to-moment tracking of social activities |

intelligence programs that will dominate the day-to-day operation of the society.

When conducted at massive scale with the intent to bring a society to its knees, these attacks would fall into the category of kinetic, physical cyberwarfare. But when undertaken gradually, piecemeal, and without attribution or even always awareness, such campaigns could degrade the target society's stability, confidence in its institutions, and morale of its people. Emerging technologies combined with the character of a digitized society create dramatic new risks of disruption of open societies, by state or nonstate actors.

## Precision Targeting of Influence

One relatively simple area of technological advance involves the further development of precision marketing techniques. Within a decade, those techniques will be significantly advanced, making possible much more consistent and targeted isolation of specific individuals with highly customized messages. These techniques will be employed primarily through social media platforms of various stripes, but also increasingly through other means of reaching individuals whose online behavior generates trails of data through their cellphones, their web browsers, and their shopping habits.

Advancements in "neurohacking," for example, will facilitate new capabilities in "neuromarketing," which targets people by manipulating their wants and desires through marketing and advertising that appeals to their mental state and emotional inclinations in real time. Facial recognition analysis technology will be able to gauge the emotions of several million users in multiple countries; emotion metric algorithms will be able to aggregate and interpret those emotions from facial recognition software.[1] Artificial agents linked to facial recognition systems and algorithms that can engage with people virtually will also become commonplace marketing tools and data collection mechanisms by 2035.[2] These techniques will empower targeted marketing on a moment-by-moment basis, reaching people at various moments of the day and during different sorts of activities, such as shopping, web browsing, or speaking on the phone.

By synthesizing active user inputs (such as user preferences, habits, behaviors, demonstrated interests, and other patterns revealed by the IoT) with facial and emotional recognition technology, and with emotional cues and sentiments derived from text conversations and social media activity, brands will be able to employ more optimized and

---

[1]   Radek Silhavy, Roman Senkerik, Zuzana Kominkova Oplatkova, Zdenka Prokopova, and Petr Silhavy, eds., *Artificial Intelligence Trends in Intelligent Systems: Proceedings of the 6th Computer Science On-Line Conference 2017 (CSOC2017)*, Vol. I, Cham, Switzerland: Springer International Publishing, 2017, p. 377.

[2]   Liesl Yearsley, "We Need to Talk About the Power of AI to Manipulate Humans," *MIT Technology Review*, June 5, 2017.

timely advertisements that appeal to an individual's mood-associated characteristics (which can be physical, behavioral, or spatial-temporal in nature).[3] The result will be a continued evolution of these tools, not merely targeting appeals by certain fixed demographic, attitudinal, or behavioral profiles, but also by changeable conditions such as mood, what people are being exposed to at a given time, health, level of tiredness, and much more. Sophisticated, AI-driven algorithms could allow the development of ultrasensitive marketing models to direct appeals to reach specific individuals at a specific time most likely to produce the desired effect.

## Artificial Intelligence

AI will be a primary facilitator of innovation over the next 10 to 15 years, affecting every industry as well as the nature of private individuals' daily activity in their physical environments and cyberspace. In this summary, we do not seek to explain or survey the full range of AI applications, but merely to provide a few examples of how AI could power the next generation of information-related social manipulation. It is possible, moreover, to exaggerate the degree of AI penetration into major economies, or what AI could accomplish in the hands of a social manipulator; its practical, real-world applications have been developing only gradually so far. In evaluating the implications for social manipulation and virtual societal aggression, therefore, it is important not to exaggerate the speed of AI advances or applications in the next decade.[4] Nonetheless, they are likely to be significant.

Simply put, AI involves the use of computing to simulate intelligent responses to inputs and processing of information, in such areas as pattern and speech recognition, strategic choice, visual perception,

---

3    CY Yam, "Emotion Detection and Recognition from Text Using Deep Learning," *Microsoft Developer Blog*, November 29, 2015.

4    The distinction between short-term and long-term applications is made in Michael C. Horowitz, "Artificial Intelligence, International Competition, and the Balance of Power," *Texas National Security Review*, Vol. 1, No. 3, May 2018, pp. 41–42.

and translation. "Artificial intelligence is the field of study devoted to making machines intelligent. Intelligence measures a system's ability to determine the best course of action to achieve its goals in a wide range of environments."[5] Machine learning is the application of algorithms or other processing instructions to evaluate and manipulate data, where the machine can iterate its performance and "learn" patterns and strategies to improve over time by processing numerous examples.

AI systems have demonstrated a growing aptitude to beat humans at games of mounting complexity, such as checkers, chess, Go, and even poker, a game in which players have only incomplete information. The first AI poker champion, called Libratus, defeated leading human players in 2017. The machine-learning potential of AI was demonstrated in the context of the game Go: A second-generation AI system, AlphaGo Zero, played 4.9 million games against itself in the span of three days, and became sufficiently competent that it then defeated the first-generation program, AlphaGo, 100 straight times.[6]

Recent studies point to a number of possible developments in AI in the next decade.[7] These developments include the use of algorithms that can process large data sets with only a single pass, or that can run on the data in unsupervised processing efforts. Machine-learning processes that simulate neural networks, developed through "deep learning," have and will continue to accelerate advancements in object and activity recognition in images and videos, and sensory perception in audio, speech, and natural language processing. When integrated with behavioral psychology, AI will begin to enable robots, artificial agents, and programs to learn by "experience-driven sequential decision-making." AI applications have already advanced natural language processing linked to speech recognition capabilities and will continue to do so, likely enabling enhanced oral communication

---

[5]   Paul Scharre and Michael C. Horowitz, *Artificial Intelligence: What Every Policymaker Needs to Know*, Washington, D.C.: Center for a New American Security, June 2018, p. 4.

[6]   Scharre and Horowitz, 2018, p. 8.

[7]   Peter Stone et al., *Artificial Intelligence and Life in 2030: One Hundred Year Study on Artificial Intelligence*, Stanford, Calif.: Stanford University, September 2016, pp. 14–17.

between humans and artificial agents or systems and real-time translation of mainstream languages.

In the related field of robotics, AI is already catalyzing a long-term push to humanize robots and produce robotic entities capable of many simple human work tasks, which will involve a synthesis of new technologies and capabilities in AI, IoT, and video and audio production. We are at the same place with robotics today that we were with the internet 20 years ago.[8] Over the next 20 years, robots are likely to begin displacing some human employees in the elderly caretaker, home services, and transportation industries, as well as the classroom and workplace, with sensory perception, object recognition, spatial reasoning and dexterity, contextual understanding, emotional understanding, and mimicry capabilities. This process will only be under way within the next five to ten years, though various studies suggest that up to half of the workforce could be displaced by robotic replacements within 20 to 30 years.[9]

In a more near-term way, AI integration with economic and social computing is likely to allow for automated systems with advanced algorithms to gauge, record, analyze, and predict social and economic choices and preferences of individuals based on their activity (both online and, increasingly, offline via wearable or implantable devices; increased use of the IoT; surveillance and "sousveillance"; and their friends', coworkers', and family's activity). The first elements of this trend are already in place in the AI-driven advertising platforms of large technology companies.

For the time being, AI is most relevant to tasks with mountains of available data and clear criteria for judging success. The primary limitation of current AI applications is that they remain heavily task- and context-dependent, not able to generalize their analytical processes. An interesting and growing challenge for AI, especially when processes involve deep learning, is that programmers cannot be sure of why AI makes the choices that it does. In some cases, AI has "gamed the

8    Alec Ross, *The Industries of the Future*, New York: Simon and Schuster, 2016, p. 28.

9    Darrell M. West, "Will Robots and AI Take Your Job? The Economic and Political Consequences of Automation," *Brookings Institution*, April 18, 2018.

system" to achieve certain outcomes, such as by forcing pauses or rule changes in games to persistently "win."[10] These unpredictable strategies of AI-driven processes may limit its applicability in some areas, such as medical technology. If an AI-driven diagnostic or treatment process were to try such end runs, it could produce dangerous results.

Through these and other advances, AI will have applications in hundreds of industries and areas. Of most relevance to the areas of social manipulation and virtual societal aggression are the ways in which AI could be able to power the automated creation of digital content and highly accurate virtual interactive experiences that mimic real life. AI is already beginning to spawn primitive automated content in the form of simple cartoons, but over time AI-driven computation will be able to generate, and populate social media with, thousands of messages and audio or video files.

A second application of AI relevant to social manipulation is lifelike interactive platforms, often known as chatbots or "conversational AI."[11] In its current form, this technology is driving the multiple interactive assistants on the market today, such as Alexa and Siri, but they remain largely question-and-response engines. To the extent that AI can create systems able to interact with users in a way that closely mimics actual human conversations and that can be replicated at scale at very little cost (one example under development is Google Duplex, discussed below), the entire social media arena, and wider infosphere, would be transformed. AI-driven platforms are likely to develop broader abilities. One AI system recently demonstrated an ability to engage in arguments by assembling parts of arguments people have made and specific facts.[12] Such conversational or interactive AI begin to suggest the risks of the technology: They could easily power hostile chatbots and seemingly human interactions in social media. Indeed, some of the major obstacles to the integration of AI into hard-edged national security applications, such as the need to provide for complex system

---

[10]  Scharre and Horowitz, 2018, p. 12.

[11]  James Vlahos, "Fighting Words," *Wired*, March 2018.

[12]  Will Knight, "This AI Program Could Beat You in an Argument—But It Doesn't Know What It's Saying," *MIT Technology Review*, June 19, 2018b.

integration of AI-driven capabilities with others, do not exist for informational applications.[13] In the national security realm, AI could be applied piecemeal, used for specific purposes as they become feasible.

Another information-based risk is that some AI applications, like most digital processes, are hackable. As two scholars argued in a recent paper, "Malicious actors who deliberately seek to subvert AI systems can potentially manipulate these AI safety problems, creating a new category of risks." The study points out that bad actors could corrupt the data on which AI calculations depend or introduce new rules for the algorithms to follow; in some cases, hackers have introduced "fooling images" that skewed the recognition processes the AI system was applying to image databases. Or they could "feed the system data that causes it to learn incorrect behaviors."[14]

## Algorithmic Decisionmaking

Another emerging area of computing technology relevant to social manipulation is the use of algorithms to process information and make decisions, forecasts or estimates. Such algorithms are most advanced in certain search, marketing, and social media platforms today. In their basic forms, they are simply scripts that involve instructions of what to do when the program encounters a given situation or pattern.[15] Google makes extensive use of algorithms to shape search results based on prior

---

13  For a discussion of these obstacles see Horowitz, 2018, p. 44. See also M. L. Cummings, Heather M. Roff, Kenneth Cukier, Jacob Parakilas, and Hannah Bryce, *Artificial Intelligence and International Affairs: Disruption Anticipated*, London: Chatham House, 2018, p. v.

14  Scharre and Horowitz, 2018, pp. 14–15.

15  Algorithmic solutions can be used as the foundation for AI applications, but simple algorithms are not AI. As one definition puts it, "An algorithm is a set of instructions—a preset, rigid, coded recipe that gets executed when it encounters a trigger. AI on the other hand—which is an extremely broad term covering a myriad of AI specializations and subsets—is a group of algorithms that can modify its algorithms and create new algorithms in response to learned inputs and data as opposed to relying solely on the inputs it was designed to recognize as triggers"; Kaya Ismail, "AI vs. Algorithms: What's the Difference?" *CMS Wire*, October 26, 2018.

patterns. Amazon employs them to make suggestions of other products that customers might be interested in buying.

Increasingly, however, algorithms are being used to generate optimal outcome decisions in many areas of social life. They are also already "being used to determine who makes parole, who's approved for a loan, and who gets hired for a job."[16] Frank Pasquale, in a study of algorithmic decisionmaking in multiple fields, concludes that the internet and banking sectors use these tools extensively. He argues that

> [t]he conclusions they come to—about the productivity of employees, or the relevance of websites, or the attractiveness of investments—are determined by complex formulas designed by legions of engineers and guarded by a phalanx of lawyers.

Pasquale concludes simply that "authority is increasingly expressed algorithmically."[17]

As Cathy O'Neil has put it, the emerging pattern is that

> oceans of behavioral data . . . will feed straight into artificial intelligence systems. And these will remain, to human eyes, black boxes. . . . These automatic programs will increasingly determine how we are treated by the other machines, the ones that choose the ads we see, set prices for us, line us up for a dermatologist appointment, or map our routes. They will be highly efficient, seemingly arbitrary, and utterly unaccountable.[18]

And they will be vulnerable to many forms of manipulation.

One area in which such decisionmaking is already beginning to have an effect is in medicine. One doctor recently argued that the emerging reality is that "the patient in the hospital bed is just the icon,

---

[16] Will Knight, "The Dark Secret at the Heart of AI," *MIT Technology Review*, April 11, 2017. See also Kartik Hosanagar and Vivian Jair, "We Need Transparency in Algorithms, But Too Much Can Backfire," *Harvard Business Review*, July 25, 2018.

[17] Frank Pasquale, *The Black Box Society: The Secret Algorithms That Control Money and Information*, Cambridge, Mass.: Harvard University Press, 2015, pp. 6, 8. See also Schneier, 2018, pp. 82–87.

[18] O'Neil, 2016, p. 173.

a place holder for the real patient who is not in the bed but in the computer. That virtual entity gets all our attention." He cites studies showing that doctors already spend more than twice as much time reviewing electronic medical records as they do in personal contact with patients.[19] Over time, this system will advance to the use of algorithms to make decisions independently of doctors. Mount Sinai Hospital in New York has used algorithmic analysis to process data in patient records and forecast disease.[20] Medical chatbots are becoming more common and have the potential to become the default interface between many people, especially those at the lower end of the socioeconomic spectrum, and the medical community.[21]

These tools pose several risks. First, to the extent that deep learning processes allow computers to discover patterns on their own, their programmers simply do not know how the algorithms actually work.[22] The result is that algorithmic decisionmaking "in human resources, health, and banking, just to name a few," is "quickly establishing broad norms that exert upon us something very close to the power of law. If a bank's model of a high-risk borrower, for example, is applied to you, the world will treat you as just that, a deadbeat—even if you're horribly misunderstood."[23] People will be rejected for loans and jobs for reasons they do not understand; more broadly, the societal pattern that could result might become a "rule of scores."[24] One example is the area of hiring, where personality tests are now being used in "60 to 70 percent of prospective workers in the United States."[25]

---

[19]   Abraham Verghese, "How Tech Can Turn Doctors into Clerical Workers," *New York Times Magazine*, May 16, 2018.

[20]   Knight, 2017.

[21]   Douglas Heaven, "Dr. Bot Will See You Now," *MIT Technology Review*, November/December 2018, p. 22.

[22]   Knight, 2017.

[23]   O'Neil, 2016, pp. 29, 51.

[24]   Pasquale, 2015, p. 191.

[25]   O'Neil, 2016, p. 108.

Another major risk is that the databases behind these tools, as well as the algorithms themselves, are typically proprietary. Companies hold the available information about how they work and do not share the basis of the results. This environment creates issues of fairness and lack of governance, as well as magnifying the overall problem of trust that is so central to a digitized, data-fueled era. People will not know the true basis on which decisions affecting their lives are being made, creating a risk of rising grievances.[26]

Finally, as with all coded information processes, these algorithms are at least theoretically hackable. States or individuals intent on causing disruption, frustration, and anxiety could go into a company's hiring algorithm, a bank's loan-approval algorithm, or a university's admissions algorithm and tweak it slightly, not enough to generate immediate evidence of tampering (especially if the algorithm is the partly opaque result of machine learning), but enough to produce results that seem random and unfair. Hackers could attempt to manipulate the data being used to train algorithms in the developmental phase.[27] Already advertisers and some others have experimented with gaming search engine algorithms indirectly by discovering their patterns and posting or designing material to take advantage of them. Future hacks may be far more direct and malicious.

## Virtual and Augmented Reality

Another area of emerging technology is the field of VR and AR. Various forms of both are coming on line even now: AR applications for cellphones are emerging, for example, that add various features to the world as "seen" through the phone's camera, as well as rapidly accelerated technologies for VR headsets. Though the technologies have been in development for decades, recent surveys of business leaders and technologists in the field suggest that they may be on the brink of

---

[26]  Pasquale, 2015, p. 25.

[27]  Kira Radinsky, "Your Algorithms Are Not Safe from Hackers," *Harvard Business Review*, January 5, 2016.

becoming mainstream.[28] One recent PwC study suggested a technology field on the verge of an explosion, projecting that there will be over 55 million VR headsets in active use in the United States by 2022.[29]

Possible uses of AR and VR are legion. Many are pure entertainment, such as more immersive experiences for movies, music, and video games. But developers are also at work on VR applications to allow people to work in collaborative networks; eventually, some proportion of the workforce is likely to use VR headsets to "be" in a working environment virtually.[30] VR can be used for design purposes and extensively in education, allowing users to "walk" through imagined spaces (such as a house design) or historical ones (such as ancient Rome).

Such technologies can empower a new field of highly targeted marketing that markets an experience rather than a specific product, service, or brand. Integrating new capabilities in AI, VR, and AR (such as smart glasses and lenses) will deliver users a new immersive realm that bridges the digital and real worlds and can be tailored to a person's individual preferences, interests, mood, surroundings, and psychological desires.[31]

The potential for aggressive social manipulation of VR and AR is obvious, though may not be straightforward. Studies have already warned that emerging VR systems could be vulnerable to hacks.[32] Hackers could insert additional details into VR environments designed to create stress or skew the results and produce frustration.[33] They

---

28   Alex Aharanov, "What Is the Future of Augmented and Virtual Reality?" *Jabil Blog*, March 27, 2018.

29   Ashley Rodriguez, "In Five Years, VR Could Be as Big in the US as Netflix," *Quartz*, June 6, 2018.

30   Peter Rubin, "You'll Go to Work in Virtual Reality," *Wired*, June 2018, p. 61.

31   Jayson DeMers, "7 New Technologies Shaping Online Marketing for the Better (We Hope)," *Forbes*, August 15, 2016.

32   Alfred Ng, "VR Systems Oculus Rift, HTC Vive May Be Vulnerable to Hacks," *CNET*, April 17, 2018.

33   Andrew J. Andrasik, *Hacking Humans: The Evolving Paradigm with Virtual Reality*, SANS Institute, Information Security Reading Room, November 2017. See also Eric E. Sabelman and Roger Lam, "The Real-Life Dangers of Augmented Reality," *IEEE Spectrum*, June 23, 2015.

could find ways to send messages subliminally, seeding users with certain views or disruptions. Broadly speaking, VR and AR offer whole virtual worlds that manipulators can hack and modify to achieve their desired goals.

## Internet of Things

The IoT refers to the increasingly dense interactive network of smart technologies in our homes, on (and in) our bodies, and in the physical environment. Within a decade, most newly manufactured objects will be able to transmit or receive data, including cars, home appliances, wearable devices, and even people: the first implantable smartphone is projected to be commercially available by 2030 and will be able to transmit real-time biological information, as well as provide communications and internet functions familiar to us today.[34]

The IoT will become one of the primary data generators, providing information on every aspect of human and machine activity, behavior, life patterns, preferences, communications, relationships, and locations. The applications and examples are nearly endless: smart food networks linking refrigerators, cabinets, stores, and producers; smart cities integrating sensor data on automobiles, pedestrians, weather, and more; precision agriculture, including livestock monitoring; smart energy management tying together thermostats, energy grids, weather forecasts, and more; and industrial IoT deployments in manufacturing. Human beings will be increasingly tied into these networks, with wearable devices, implanted sensors, and environmental sensors feeding reams of data about our location, heart rate, temperature, pulse, emotional state, and much more.

"Smart city" technologies being developed today are likely to run on a series of IoT-connected sensors that record, interpret, respond to, and predict activity in real time in urban transportation, security,

---

[34] Global Agenda Council on the Future of Software and Society, *Deep Shift: Technology Tipping Points and Social Impact*, Cologny, Switzerland: World Economic Forum, 2015, p. 8.

energy, public health, and critical infrastructure.[35] Smart lights (street lights and traffic signals equipped with motion sensors and receptors) will turn on or off, red or green, or adjust to report delays or issues to IoT-linked cars and pedestrians. Similar IoT sensory capabilities linked to parking meters and parking lots will alert IoT-linked cars to open spaces.

Smart vehicles will eventually include self-driving cars, though even before fully driverless cars and trucks become common, vehicles linked to the IoT will be able to detect, diagnose, report, and eventually self-repair mechanical problems; call 911 and solicit emergency response units when accidents occur; synchronize Global Positioning System (GPS) capabilities with smart city sensory systems and other vehicles to optimize driving time, route, and parking; and connect to personal IoT networks at home and the office to alert other devices to turn on or off in anticipation of a person's next movement or activity. Meanwhile, smart cameras will provide omnipresent and real-time video surveillance and new emergency response capabilities.

Estimates suggest that by 2030 there will be over a trillion sensors connected to the IoT, accounting for half of all internet traffic to and from homes.[36] The overall market for IoT-enabled devices may exceed $1 trillion in that same time frame, with an additional $750 billion spent on IoT connectivity modules. The emergence of this dense network will also propel the expansion of new network technologies that increase bandwidth: Continuous and high-quality streaming access will become a requisite function and standard technology in homes, offices, and public spaces to support the IoT.[37]

There is sometimes a tendency to think of the IoT as primarily linking devices in the home or businesses, but it will also increasingly integrate human beings, including their wearable or implanted sensors. IoT "mindshare technologies" are being developed to connect people to their devices, as well as their devices to other devices, by facilitating and

---

[35] Codrin Arsene, "IoT Ideas That Will Soon Revolutionize Our World in 8 Ways," *Y Media Labs*, November 24, 2016.

[36] Global Agenda Council on the Future of Software and Society, 2015, pp. 7–8.

[37] Global Agenda Council on the Future of Software and Society, 2015, p. 7.

managing their data exchanges and communications. A person's blood pressure sensor will be linked to his or her refrigerator, smart toilet, and environmental sensors of mood and stress; the latter can be tied to virtual personal assistants to guide the suggestion of entertainment.

The emergence of an IoT obviously carries enormous potential for both classic cyberaggression and social manipulation. Schneier has written of the security vulnerabilities inherent in the fact that "everything is becoming a computer." He argues that the United States and other advanced economies are "reaching a fundamental shift that is due to scale and scope . . . . Everything is becoming one complex hyperconnected system in which, even if things don't interoperate, they're on the same network and affect each other."[38] He catalogs dozens of such interconnection vulnerabilities, such as attackers getting into people's Gmail accounts through their refrigerators; ransomware being inserted into the software controlling home thermostats, effectively holding the dwelling hostage; and using insecure systems to access hotel electronic door keys. Schneier explains that one problem is that the imperfect but critical practice of information security monitoring, updating, and patching characteristics of the software industry will not be followed by manufacturers for whom software is an appendage—toilets, cars, home security systems—leading to far greater vulnerabilities even than in traditional software.

In more extreme forms of attack, aggressors could seek to bring down major components of the IoT, undermining the networks of information, sensing, decisionmaking, and supply that it will come to represent.[39] But in more nuanced forms of social manipulation, states or nonstate actors could merely seek to introduce wide-ranging disruption and inefficiencies, as well as work to undermine trust in social systems. They could change the settings on sensors or distribution channels, making people get the wrong sort of groceries or home supplies. In more sinister versions, aggressors could alter the medical data

---

[38]  Schneier, 2018, pp. 3, 7.

[39]  On the risks of both large-scale digital infrastructure and IoT attack, see Justin Sherman and Deb Crawford, "Securing America's Connected Infrastructure Can't Wait," *War on the Rocks*, December 4, 2018.

being collected so that algorithms in the system make incorrect diagnoses of illnesses and prescribe or supply incorrect medicines. They could change settings in traffic systems or automated cars to reduce rather than increase the efficiency of traffic patterns, or cause accidents and even deaths. They could change settings or issue destructive commands to research robots in laboratories or personal homes around the world.[40] Examples of attacks already include hacking of self-driving cars, malware that took control of internet-enabled cameras, and many more.[41]

The IoT is gradually coming to represent a dense network of sensing, information exchange, and decisionmaking that will provide the essential data collection and networking scaffolding of advanced societies. As such, it will represent one of the most elaborate opportunities for social manipulators seeking the ability to undermine trust and faith in social institutions and degrade people's larger sense of ontological security.

## Voice-Enabled Interfaces

The explosive growth of voice-activated assistants—such as the Amazon Echo (Alexa), Google Home, Apple Siri, and SONOS One—is changing the way people interact with the technologies around them. Especially when paired with increasingly effective AI capable of human-like interactions and even conversations, these voice-activated systems will become the default means by which people search for information, direct the operations of the surrounding IoT, and even make decisions. While they are in some sense merely a subset of other technological categories, they will become such a critical gateway between citizens and the larger infosphere that their implications—and vulnerabilities to manipulation—should be understood on their own terms.

---

[40]  Will Knight, "Hordes of Research Robots Could Be Hijacked for Fun and Sabotage," *MIT Technology Review*, July 24, 2018c.

[41]  Adam Segal, *The Hacked World Order: How Nations Fight, Trade, Maneuver, and Manipulate in the Digital Age*, New York: PublicAffairs, 2016, pp. 99–101.

Recent estimates suggest that voice-powered speakers will reach more than half of U.S. households by 2022, with over 175 million such speakers in operation. But voice-activated assistants will mostly be deployed in other systems: Some five *billion* such assistant interfaces will be operative worldwide by 2022, mostly working through cellphones. In the United States alone, the total number of such assistant-powered devices is expected to roughly double between 2017 and 2022, reaching 870 million, or more than two for every American.[42]

Such interactive systems depend on voice recognition technology, and it has been developing as rapidly as the physical interfaces. A major challenge has been to develop systems capable of easily understanding "natural language": the often-idiosyncratic ways in which people phrase common ideas or requests. Nonetheless, voice recognition software can now operate with less than a 5 percent error rate.[43]

The interactive engine—essentially, the voice on the other end of the conversation with a voice-activated assistant—is being powered by increasingly sophisticated AI that is becoming more and more adept at sounding like an actual human interlocutor. (This is the same family of AI applications that will increasingly be used to power advanced chatbots, such as interactive therapeutic systems.) One example of such an emerging technology is Google Duplex, a natural-language system powered by AI and being developed to power telephone and other audio interactions. It is capable of carrying out interactive conversations with tremendous degrees of apparent human-voice accuracy in closed domains, such as setting appointments.[44]

There remain strict limits to the effectiveness of such technologies. Several companies have been trying to develop an AI-driven chatbot capable of the seemingly prosaic task of scheduling a meet-

---

[42] Sarah Perez, "Voice-Enabled Smart Speakers to Reach 55% of U.S. Households by 2022, Says Report," *TechCrunch*, November 8, 2017. See also J. Walter Thompson Intelligence, *Speak Easy*, New York, June 2017.

[43] Clark Boyd, "The Past, Present and Future of Speech Recognition Technology," *The Startup*, January 10, 2018.

[44] See Yaniv Leviathan, "Google Duplex: An AI System for Accomplishing Real-World Tasks Over the Phone," *Google AI Blog*, May 8, 2018.

ing, and the task has proven exceedingly difficult, with AI unable to distinguish basic common-sense implications of people's requests.[45] A standing technology challenge to create a chatbot that can fool a panel of human judges—by making them believe they are interacting with a real person—has not yet come especially close to success. Yet people report significant degrees of emotional attachment even to the relatively primitive chatbots that exist today, and chatbots already dispense medical and legal advice and serve as the initial gateway to many customer service interactions.[46] As the technology improves, it will be paired with voice-enabled interfaces to create a fundamentally new interactive experience.

Increasingly, these systems are achieving the ability to sense people's emotional states. Amazon is developing voice analysis capabilities to allow its Alexa concierge to understand the speaker's emotional state. SONOS has "filed a patent for technology that could customize playlists based on the emotion in [a listener's] voice or biometric data obtained from a wearable device, like perspiration or heart rate, all cross-referenced" with the listener's music history.[47]

Over time, these portals are likely to shift from a distinct category of curious (and often inaccurate) computerized ask-and-response technologies to become the basic portal through which people conduct most of their interactions with the larger technology systems around them. (Industry leaders have begun to refer to this trend as the creation of "ambient computing."[48]) Many activities, including dictating term papers, making internet searches, ordering take-out, setting thermostats, dictating the parameters of diet (and the orders sent to grocery stores), and having dialogues about medical diagnoses, will take place

---

45   John H. Richardson, "AI Chatbots Try to Schedule Meetings—Without Enraging Us," *Wired*, May 24, 2018.

46   See, for example, Arielle Pardes, "What My Personal Chat Bot Is Teaching Me About AI's Future," *Wired*, November 12, 2017.

47   Nitasha Tiku, "We'll Share Our Emotional State as Willingly as We Share Our Photos," *Wired*, June 2018, p. 55.

48   Paul Cutsinger, "Mark Cuban: Voice, Ambient Computing Are the Future. Developers Should Get in Now," *Amazon Alexa Blog*, March 25, 2019.

through this portal. The essential interactive medium between people and technology, in other words, is in the process of shifting from digital input (typing, point-and-click, and touch screens) to verbal.

The rise of voice-enabled interfaces will create multiple opportunities for hostile actors to intervene in the process and create social disruptions. They could simply degrade the effectiveness of software driving the AI interface, generating frustration on the part of the user. In more sinister scenarios, manipulators—with scalable interventions, themselves powered by AI—could hijack the interfaces and have them deliver responses that range from inaccurate (an invalid response to a simple information query), to disruptive (giving incorrect information about the location of a restaurant), to actively hostile (persistently judgmental or dismissive responses to queries). To the extent that social manipulators could gain even partial control of this emerging voice-enabled "ambient computing" environment, they will be able to shape a society's default interactive channels with the technologies that dominate its lives.

## Blockchain and Distributed Ledger Systems

Distributed ledger technology will emerge as the primary technology for tracking when, how, and with what or whom devices communicate, interact, or transact. It will enable automated peer-to-peer, device-to-device contractual behavior and provide the platform for trustworthy digital infrastructure.[49] A *blockchain* is a decentralized, distributed, and mutually verified ledger that could reflect many sorts of exchanges: money (such as Bitcoin), equity certificates, or instructions, for example. The goal is to "drastically reduce the cost of trust by means of a radical, decentralized approach to accounting—and, by extension, create a new way to structure economic organizations."[50]

---

[49] "Blockchain and the Internet of Things: The IoT Blockchain Opportunity and Challenge," *i-SCOOP*, September 2016 (updated February 2018).

[50] Michael J. Casey and Paul Vigna, "In Blockchain We Trust," *MIT Technology Review*, April 9, 2018.

The real value in current digital and cryptocurrencies, such as Bitcoin, is not actually the currency but the idea of a public ledger that logs all transactions with decentralized regulation and involves no central bank, nation-state, or any central institutional control of any kind.[51] By 2030, monitored blockchains (enhanced by AI algorithmic monitoring and analysis systems) will provide the basis for financial oversight, tracking, reporting, and surveillance. Nearly three-fourths of respondents to a 2015 survey of information and communications technology executives and experts said they expected that, by 2025, tax will have been collected "for the first time by a government via a blockchain."[52] If such systems work as intended, they ought to reduce the potential for social manipulation of shared ledgers of information: Because of the intense cryptography and especially the ongoing mutual verification by distributed users, it ought to be very difficult for hackers to alter blockchain records.

But blockchain technology also opens the door to an increasing virtualization of economic value in society, which could render nations much more vulnerable to outside tampering with their infospheres. Blockchain technology creates the potential for *digital assets*: uniquely identifiable, noncopyable assets that exist only in digital form, such as Bitcoin. Any form of value can theoretically be digitized by such technologies. Yet if we follow the rule that anything that is programmable is also hackable, the potential for hostile social manipulators to find ways past the cryptography and distributed controls of a blockchain to alter these instructions must be taken very seriously.

## Video and Audio Fakery

A critical area of emerging technology that can complement current efforts at social manipulation, particularly in spreading misinformation or disinformation, is the capability to generate audio and video

---

51  Ross, 2017, pp. 98–103; Global Agenda Council on the Future of Software and Society, 2015, p. 24.

52  Global Agenda Council on the Future of Software and Society, 2015, p. 26.

images that represent false events as real. It is easy to imagine the potential for such technologies to fuel next-generation manipulation campaigns: distributed audio of private statements of national leaders; video of explosive events designed to prompt public outrage; or audio and video designed to remove the culpability of an aggressor by providing alternative versions of events (such as a video that "proved" Chinese vessels had not rammed a fishing boat of another claimant in the South China Sea). We stand at the cusp of an era when it will be extremely difficult for average people to distinguish what is real from what is invented in the audio and video information they encounter.

## Fabricated Audio

Computer-generated audio is not a new phenomenon. There are a wide variety of services, from online translators to applications on mobile phones, that provide computer-generated audio by linking a collection of short recorded speech fragments to create a sentence.[53]

Digital voices like these however, are currently limited by the sentence fragments memorized and the absence of natural tendencies found in speech, such as emotion and sentence flow, often leading the voice to sound a bit synthetic.[54] This limitation makes discerning between the audio of a real person versus that produced by a computer simpler. In comparison, audio generation technology that is currently being developed works differently, using recent breakthroughs in neural networks to learn and mimic the properties of human speech in an effort to create a more natural-sounding voice.[55] In addition to improving the overall quality of computer-generated speech, technology is under development to replicate any given individual's voice from scratch, which could be used to make anyone say anything that the manipulators want. One example of this software is being developed by Adobe, which in 2016 presented a technology demo of a software called VoCo. Referred to as the Photoshop of audio, the software

---

[53] "Fake News: You Ain't Seen Nothing Yet," *The Economist*, July 1, 2017.

[54] "Fake News: You Ain't Seen Nothing Yet," 2017.

[55] Avi Selk, "This Audio Clip of a Robot as Trump May Prelude a Future of Fake Human Voices," *Washington Post*, May 3, 2017.

demonstrated the capability to delete words from an audio recording or add words by entering new text, which the software then generated by mimicking the speaker.[56] According to one of the developers, the software requires a 20-minute recording to be able to understand the makeup of the voice, after which it can replicate and modify the recording.[57] Though there is no time estimate for when the company may release the technology, the software demonstrated the capability to modify audio, and journalists in the field expect this capability only to improve.

The firm Lyrebird is developing similar capabilities. Lyrebird's software uses artificial neural networks to learn "the pronunciations of characters, phonemes, and words in any voice by listening to hours of spoken audio. From there it can generate completely new sentences and even add different intonations and emotions."[58] But whereas Adobe's VoCo requires 20 minutes of audio, Lyrebird's system can adapt to any voice based only on one-minute samples after learning how to generate speech.[59] As far as time estimates, Lyrebird states that its technology will likely become widespread within a few years, as it plans to make the software available to anyone.[60]

In some cases, the time estimate may be even shorter. VivoText, a voice-replicating firm based in Israel, has developed applications that allow users to "select the emphasis, speed and level of happiness or sadness with which individual words and phrases are produced," and also to clone any voice and use it to say anything the user wants.[61] This effort would enhance the ability to capture the emotional component of voice that current computer-generated audio critically lacks. Google,

---

56   "Let's Get Experimental: Behind the Adobe MAX Sneaks," *Adobe Blog*, November 4, 2016.

57   Adobe Inc., "#VoCo. Adobe MAX 2016 (Sneak Peeks)," November 4, 2016.

58   Bahar Gholipour, "New AI Tech Can Mimic Any Voice," *Scientific American*, May 2, 2017.

59   Gholipour, 2017.

60   Lyrebird, "With Great Innovation Comes Great Responsibility," undated.

61   "Imitating People's Speech Patterns Precisely Could Bring Trouble," *The Economist*, April 20, 2017. See VivoText's website for more detail on its emerging products.

among other large technology companies, is also working on software to enhance the quality of its audio service, which, according to recent tests, is rated considerably similar to human speech.[62]

Companies, including Lyrebird, have indicated that the intention of their software is to be used for such services as personal AI assistants and speech synthesis for people with disabilities, but have acknowledged that their software could potentially have negative applications.[63] At a time when public trust in information is at risk, the potential for sources that retain inherent trustworthiness, such as audio recordings, to become unreliable could have significant implications. For example, given the availability of audio recordings for a number of prominent political figures, these advancements could make putting words in the mouth of a leader as easy as feeding a computer recordings and then telling the software what that person should say. How convincing will these computer-generated audio files be? According to a 2017 interview with Gregory Allen, an adjunct fellow at the Center for a New American Security, in one to two years, technology will allow computer-generated audio to be able to fool the untrained ear, and in five to ten years, technology will enable audio forgeries "to evade certain types of forensic analysis."[64]

Adobe, among others, has noted its interest in developing digital solutions, such as watermarking, to help identify audio manipulations, though it is unclear how long the forensics and verification process would take. Overall, the advancement of these technologies could shift the balance from technology favoring the documentation of the truth to favoring the fabrication, making the risk of encountering a false audio clip the new reality.[65]

---

[62]  Aäron van den Oord, Tom Walters, and Trevor Strohman, "WaveNet Launches in the Google Assistant," *DeepMind Blog*, October 4, 2017.

[63]  Gholipour, 2017.

[64]  Rob Price, "AI and CGI Will Transform Information Warfare, Boost Hoaxes, and Escalate Revenge Porn," *Business Insider*, August 12, 2017.

[65]  Gholipour, 2017.

**Fabricated Video: The Rise of "Deep Fakes"**

Generating or editing pictures is a feature that technology has been capable of for several years. The social content website Reddit, for example, hosts friendly competitions to see which users can create the best picture using image manipulation software. The ability to generate high-quality realistic photos or videos, however, has been a more challenging obstacle. Recently, software tools have been introduced that are playing an essential role in overcoming this challenge.[66] One such tool is known as generative adversarial networks (GANs), which work by integrating a competitive function into software, with one network seeking to generate an item, such as an image or video, while the other network judges the item to determine whether it looks real.[67] As the first network continues to adapt to fool the adversarial network, the software learns how to better create more realistic images or videos.[68] With these types of machine-learning tools, Allen asserts, "In the near future, it will be possible even for amateurs to generate photorealistic HD [high definition] video, audio, and document forgeries—at scale."[69]

In the case of images, GANs in combination with other tools have demonstrated that generating realistic images is not only possible but will dramatically improve over the next several years. For example, a machine-learning artist at Google has been able to "generate images of imagined faces with a resolution of 768 pixels a side, more than twice as big as anything previously achieved."[70] In October 2017, a

---

66  Lee Ferran, "Beware the Coming Crisis of 'Deep Fake News,'" *RealClearLife*, July 27, 2018. See also the discussion at the Heritage Foundation, "Deep Fakes: A Looming Challenge for Privacy, Democracy, and National Security," panel discussion, Washington, D.C., July 19, 2018.

67  "Fake News: You Ain't Seen Nothing Yet," 2017. See also Ferran, 2018.

68  Faizan Shaikh, "Introductory Guide to Generative Adversarial Networks (GANs) and Their Promise!" *Analytics Vidhya*, June 15, 2017.

69  Greg Allen and Taniel Chan, *Artificial Intelligence and National Security*, Cambridge, Mass.: Belfer Center for Science and International Affairs, Harvard Kennedy School, July 2017, p. 29. See also Will Knight, "These Incredibly Realistic Fake Faces Show How Algorithms Can Now Mess with Us," *MIT Technology Review*, December 14, 2018e.

70  "Fake News: You Ain't Seen Nothing Yet," 2017.

graphic processing unit company called NVIDIA demonstrated the capability to generate HD images of people and objects by using GANs to train software on a database of image samples.[71] Though some of the generated images were distorted, the company was able to create high-quality images of people and items, such as vehicles, rooms, and entire buildings, leading the research team to believe that generating highly realistic photos is within reach.[72]

Researchers have also recently been able to develop small but photo-realistic images by converting text descriptions into images. The software is able to produce a variety of images based on sentence descriptions, such as "The small bird has a red head with feathers that fade from red to gray from head to tail" and "A group of people standing around and posing for a picture."[73] Future developments will seek to improve the resolution and size to generate full HD images, which, according to Jeff Clune, an assistant professor of computer science at the University of Wyoming who works on generating images using neural networks, "is likely on the order of years, not decades."[74]

Though the capability to create computer-generated images is further along than video production, there have been several recent developments that indicate generating realistic videos could be possible soon. One example of these developments is the software produced by U.S. and German researchers that, in combination with a common webcam, can allow a user to change the facial movement of any person

---

[71] Tero Karras, Timo Aila, Samuli Laine, and Jaakko Lehtinen, "Progressive Growing of GANs for Improved Quality, Stability, and Variation," *Sixth International Conference on Learning Representations, Conference Proceedings*, Vancouver, Canada, 2018; Hillary Grigonis, "A.I. Creates Some of the Most Realistic Computer-Generated Images of People Yet," *Digital Trends*, October 30, 2017.

[72] Karras et al., 2018.

[73] Han Zhang, Tao Xu, Hongsheng Li, Shaoting Zhang, Xiaogang Wang, Xiaolei Huang, and Dimitris Metaxas, "StackGAN: Text to Photo-Realistic Image Synthesis with Stacked Generative Adversarial Networks," *IEEE International Conference on Computer Vision, Conference Proceedings*, Venice, Italy: Institute of Electrical and Electronics Engineers, October 2017, pp. 8–14.

[74] James Vincent, "Artificial Intelligence Is Going to Make It Easier Than Ever to Fake Images and Video," *The Verge*, December 20, 2016.

in a recorded video in real time.[75] Using this software, a recording of a prominent figure's facial expressions can be modified in real time to match a user's facial expressions, producing a new video in which the prominent figure appears to be mouthing whatever the user wants.[76]

Another example is the software being developed by researchers at the University of Washington that seeks to convert audio clips into realistic video by training software to generate matching mouth shapes on a speaker.[77] The software currently is designed to learn the speech patterns of one person at a time, but the team identified future developments, including helping the software widen its capability to recognize speech patterns and doing so with less data.[78] In addition, there have been technological developments to generate videos from text commands, such as "swimming in a swimming pool" or "playing golf."[79] For now, the capability is limited in the duration, resolution, and motion that a generated video can produce, but future steps include generating human pose and skeleton features to improve the quality of human activity in generated videos.[80] The potential for achieving this capability is certainly possible in the next ten to 15 years, as there is already some preliminary research on how to address these two steps.[81]

---

75  Adario Strange, "Face-Tracking Software Lets You Make Anyone Say Anything in Real Time," *Mashable*, March 20, 2016.

76  Jutus Thies, Michael Zollhöfer, Marc Stamminger, Christian Theobalt, and Matthias Nießner, "Face2Face: Real-Time Face Capture and Reenactment of RGB Videos," *IEEE Conference on Computer Vision and Pattern Recognition, Conference Proceedings*, Las Vegas, Nev.: Institute of Electrical and Electronics Engineers, 2016.

77  Jennifer Langston, "Lip-Syncing Obama: New Tools Turn Audio Clips into Realistic Video," *UW News*, July 11, 2017.

78  Langston, 2017.

79  Yitong Li, Martin Renqiang Min, Dinghan Shen, David Carlson, and Lawrence Carin, "Video Generation from Text," *Thirty-Second AAAI Conference on Artificial Intelligence, Conference Proceedings*, New Orleans, La.: Association for the Advancement of Artificial Intelligence, February 2018, pp. 3–6.

80  Li et al., 2018, pp. 5–8.

81  Haoye Cai, Chunyan Bai, Yu-Wing Tai, and Chi-Keung Tang, "Deep Video Generation, Prediction and Completion of Human Action Sequences," *European Conference on Computer Vision 2018, Conference Proceedings*, Munich, Germany, September 2018, p. 8.

It is not difficult to imagine how the ability to generate realistic images or videos could pose dangerous consequences. As technology improves the quality of this production, it will likely become more difficult to discern real events from doctored or artificial ones, particularly if combined with the advancements in audio software. The result could be footage of prominent figures saying and doing whatever a particular person would want, eroding social trust in information.[82] Ian Goodfellow, the research scientist who introduced GANs, asserts that creating very convincing YouTube fakes could be possible by 2020.[83] In addition to creating information, these advancements could create an atmosphere in which audio, images, or videos of real events can be claimed to be doctored fakes. "What I think we'll see, in a couple of years," predicts Matt Turek, project manager of a Defense Advanced Research Projects Agency (DARPA) effort on media forensics, "is the synthesis of events that didn't happen. Multiple images and videos taken from different perspectives will be constructed in such a way that they look like they come from different cameras."[84]

Moreover, the bar may not be as high as completely realistic and accurate images. Many videos and images online are already muddy or distorted, sometimes as the result of a need to compress file sizes. The performance of these systems may not actually need to improve to crystal-clear synthesis in order to convince many viewers of their product's authenticity.

Over time, computer-generated imagery (CGI) and similar technologies with the potential to create fairly realistic moving images will penetrate consumer markets, allowing for widespread use of hyper-realistic computer-generated imaging and video production by private companies and individuals. Bots with advanced AI capabilities will resemble human beings (physically and visually) on social media plat-

[82] Vincent, 2016.

[83] "Fake News: You Ain't Seen Nothing Yet," 2017.

[84] Quoted in Joshua Rothman, "Afterimage," *New Yorker*, November 12, 2018, p. 40.

forms and VR and AR spaces well enough that we will not be able to distinguish real from CGI beings.[85]

## Surveillance Systems

Almost every new technology linked to the cloud or IoT will be able to serve some kind of surveillance or "sousveillance" purpose by sometime between 2030 and 2035. (*Sousveillance* refers to the capturing of activity from "below," in such ways as capturing data on people's internet habits, recording their movements through cellphone locations, recording of audio by home-based sound-activated assistants, and more.) Visibility and oversight of a person's or group's activity will necessarily involve monitoring their movements, communications, transactions, and behaviors. Indeed, what is arising is a sort of *ambient surveillance system* in which vast troves of data are being gathered and processed and theoretically available to governments and other actors, in ways theoretically designed for helpful or commercial purposes but which nonetheless reflect a degree of data collection on individuals that would have been unthinkable for even the most authoritarian government just a generation ago. At the same time, the advance of AI is creating a demand for ever-increasing data collection to provide the essential fuel for training these systems, producing additional financial incentives for vacuuming up huge swaths of information about Americans.

By 2030, motion-magnifying and microscope software (called Eulerian Video Magnification [EVM]) will be standard in surveillance and smartphone cameras and video recordings; these tools reveal details that would otherwise be invisible (e.g., tiny movements in eye muscles, blood flow, microscopic movements in seemingly stable objects). There will also be at least 1 billion drones on earth, most of which will carry

---

85   Jesus Diaz, "The Weird, Wild Future of CGI," *Fast Company*, October 19, 2017.

surveillance equipment and have the ability to receive and transmit data.[86]

Most nanotechnologies will come from advanced life sciences (e.g., surgical precision tools and cellular-level technology). The push to create smaller devices with precision capabilities and HD imaging and video will aid similar efforts in future surveillance hardware. The smallest surveillance drones today are roughly the size of a small insect and still in early development.[87]

The role of sousveillance is growing rapidly. Recent debates about the information collected by Google and Facebook on individuals is only the beginning of a much larger discussion of the sousveillance challenge. Within ten to 15 years, 90 percent of the global population will have an internet presence; 80 percent will have free and unlimited data; over 50 percent of internet services to homes will be through appliances and home devices linked to the IoT; 1 trillion devices will be linked to the IoT; and surveillance will be a matter of access to devices and networks, as well as big-data management, mining, and analysis.[88] Wearable devices and implants that judge health and emotional states will provide a remarkable degree of fidelity in reporting people's mood and outlook.[89]

Already, concerns are rising about how hackers and aggressors can employ stolen data from the rising ambient surveillance system. In such instances as the theft of Office of Personnel Management records, Cambridge Analytica's acquisition of friend and contact data through Facebook, and other cases of database theft and hacking, states and organizations have used access to such data for coercive purposes or competitive advantage. That potential avenue to effective social manipulation will only grow as the process of ambient surveillance deepens.

---

[86]  Hao-Yu Wu, Michael Rubinstein, Eugene Shih, John Guttag, Frédo Durand, and William Freeman, "Eulerian Video Magnification for Revealing Subtle Changes in the World," *ACM Transactions on Graphics*, Vol. 31, No. 4, 2012.

[87]  Gareth Evans, "Robotic Insects Add Whole New Meaning to 'Fly-on-the-Wall' Surveillance," *Army Technology*, March 16, 2015.

[88]  Global Agenda Council on the Future of Software and Society, 2015, p. 7.

[89]  Tiku, 2018, p. 55.

Example techniques include several already well established—such as new versions of "doxfare" (stealing documents with personal or confidential information and using them for blackmail purposes and other ways of interfering in another state's political process),[90] as well as direct political manipulation through increasingly powerful inferential models of preference—but also new approaches that employ collected data on location, mood, behavior, friends, connections, and much else to power strategies of social disruption and degradation of trust.

## Conclusion: A Rapidly Changing Infosphere

This complex and, in many ways, interlinked suite of technologies holds the potential to accelerate the transformation of the infosphere in advanced economies. It would be too simplistic to project current trends in the spread or capabilities of these technologies, or to assume that their effects will be linear. For example, video fakery need not create a future in which no one has a clear sense of whether anything he or she sees is real or not; the Internet of Things could provide a sort of networked resilience as much as or more than new vulnerabilities; and governments—even autocratic ones—might be forced to limit the employment of surveillance systems. Assuming worst-case, dystopian outcomes from the continued emergence of these technologies would be as wrong as assuming the most optimistic results.

Nonetheless, this brief review does make clear the significant and arguably growing risks to the stability and coherence of advanced societies from the potential for outside actors to manipulate, disrupt, and commandeer these technologies and systems. These technologies also contain built-in potential to change the character of the infosphere itself, even absent intentional manipulation, in ways damaging to social cohesion and democratic governance: accelerating the decline of a shared reality, strengthening systems of institutional dominance

---

[90]  Ido Kilovaty, "Doxfare: Politically Motivated Leaks and the Future of the Norm on Non-Intervention in the Era of Weaponized Information," *Harvard National Security Journal*, Vol. 9, No. 1, 2018.

over individuals, and exacerbating the sense of alienation on the part of average citizens. Perhaps the dominant lesson to be taken from this review is that the United States and many other nations confront a transitional moment. The collective effect of these technologies could be transformational, and societies and governments are likely to confront the requirement to be increasingly self-conscious and directive in their efforts to shape their effects.

The following three chapters provide some context for that requirement by offering three potential scenarios for the evolution of these technologies and the potential they offer for hostile social manipulation. Each scenario describes the opportunities and hopes that give rise to the trends it imagines, but each is admittedly designed to highlight risks. They are not offered as forecasts; the emphasis is specifically on ways in which the combined effect of these advances can pose dangers, and real outcomes are likely to reflect a somewhat different range of influences. Nonetheless, each of these scenarios is entirely plausible, given the character of emerging technologies.

# CHAPTER FIVE

# Future 1: The Death of Reality (2025 Scenario)

## A Note About Methodology

To investigate possible scenarios for how hostile social manipulation could unfold, we relied on the trends and data surveyed in the past three chapters: research on the evolving landscape of the infosphere; social science findings on attitudes, attitude change, persuasion, and social trust; and the evolving character of specific technologies. These scenarios are designed to illustrate three possible futures for the role of information in society, which we refer to as the infosphere. In each case, we describe how information-based aggression could use the elements of each scenario to attack democracy.[1]

We term these narratives "futures" because they are general descriptions of a world that could emerge rather than specific, event-driven scenarios. Chapters Five, Six, and Seven each describe one of these futures through an initial summary of the future, one or more sections on specific elements of that future, and a concluding section describing the risks of social manipulation in that environment. Each chapter includes some discussion of the technological, social, and political factors that contribute to the future. The futures are dramatized and include many invented potential future developments, but events are grounded firmly in research on current trends. Their purpose is in

---

[1]  For a description of the ways in which multiple autocratic regimes are using these technologies for domestic and international influence, see Juan Pablo Cardenal, Jacek Kucharczyk, Grigorij Mesežnikov, and Gabriela Pleschová, *Sharp Power: Rising Authoritarian Influence*, Washington, D.C.: National Endowment for Democracy, December 2017.

part to bring to life a series of images about the unfolding future of the infospheres of advanced democracies in narrative ways.

These futures are not predictions. In outlining them, we are not suggesting that the specific combination of factors reflected in any one of these futures is likely to emerge as described. They are illustrative and suggestive, designed to provoke discussion about the potential future trajectory of hostile social manipulation and virtual societal warfare. But each is deeply grounded in research on the changing infosphere, the social science of influence and trust, and the character of emerging technologies. The scenarios are designed to illustrate three possible dangers inherent in emerging technologies. There are some contrary trends under way—such as the growing, if still incomplete, efforts by social media platforms to counteract fabricated information—that are likely to moderate some of these outcomes. But the scenarios described below remain plausible given emerging technologies and *if* the governments and institutions in many nations do not actively work to shape the character of the evolving infosphere.

Furthermore, these three futures are not presented as mutually exclusive possible outcomes. Each is built around a single leading variable drawn from trends in the infosphere: One focuses on the decline of any firm and objective sense of the distinction between real facts and events and fabricated or incorrect ones; one focuses on the rise of echo chambers and the collapse into a fragmented information reality of self-reinforcing silos of belief and information; and one focuses on the growing role of algorithmic decisionmaking. Any actual future is likely to involve some degree of all of these main drivers, and they overlap to some degree; a world of information silos is also a world in which the objective sense of reality has faded. By focusing on each in turn, the futures allow us to investigate various aspects of an emerging infosphere in detail.

Finally, we have proposed that these futures could arrive between the years 2023 and 2028. The dates chosen are somewhat arbitrary, though they have been assigned these dates based on how close the infosphere appears to be, in terms of technology and structure, to these futures. But the dates are not meant as predictive.

## The General Future

"Reality" died in 2023.

It is perhaps audacious to attach a specific date to such a gradual and ambiguous process. Yet many developments that year, two seemingly long and eventful years ago now, suggest that it will be seen as the threshold of a new post-truth, post-fact, post-reality era in human life. The very notion of an objective, singular, identifiable reality is already being mocked in many corners of society and referred to as a charming anachronism.

What, precisely, happened in 2023 to justify this bold claim? Several things, each of which reflected the apotheosis of trends that had been maturing for a decade or more. The first and most encompassing of these developments comprised the essential feature of the information environment as we now know it: Simply put, the ability to manufacture seemingly tangible reality from scratch has now become commonplace.

In some ways, this is the natural outcome of the empirical trends toward a "postmodern" reality that had been expected for decades, in which the meaning and significance of events are not universal and agreed upon but contingent and debated. The trend had roots in some creative and hopeful efforts to break down narrow and conventional ways of thinking and to provide individuals with an unprecedented opportunity for expression. The fundamental motive and much of the effect of these trends—the right to have a subjective take on events—it must be remembered, has been empowering. It has emerged in ways closely intertwined with the broader trajectory toward the empowerment of the individual against constraints and oppression, whether from governments or social consensus. Many of what are now described as reality-bending (or reality-destroying) expressions, including several modern schools of artistic expression, the gradual decay of societal constraints on thought and certain forms of behavior, and reality-mixing forms of entertainment, have grown out of this more fundamental expression of the individual perspective against the universal.

But as the critics of postmodern ideas have long warned, it has proved difficult to slow the momentum of this subjectification of human perception. When no one dominant narrative or conventional wisdom can be true or valid, it is now clear, to some, how *any* generalized truth claim can aspire to such a status. Technologies and outlooks that allowed individuals to offer a unique voice on events soon offered that opening to millions of individuals. Reality became personalized as much as shared, a trend accelerated by some major institutions in society, including businesses, which sought to claim their own right to interpret events.

From a longer-term perspective, in fact, the general trend was nothing new, because the substitution of metaphorical for verbatim truth has a long history. During the 20th century, the literalness of painting gave way to abstraction and expressionist interpretation of life rather than direct representation. Nonfiction writing and journalism came to embody new forms that stretched the veracity of the facts. The concept of a verifiable, authentic memoir gave way, at least for a time, to forgeries passed off as legitimate; the devotion to historical accuracy in "biopics" gave way to artistic license. Many of the most popular television shows built drama out of stage-managed claims of verisimilitude—i.e., "reality" shows constructed from narrative-driven invention.

This most fundamental trend had its roots in decades of corporate efforts to manipulate facts and reality. Arguably the source code for all such efforts was the tobacco lobby's efforts to destroy faith in scientific research suggesting that smoking caused cancer. The industry launched a massive effort with all the hallmarks of past programs: attacking the legitimacy of scientists and institutions behind the research; hiring friendly scientists to generate countervailing research, much of it fatally biased; paying for massive public relations campaigns to shape public opinion; and recruiting famous sports stars and television personalities to endorse its message.[2] The goal was to frame the issue and shape the narrative, controlling how at least a significant minority of the population understood the issue.

---

[2]   For a comprehensive assessment of a number of these campaigns, see Ari Rabin-Havt, *Lies, Incorporated: The World of Post-Truth Politics*, New York: Anchor Books, 2016.

In this sense, more of human life has come to reflect the artistic, the created, and the imagined rather than the literally "true"—the Hollywoodization of life, in a much more ontological sense rather than the cultural sense that was once imagined.[3] (It was Picasso who said that "[a]rt is not truth; art is a lie that enables us to recognize truth."[4] He could not have imagined how seriously many in the entertainment business would take that sentiment.) The story of the late 20th and early 21st centuries was already one of a declining barrier between true and fake, real and unreal. Several powerful technologies have now accelerated that blending in dramatic ways.

These emerging patterns have been fueled in part by an uncomfortable but unavoidable truth: Human beings favor comfort and pleasure over facts. "Only to a limited extent does man want truth," Friedrich Nietzsche argued in a prescient forecast of the current trends in reality-bending. "He desires the pleasant, life-preserving consequences of truth; to pure knowledge without consequences he is indifferent, to potentially harmful and destructive truths he is even hostile." Human consciousness, Nietzsche believed, is "an apparatus for abstraction and simplification—designed not for knowledge but for *gaining control* of things."[5]

Over the last few decades, corporations, news media, and the entertainment industry increasingly have decided to accept and work within this basic aspect of human nature rather than fight it. They are giving people what they want, and at a time of social disruption, slowing growth, rising inequality, and alienation in the face of increasingly impenetrable institutions, what they want is perceived, more often than not, to be sensational, extreme, and targeted against some sort of out-group that allows the audience to deepen its sense of social membership.

---

[3]   Stacy Schiff, "The Interactive Truth," *New York Times*, June 15, 2005.

[4]   David Shields, *Reality Hunger: A Manifesto*, New York: Knopf, 2010, pp. 14, 32, 34–35, 40–42.

[5]   Friedrich Nietzsche, *On Truth and Untruth: Selected Writings*, trans. and ed. Taylor Carman, New York: Harper Perennial, 2010, pp. 24, 121.

An important contributing trend to this future has been the continued, and indeed accelerating, collapse of institutions and authorities that mediate reality. The first event in 2023, coming just a few days into the new year, was the announcement that Facebook had acquired the *New York Times*. It was generally viewed as an act of charity and social responsibility; rocked by a series of scandals, consistent attacks from skeptical populist hackers, and the decline of several nonpublishing ventures that had been keeping the parent company alive, the *Times* had announced in 2021 that it was headed for eventual bankruptcy without significant new investments. (General newspaper revenue has been falling 4 percent to 5 percent a year since about 2010.[6]) Facebook billed the act as a continuation of its efforts, begun in 2017, to combat fabricated or biased information on its platforms. Though the company and its founder, Mark Zuckerberg, quickly insisted on their devotion to investigative journalism—much as Jeff Bezos had done when acquiring the *Washington Post*—they also announced a host of plans to fully digitalize (or virtualize) the *Times* and integrate it into Facebook's user-driven interface. "Your Facebook News Feed will now be—literally—the *New York Times*," Zuckerberg proudly announced. "They will be one and the same."

The problem, of course, is that Facebook planned to filter the resulting feed to a significant degree through the same algorithm-governed model that decided what people would "want" to read. Its business model relied on clicks and preferences, not telling people what they "should" know. Readers can still access the *Times* in its entirety through direct browsing, but many do not take the time. The result has been to fragment one of the few remaining national-level shared channels of collective awareness. The *Times*—the "paper of record" for the nation—was now nothing more than a brand name attached to a completely user-driven algorithm. Reporters would still work in newsrooms generating stories, some of them "investigative" reports. But who read them would be contingent upon preferences. This devel-

---

6   Regina Joseph, "A Peek into the Future: A Stealth Revolution by Influence's New Masters," in Weston Aviles and Sarah Canna, eds., *White Paper on Influence in an Age of Rising Connectedness*, Washington, D.C.: U.S. Department of Defense, August 2017, p. 11.

opment represented another step in the continued decline of trusted intervening institutions, which can provide some baseline of essential fact claims, in the public media.

The trend has affected far more institutions than just the media. Another prominent target of the rising skepticism toward authorities is academia. Conservatives in the United States had long viewed universities as bastions of liberalism, and this perception intensified in the past several years as a few schools, supporting speech-constraining ideas of identity politics, fought for the right to fire professors for expressing supposedly offensive views that conservatives found to be perfectly reasonable. At the same time, the reliability of social scientific research in higher education has been called into question by a persistent "replication crisis," a term for the fact that many high-profile "findings" in social science research simply cannot be replicated. The result has been to cast doubt on any new study. By 2022–2023, polls were finding that only 15 percent to 20 percent of Americans had "high confidence" that universities were upholding their mission as "places for the objective pursuit of truth."

That trend is part of a larger one: the rise of anti-intellectualism.[7] Faith in all manner of experts and expertise has plummeted. Polls in 2018–2020 showed "faith in experts" dropping into the single digits, and the numbers have recovered only slightly since then. Many people now view the very idea of objective knowledge as elitist.[8] Increasingly, the idea of "expertise" has given way to a perception that "everyone has their viewpoint," the Nietzschean idea that perspective is everything.[9]

Broadly speaking, these challenges to faith in facts and knowledge are a symptom of something more profound: A sense that collective institutions of governance and social capital have proven unequal to the task of managing postmodern life. They are too big, too impersonal, too bureaucratic to be trusted. Postmodern society has become so complex that no one can understand even a fraction of it, and the resulting unease is reflected back at public institutions as a form of

---

[7]   Tom Nichols, "How America Lost Faith in Expertise," *Foreign Affairs*, March-April 2017b.

[8]   Lewandowsky, Ecker, and Cook, 2017, p. 354.

[9]   Lewandowsky, Ecker, and Cook, 2017, p. 356.

frustration and, in some cases, anger. Trust is based in a sense of safety and some level of shared truth,[10] and as those things have ebbed, levels of social trust have declined, as well. More accurately, the divergence between trust in local things (neighbors, businesses, and school boards) and national or international institutions has exploded. Measurable levels of anxiety in the United States have been on a steady rise since the early 2000s.

## A Future of Virtual and Invented Reality

The death of reality has been midwifed by the explosion, over the past five to seven years, of astonishing developments in a critical area of technology: lifelike audio and video and the associated technologies of fakery that continue to blur the boundaries between "true" (verifiable) and invented content.[11] People have been making replicas and fake content for decades, but the difference now is that these fakes, whether images, audio clips, or videos, are of such high fidelity that they make it almost impossible for anyone to verify their authenticity without time-consuming and, in some cases, very extensive investigation.[12] The same technologies, combined with advanced robotics and AI, are just beginning to cross the line into the long-awaited future of humanlike robots, though even now that threshold remains to be crossed in a meaningful way.

The first to come along was simple image creation. The very term "Photoshop" became a universal term to denote the faking or modification of a still image. In 2025, the programs, some driven by machine-learning processes, are so good that would-be fakers can assemble images—by voice command—of just about anything they want.[13] As long ago as 2015, the website Reddit was hosting competitions in image

---

[10]   See the discussion by Simon Sinek in National Public Radio, "Trust and Consequences," *TED Radio Hour*, May 15, 2015.

[11]   "Fake News: You Ain't Seen Nothing Yet," 2017.

[12]   Kevin Roose, "Here Come the Fake Videos, Too," *New York Times*, March 4, 2018.

[13]   Vincent, 2016; Karras et al., 2018; Grigonis, 2017; Zhang et al., 2017.

manipulation, giving awards for the most impressive ability to create fake reality in a still photo. By 2018, the most advanced artificial image creation programs, using competitive AI programs to build and then test the veracity of pictures, were generating high-resolution images of entirely fictional people that were completely indistinguishable from real photos.[14] The fidelity of the images now matches the resolution of high-end digital cameras from 2018.

People can now create images from scratch of whatever they like, integrating elements from as many other images as they need. Firms that specialized in stock images quickly got into the act: People interested in manufacturing images can buy massive databases of manipulatable files, and simply call up whatever components they like and assemble them into the finished image they intend. And the process can easily be automated: AI married to image generation programs can be used to produce as many images of whatever kind the user needs.

Thousands of prank and serious imposter photos have already begun to flood the internet. Some of the images are historical, such as the infamous fake circulated in 2021 that appeared to be a shot, taken by Federal Bureau of Investigation (FBI) surveillance, of John F. Kennedy in an intimate setting with Marilyn Monroe. Others are clearly designed to discredit, such as images of national leaders with prostitutes, using drugs, or abusing their children.

Another well-established area is digital audio, because the technology has been under development the longest and is the easiest, technologically, to mimic.[15] Adobe's VoCo system was one of the best known but has been joined by a dozen other programs, such as Lyrebird and VivoText.[16] All a user needs is a high-quality audio recording of as much as 20 minutes—or as few as one or two—of the target individual, and they can create a digital replica of the voice that can be programmed to say anything the user likes. The result can only

---

[14]  Cade Metz and Keith Collins, "How an AI 'Cat-and-Mouse Game' Generates Believable Fake Photos," *New York Times*, January 2, 2018.

[15]  Selk, 2017.

[16]  "Let's Get Experimental: Behind the Adobe MAX Sneaks," 2016; Adobe Inc., 2016; "Imitating People's Speech Patterns Precisely Could Bring Trouble," 2017.

be distinguished from a "real" recording with complex analysis of the digital files.[17]

One of the best known of these audio platforms is Lyrebird.[18] It became famous in 2019, when three high school students used it to create a parallel State of the Union Address from the U.S. president—complete with background applause and sound effects from a virtual congressional audience—and posted it on various blogs. The posts garnered 35 million views within a week, and later surveys suggested that between 30 percent and 40 percent of the Americans who heard these fakes believed they were listening to the real speech.

By 2020, digital audio manufacture was joined by high-quality digital video. The origins of the field lay in digital capture technologies, such as the ones used in Hollywood in such films as *Avatar* and *Planet of the Apes*, which transformed an actor's expressions into a digitally created character. Important work was also done by the video gaming industry, which sought increasingly realistic representations of character and setting. Researchers, such as those at the University of Southern California's Mixed Reality Lab, and CGI studios used the technology to create digital representations of actual people, and then made the resulting program flexible enough to say and do anything they wanted.

Even by 2017, primitive versions of the technology had been used to create obviously fake—but still shockingly good—virtual versions of several national leaders.[19] By 2020, several programs began to incorporate a reliable function through which users could simply key in words or phrases ("cat jumping on box"), and the system would generate high-quality digital video describing such a scene.[20]

Increasingly, the field of virtual image, audio, and video creation is being driven by machine learning in the form of GANs, which involve, essentially, programming one AI system to hunt for fakes, and forcing

---

[17]  Price, 2017.

[18]  Gholipour, 2017; Lyrebird, undated.

[19]  Strange, 2016; Thies et al., 2016; Langston, 2017.

[20]  Li et al., 2018; Cai et al., 2018.

a second program to try to spoof it.[21] The action-reaction iteration in such systems vastly exceeds the speed with which human programmers could enhance the fidelity of manufactured video. By 2021, such efforts had crossed the threshold of generating images that over 95 percent of people could not visually distinguish from reality. The GAN systems have surpassed the task of fooling human perception and are exclusively working to spoof high-quality digital forensics, which they can do in many cases. Because of such advances, all that aspiring digital fakers need is an hour or two of video of their intended target, and they can use one of the major commercial programs on the market to create a digital representation that can be manipulated at will—and dropped, *Zelig*-like, into existing scenes.[22]

Some of the results have been benign. The fact that people can now pay a fee to engage in a personal conversation with Margot Robbie any time they like by having a video chat with a digital replica that converses naturally, with the proceeds of the fee donated to charity, is merely a curiosity. The first time the mobile hologram of James Franco appeared next to customers at a Target, calling them by name and speaking in personal terms by accessing massive online databases about them, it seemed magical and spurred a spike in sales; within a few months, people largely ignored such obvious salesmanship. A host of young filmmakers have been empowered by the ability to create whole movies essentially in their basements, generating and manipulating characters at will—the digital video equivalent of electronic music.

Other applications of these seemingly magical technologies, however, have been designed to create harm and chaos, substituting invented realities for real ones. People can now generate seemingly persuasive evidence for any claim they want to make: historical conspiracy theories, attacks on the credibility of political leaders, or occurrences of world events. Global warming skeptics circulate video "proving" that the ice caps are not melting. Human rights activists, lacking real evidence, have generated fake audio and video of mass genocide to spark popular outrage. The issue in many cases is that it is not as though

---

[21]  Metz and Collins, 2018; Shaikh, 2017.

[22]  See the discussion of fakes in Simon Adler, "Breaking News," *Radiolab*, July 27, 2017.

there is no identifiable reality to establish, but that a third or more of Americans on many issues simply have a much stronger *appetite* for a skewed reality that agrees with their expectations than for "reality" per se, and that new technologies have empowered motivated reasoning in unprecedented ways.

One of the most sinister plots emerged in 2024, with the massive, coordinated effort—believed to have been masterminded by a foreign government—to release "evidence" that the 9/11 attacks had indeed been a U.S. government plot, as long claimed by conspiracy theorists. The faked evidence included top-secret U.S. Department of Defense memos, audio recordings of then–Secretary of Defense Donald Rumsfeld "talking" about the plot with Vice President Richard Cheney, video footage of the supposed missile that hit the Pentagon, and much more. Dubbed "the Pentagon Papers of 9/11" by several alt-right websites, the flood of information has continued with more supposed releases to keep the issue percolating. Despite the fact that websites devoted to unmasking such fakes immediately applied fake-detection software to debunk the claims, polls suggest that a third of Americans now either believe the claims or have "serious questions" about who launched the attacks.

A related problem is that the creation of such digital fakes has now been automated. Content creators have used AI to generate automated content for years,[23] but the marriage of much more capable AI and world-class digital manufacture techniques has sparked an explosion of images, audio, and video that is completely artificially generated. Most electronic music is now created by AI without the involvement of any human beings—no musicians, producers, or singers—and increasingly the pattern is spreading to orchestral, pop, and rock genres.[24] Most television commercials are created that way, without any human actors;

---

[23]  Matt Chessen, *The MADCOM Future*, Washington, D.C.: Atlantic Council, 2017b.

[24]  Jazz listeners held out for years, rejecting the artificiality inherent in the digital generation of music, until 2023, with the release of "Waterfront Lullaby," an album of avant-garde jazz first attributed to a human group called "The Fusion Collective" and quickly declared by *The Jazz Review* to be "a new classic, the greatest expression of the genre in a decade if not more—and yet more proof, if anyone needs it, that we need human intuition, craft, and, yes, *soul* behind the creation of true jazz." When "The Fusion Collective" was revealed to be a

all print ads are AI-generated. In 2024, the first theatrically released major motion picture emerged that had been created entirely inside a computer. Appropriately enough, it was a science fiction tale about a future society dependent on a massive central information nervous system. It starred a combination of images of real actors (the rights to which were purchased) and several entirely fictional digital creations. It cost about $18 million to make—ten cents on the dollar to the cost of actual, physical films.[25]

Efforts to counter these technologies, and to re-establish a stronger sense that people can distinguish real images from fake, have been under way for some years. The U.S. Department of Defense sponsored work that used AI to help assess images and call out fabricated video.[26] These systems provided some degree of accuracy in catching early-generation video fabrications by using simple rules of thumb, such as searching for videos in which the people do not blink. But forgers, some state-sponsored, have moved well past earlier versions of easily detectable fakery to far more sophisticated, AI-supported techniques. And while existing software filters could theoretically help determine accuracy, most people simply do not use them, and faked video and audio files that agree with the pre-established beliefs of segments of the population are widely accepted even though easily debunked. The pattern with such fakes thus has continued the trend established with basic facts: Invalid claims that could and should be countered through straightforward correction can still persuade significant proportions of the population.

These technologies of image, audio, and visual fakery have evolved in parallel and have largely now merged, with dramatic advances in

---

new Amazon-sponsored, jazz-manufacturing AI program called Marsalis, many jazz listeners shrugged and bought its next album. It came out 96 hours after "Waterfront Lullaby."

[25]   One of the invented "actors" who appeared in the film, Aiden Williams, quickly became one of the highest-paid celebrity endorsers, appearing in over 40 commercials in the year after the film's release.

[26]   Will Knight, "The US Military Is Funding an Effort to Catch Deepfakes and Other AI Trickery," *MIT Technology Review*, May 23, 2018a; Will Knight, "The Defense Department Has Produced the First Tools for Catching Deep Fakes," *MIT Technology Review*, August 7, 2018d.

two related areas: VR and AR. In emerging AR applications, for example, as people pass through their daily life, their perceptions of things are curated in unprecedented ways. Everything, including the appearance and contents of their office, the appearance of people they pass in the street, and the advertising in the surrounding environment, has become customizable and customized.[27] Such continual modification of the perceived quality of objects has tended to weaken the hold of a shared social experience. In many ways that we have taken for granted for essentially all of human social existence, such a shared objective experience will no longer exist. People will see the world quite literally through a set of self-programmed filters.

People now experience everything brought to them as essentially real. It began with AR-powered entertainment characters and news stories,[28] and continued with a thousand examples of companies, organizations, and individuals offering every manner of image to populate a person's smartphone display or AR headset.

Finally, growing applications of robotics also help blur the boundary between the real and the artificial. AI- or human-driven online bots or physical robots comprise a significant new market for therapy, in-home care, and other interactive applications, and these also soak up more information about massive numbers of people. Five years ago, a firm called CareCoach began deploying avatars to monitor elderly patients in home care settings. The avatars are driven, in this firm's case, by carefully hired and well-trained human operators. The systems can monitor someone all day and be aware of dozens of pieces of information, building strong personal bonds with the customers. Many of them have come to view the little puppies or other avatars as close friends and take them on hikes or boating trips to continue the conversation.[29] The line between human and artificial relationships is becoming increasingly unclear.

---

27   David Pierce, "Enjoy Your New Virtual Office," *Wired*, February 2018, p. 43.

28   Graham Roberts, "Augmented Reality: How We'll Bring the News into Your Home," *New York Times*, February 1, 2018.

29   Lauren Smiley, "Something to Watch Over Me," *Wired*, January 2018.

## The End of a Shared Picture of the World

The result of all this has been the decline of public adherence to anything like a generally accepted set of facts on major social issues.

Not all "facts" are disappearing or have become irrelevant. Certain prosaic, scientifically based, and personally attested facts persist. Bacteria are still understood to cause infections and are treated with antibiotics. Engineers are still able to calculate the support requirements for a new home or bridge.

Yet even in the realm of supposedly scientific assessments of truth, more and more issues are contended. The debates over climate change and vaccines are perhaps the leading examples, with most Americans no longer confident of any meaningful reality in either area outside the perceptions of their echo chambers. This trend has spread to other issues on which there ought to be some basis of objective agreement, such as the level of crime in society, the health threat posed by recreational drugs, and the reliability of treatments for various diseases. In these and other cases, shadowy campaigns have employed multiple means of disinformation and fakery to undermine any potential for consensus. The result has been to paralyze government policy responses.

The challenge is even more intense for major social and political issues that are in contention, as the basis of objective information that people can use to resolve and render judgments about them is called into question. The real trend is therefore more specific than the death of truth: The problem now appears to be that *the meaning of major social issues and events is becoming increasingly indeterminate.* Whether on questions about vaccinations, climate change, crime, the effects of certain economic policies, or a hundred other issues, it is increasingly impossible to settle on any agreed-upon truths to support general judgments among the body politic.

As much as a decline in concern for truth, the era represents an explosion of the sort of cynical, hard-edged irony that has long been resident in the 4chan community and other online communities that refuse to take anything seriously. Increasingly, the online aesthetic is one of parody, pranksterism, and a comprehensive spirit of nonconformist mockery designed to tear down established values and institutions.[30] The worst sins in such communities are to accept anything at face value, to take the establishment's word for anything, or to take any value or tradition seriously. The character of the era has gone well beyond the death of truth to something more: the death of significance or shared meaning under the assault of the relentlessly ironic.

Indeed, the very value of honesty as a social norm has come under increasing stress, as the information environment seems so determined to discount its significance. The "hacker's creed," *Wired* magazine suggested back in 2018, has long been that "[e]nlightened cheating is the highest form of gameplay." Disobedience trumps compliance as a value.[31] This emerging belief system has become more and more common, especially in technical and information-related fields.

The first glimmers of a rebellion against these trends have been under way for decades, as people thirst for authenticity and begin to express a rebellion against the invented fakery of a post-reality world. Already by the 1980s, significant strains in U.S. literature reflected a disquiet with people who, "bombarded by mall culture and mass media," come to believe that "they have 'McLives' rather than lives."[32] The desire for signs of the authentic—for craft-based businesses, rural living and log homes, living "off the grid," natural and organic food, and much more—is now a significant theme, especially among younger Americans. But it has not arrested the basic trends in information characteristics of the new era.

## Information Aggression and Manipulation in the Death of Reality

As these trends and realities have emerged, specific forms of information-based aggression have come to characterize the "death of

---

30  For a discussion of the trend as of 2017, see Angela Nagle, *Kill All Normies: Online Culture Wars from 4chan and Tumblr to Trump and the Alt-Right*, Winchester, United Kingdom: Zero Books, 2017, especially pp. 5–7 and 28–29.

31  Virginia Heffernan, "Twilight of the Hackers," *Wired*, February 2018, p. 14.

32  Shields, 2010, p. 25.

reality." Most notably, the accelerating "breakdown of a shared public reality," as one commentator put it as far back as 2018,[33] has created opportunities for manipulators to work within this increasingly virtual, imagined, postmodern landscape to create perceptions among specific sectors of the population. And they have had more effective tools with which to do so, with the ability to manufacture audio, video, still images, and VR programs that depict just about anything they want with great fidelity. Manipulating code is no longer about screwing up the operation of a computer system; it is about tweaking the nature of the reality people encounter.

By about 2021–2022, it had become commonplace for significant numbers of provocative images, videos, and audio "recordings" to fly around the political landscape of advanced democracies in the weeks before elections or referenda. Politicians were "seen" accepting bribes or having affairs, heard insulting major groups of the population, and shown in collusion with figures from organized crime or hostile foreign powers. Political leaders, "reputable" news sources, and others have worked hard to counteract these attacks, but their efforts are always incomplete and sometimes too late to make a difference: Skilled manipulators know how to time their attacks on the cusp of an election or vote. In many cases, politicians have been discredited by such attacks; several elections have clearly been affected.

At the same time, manipulators have been working hard to preempt the responses to these attacks by destroying the potential for a shared social reality in the target countries. To counteract the effects of fact-checking websites and other "objective," web-based sources of information, they have been using AI to produce dynamically generated content to overwhelm the objective information on the web. They also have been actively shaping online resources, such as Wikipedia pages, and directly hacking some of the objective sites to plant the false stories. (In an infamous case, the *Financial Times* webpage carried a planted, entirely fabricated story about a British politician's financial

---

[33] John A. Gans., Jr., "Governing Fantasyland," *Survival*, Vol. 60, No. 3, June-July 2018, p. 200.

misdeeds. It was up for two days before the politician got wind of it and brought it to the attention of the paper's editors.)

Efforts to shape perceived reality through social media have been turbocharged in recent years. AI-driven bots now dominate the competition on these platforms; they can detect countervailing posts and argue in response in ways largely indistinguishable from human beings. Combined with massive data theft and the establishment of Facebook- or Google-sized databases on individual Americans (and to a lesser extent Europeans) by hostile powers, an information aggressor in Moscow or Beijing can now target ads, messages, and information as precisely as any platform company. Recent reports suggest that China has devoted tens of thousands of highly trained, social media–savvy, English-speaking trolls to a persistent, ongoing campaign with specific goals in terms of shifting perceptions and achieving specific behavioral outcomes in the U.S. public.

Often the goals of such campaigns are not to make people believe a certain narrative as much as to feed existing belief systems and prompt alienation, outrage, and conflict. Aggressors are fabricating videos designed to appeal to the most paranoid instincts of fringe groups and to harden political polarization generally. Republicans receive a constant dose of videos showing Democratic politicians saying and doing awful things; Democrats receive similar videos of Republican politicians.

Beyond simply affecting information accuracy and flow, information aggressors are increasingly experimenting with ways to grab control of parts of the increasingly created reality that confronts Americans in their daily lives. There are verified cases of manipulators hacking into chatbots that serve military posttraumatic stress disorder (PTSD) patients and giving counterproductive advice. In a few cases, it appears that sophisticated hackers have begun to alter VR streams, slightly changing the events in videogames being played on VR headsets; hacking into VR-hosted workplace discussions to implant provocative audio; or adding disturbing images to the AR apps on cellphones. An increasingly common tactic appears to be the insertion of subliminal messages into any VR or AR streams they can access.

The effects of this persistent assault on reality are only beginning to be felt, but already they appear to be worsening the challenging aspects of the infosphere that were already problematic for democracy. So many advanced democracies have become obsessed with shoring up the "real" that they have little time or energy left for productive policymaking. These attacks are deepening the polarization of democratic societies in ways that make the creation of a new bipartisan consensus on reform and change almost impossible.

What has turned out to be especially pernicious is the habit of discrediting individuals or groups who rise up to help improve this situation. When new fact-checking groups crop up, a dozen reports will emerge that they are tied to some unsavory criminal, funded by partisan donations, or generally corrupt. Any politicians who stand up for factual accuracy receive particularly brutal virtual assaults.

In some cases, in the United States, the effectiveness of such attacks has been aided and abetted by the long-term process of gerrymandering and polarization of representation districts and states. Many representatives now rely, especially in the primaries, disproportionately on narrow slices of the population to remain in office. Manipulators can affect the perceptions of those slices more effectively than a population as a whole. The effect is not unlike a political party that becomes dominated by one ideological subgroup and has a general chilling effect on political action, with most leaders simply unwilling to stick their necks out.

Most generally, these attacks are having the effect of further eroding social trust, the essential glue that keeps advanced societies of all sorts, democratic and otherwise, working efficiently. The mediating institutions of social reality, from the media to government, had already experienced a significant decline in trust by 2018. Now the very idea of a trusted objective reality is in real jeopardy. There is evidence that this trend is cascading through other elements of social trust, as would be expected when a constant flow of fabricated attacks is churning through a society that are designed to ruin trust in specific individuals and institutions. Over the last decade, long-term trends serving to weaken the sense of an objective, verifiable reality have accelerated, under the influence of a range of technologies that have deeply affected the infosphere of the United States and other developed economies. Some of the reasons for the trend and the justification for individual technologies are hopeful and creative, but the effect has been perilous for social coherence and democratic stability in a number of countries. And as the trend has accelerated, it has become less and less clear how it can be reversed or even moderated. The "death of reality" seems to be a self-reinforcing process; with each passing year, reaffirming a shared vision of facts and events seems less and less plausible.

# CHAPTER SIX

# Future 2: Silos of Belief (2024 Scenario)

## The General Future

It is 2024, and people have retreated ever further into closed, mutually suspicious information environments. Multiple groups of people in the same country are now essentially living in different realities.

Over time, the ability and inclination of people to closet themselves off into tightly self-referential communities of knowledge has only accelerated. The outlets that served as sources of shared fact and meaning, such as network news, major daily newspapers, and a bipartisan core of political leaders, have continued to give way to more discrete, bespoke, and often partisan sources of information. This shift has been partly a function of changing economics and the continued atrophying of respected information filters. In one recent example of this trend, *Washington Post* owner Jeff Bezos declared that the newspaper's business model was "irretrievable" and he could not continue to subsidize its operations with tens of millions of dollars per year. The paper's staff has developed a plan to transition to an exclusively online format and to shrink the size of the reporting staff, resulting in fewer stories and a stream of just one or two investigative reports per month.

But the paper's editors also made a fateful decision that reflects the spirit of the age: After several years of a largely failed appeal to a general readership, this famed major daily newspaper is now billing itself as the "essential guide for the thoughtful progressive." It is explicitly appealing to a specific demographic, trying to make itself the dominant player in one mega-silo rather than drawing people together from various belief groupings. This practice is now the norm for content creators of every variety. The name of the game is to find a silo and dominate it—with a product, a channel of information, or a perspective—rather than gain broad appeal.

These trends and this future began with the best of intentions. People were seeking out those with similar interests for discussion and shared ideas, whether regarding their hobby, their profession, or issues of concern. They sought to align with those who had similar ideas in order to marshal action on issues of shared importance. Such virtual communities have proved important in shoring up people's sense of belonging and ontological security in an era of massive, often homogenized societies, which carry the risk of submerging individual identities in abstract patterns and trends. By allowing people to seek out similar individuals, social media platforms and other forms of engagement offered an important psychological reassurance.

They also offered another form of empowering individual expression. With these capabilities, people could leapfrog the constraints of their immediate surroundings and connect with people of similar belief, experience, preference, or other shared identities or views. Those facing bias or repression could connect with others in a comparable situation and be strengthened and supported. People whose beliefs have been repressed by their community could find support through these means.

The *siloization* of the information space is, in part, the natural consequence of an era of individualization. Marketing campaigns are now almost entirely personalized; the ads one person gets, even down to their specific claims, are customized based on thousands of data points available to the advertisers. The idea of appealing to broad swaths of the population in one massive appeal now seems as primitive as a 1950s cigarette advertisement. Marketers today are pushing buttons on AI-driven engines that scoop up troves of information from databases and reach out to small groups or specific individuals with highly tailored messages.

But the challenge, as with many trends associated with the modern infosphere, has been to keep such a capability from running out of control and being expressed in ways that are socially destructive rather than individually empowering. The fragmentation of the marketplace characteristic of marketing to narrow groups has now been joined by a fragmentation across society, in political, social, and informational terms.

In terms of information access for individuals, it has simply become an accepted way of life for people to operate within self-defined groups. These can be professional, ideological, ethnic, or otherwise, but the essential guideposts of people's identities are now the distinctive echo chambers to which they belong. People wear clothes, put stickers on their cars, and otherwise self-identify with signifiers of these silos. The habit of operating in subgroups, with much less affiliation to the larger society, is by now firmly established.

The same technologies have provided avenues—for those with the time and appetite—to break *out* of their silos even more fundamentally than in the past. This has long been an opportunity resident in the internet and more comprehensive infosphere. People have an immense menu of opinions, approaches, and beliefs to sample from. But the overall result has nonetheless been a gradual fragmentation of people's information diet, and this appears to have catalyzed intervening psychological needs and reactions that cause at least some proportion of society to seek refuge ever deeper into limited silos of belief. Some social media platforms, for example, have adopted suggestions to intentionally expose people to attitudes from outside their algorithmically established preferences via their news feeds. And while some percentage of users take them up on the offer, experience suggests that between 30 percent and 60 percent (depending on the subgroup and the timing) do not; they simply ignore headlines that run obviously against the essential beliefs of their silo.

## A Fragmented Society

The existence of information silos builds on more profound social and economic trends, notably the division of society into more distinct and less permeable class, regional, and, in some cases, ethnic and racial segments. This division is the natural extension of the political polarization that has been growing in the country, supercharged by information silos that allow citizens to believe essentially whatever they want to believe and constantly discredit those who believe anything else. The emergence of these powerful information bubbles has deepened the polarization that was already under way and that made it impossible to enact any meaningful reforms.

In 2023, as just one example, the latest in a series of entitlement program reforms—designed to address the ballooning federal deficit and debt—collapsed before it even came to the floor of the House or Senate for a vote, irrevocably shattered by the competing grass-roots campaigns of a handful of social media information entrepreneurs spreading wild rumors and conspiracy theories within carefully selected silos about what the legislation would produce. Fundraising for charity is increasingly based on silos (asking for donations to help others in such narrowly defined groups), which are not always related to ethnicity, race, nationality, profession, or interests, but increasingly appeal to a person's identity as the member of a specific group. National bipartisan consensus on major policy issues has been, in a sense, overtaken by social events: It simply no longer exists, or can exist, in any measurable way. Political leaders hopeful of making national progress on any issue must now knit together bits and pieces of agreement from dozens of silos.

A common theme governing many of these silos is that the slices of information pouring into people's realities have become highly sensationalistic: violent, full of sexual content, and built on gossip and innuendo. Over time, information marketers have discovered the precise human information appetites that most attract attention. Different forms of information and content are tastier than others to the human brain; we have a neurobiological predilection for the extreme and the titillating.[1] Some people have become trapped in self-reinforcing silos of such content, and thousands have suffered significant emotional trauma and psychological injuries as a result. Therapeutic treatment centers for the "information traumatized" have sprung up across the country.

---

[1]   Pariser, 2011, p. 14.

The idea of what might be called a *unified social experience* has become passé. A popular term among the young for older Americans is "totalists," referring to people with a nostalgic desire for experiencing universal forms of information, experience, and truth. People attending the same concert now have dramatically different experiences, courtesy of the AR goggles they can purchase to add light shows, advertisements, and even guest artists. More significantly, there is no longer a single set of "news" to which all Americans are exposed. Newspapers are now almost entirely digital, and the feeds have become as algorithmically directed as web searches or Netflix recommendations. Major papers gather data on what readers are likely to *want* to see and feed them those stories first. The same has become true of television news broadcasts, which are now often "hosted" by AI-driven VR avatars that can be programmed to give specific viewers the news that will draw their attention.[2]

One associated problem is that people do not *think* they are in closed realities. Polls consistently show that people assume they are accessing a wide range of information, and they discount the degree to which their interaction with the world takes place with blinders on. They do not appreciate how cut off they are from a wide range of opinions.

In this emerging reality, herd behavior turns out to be more common within fragmented silos of social interaction than in society as a whole. Human beings are subject to panics and herd behavior in general, but the larger and more diverse the social entity, the more dampeners theoretically exist to constrain the herd rush in a certain direction. Within an ideologically, nationally, ethnically, racially, or politically homogenous silo, however, the dynamics of herding have proven to be extreme and inevitable.

---

[2]  Pariser, 2011, p. 45.

## The Wars of the Silos

Over time, these increasingly suspicious silos, along with broader social trends of fragmentation and ideological polarization, have produced an increasingly hostile series of aggressive actions between opposing groups. These actions have included trolling, cyberbullying, identity theft, distributed denial-of-service (DDoS) attacks, and floods of emails and prompts that overwhelm a computer or system. These wars—though among virtual communities—pit states against states, states against nonstate actors, and networks of nonstate groups against similar networks. Billionaires fund information to reinforce the beliefs of particular silos, and they help launch information wars—sometimes aimed at persuasion, often morphing into vicious cyberbullying—on others.

The wars also focus on debates over facts. Conservative groups skeptical of global warming funnel a constant stream of often misleading information into receptive bubbles, as do some progressive groups that are anti-vaccine or anti–genetically modified organisms (GMOs). Wealthy individuals or political action committees can simply decide that they want to believe something and, if that claim roughly agrees with preexisting ideological convictions, they can generate information—usually a mix of real and fabricated—to foment such beliefs.

Because of the fragmentation of the infosphere, these campaigns have limits and can never achieve majority support. But the nature of a fragmented society is such that they do not have to. A major lesson of the last two decades is that, in a highly polarized situation in which two political parties are in a gridlock, mobilizing even 30 percent of the population against a major policy idea is enough to kill it. This is especially true if most of that 30 percent lies within the base constituencies of the two parties, and thus strike special fear into the hearts of elected officials worried about primary challenges. In the past, when such minorities opposed policy ideas—civil rights reforms, for example—a larger bipartisan majority was available to override the political obstruction. That is no longer the case.

And this result has now been locked into place by the reality of information bubbles. There does not seem to be any prospect of re-creating a broad bipartisan majority on any issue, because no broad collection of Americans can be assembled for *anything*. Information professionals, whether corporate marketers, campaign managers, or issue entrepreneurs, have in fact given up trying. They are now entirely in the segmentation and specialization business. The problem for democracy is that this business works very well to persuade small numbers of people of something that fits into their preconceptions, but it is self-cancelling when it comes to building large-scale social consensus.

An accompanying trend is the fragmentation of expert communities, or *epistemic communities*, that had played some role in drawing together scientific knowledge. There are well-established, competing subgroups in most expert fields that regularly attack one another through social media, wars that are spilling over into academic journals and other forums. In some cases, the visions seem relatively arbitrary; they are not all ideological, and some subgroups seem to form around specific personalities or academic theories. Increasingly, the focus of academic activity is to discredit competing academic silos; specific departments are associated with one or another silo, as they previously had been associated with a school of thought.

There are parallel silos at the global level. Some autocratic states have had success sustaining national-level narratives with at least some residual appeal amid the fragmentation—far more so than democratic societies. Major autocracies are making use of these trends by trying to create and then wall off massive echo chambers that equate to their national or ethnic populations, including their diasporas. One way they are exporting their narratives is by forcing conditions on foreign companies and organizations for the right to engage with them. Even by 2018, for example, China had forced over 500 academic journals to blot out a handful of selected words—including "Tiananmen," "Dalai Lama," and "Tibet"—from their articles.[3] (The online versions of the

---

[3]  China's censorship efforts in this area are recounted in Evan Osnos, "Making China Great Again," *New Yorker*, January 8, 2018.

articles now come complete with retractions, as if they are declassified government documents.)

## A Burgeoning Landscape of Cyberharassment

One trend closely associated with the growth of echo chambers has been the explosion of the trolling ethic: widespread cyberharassment that characterizes the "wars of the silos." Despite growing efforts by several social media platforms, websites, and governments, the infosphere has become, in this reality, a notably crueler and more intimidating place.[4]

Cyberharassment and bullying have their roots partly in the massive trolling community that emerged a decade ago, on sites where angry, ironic bands of self-styled mischief-makers gathered to launch massive campaigns against any target that sparked their ire. One of the most infamous campaigns was Gamergate, in which women in the gaming community were subject to vicious, misogynistic, and sometimes brutally threatening online attacks.[5] These communities of cyber storm troops have both fragmented and metastasized, and the web is increasingly a place of anarchic wars of all-against-all in which waves of cyberattack are met with equally comprehensive ripostes.

A decade ago, conducting such an attack was a laborious act of cybercraftsmanship. Each step had to be hand coded. Today, such attacks are driven by AI engines custom-built to destroy people's lives using cyber means. These *attack bots* have a repertoire of thousands of potential actions to take and align an initial strategy with a target's seeming vulnerabilities, using various algorithmic guidance. They then track responses, such as public statements by or about the targets, evidence of actions they have taken, and the changing shape of available data about them, and escalate or tailor the ongoing campaign to what

---

4   To be clear, cyberharassment and bullying were likely to become significant components of any potential future information scenarios; they are inherent to a shared infosphere. But in an era of highly fragmented and often warring subcomponents, the echo chamber future has proven especially vulnerable to an explosion of these practices.

5   Nagle, 2017, pp. 15–17, 24–25, 35.

they see. All it takes now is for an official in one of the cyberaggressor countries to push a button, and a life is effectively destroyed. And because of the sophistication in spoofing and other means of concealment, AI-conducted cyberattacks are exceptionally difficult to trace.

Many of these attacks increasingly make use of the IoT as an avenue for harassment. An especially prominent commentator on one side of a silo war may come home to find that the WiFi-connected thermostat has been reprogrammed to overheat his or her house, or that the smart refrigerator has ordered a hundred gallons of milk. More sinister attacks have gone after the health of the targets, manipulating the settings of their web-enabled pacemaker or insulin pump and modifying the algorithm at their doctor's office that processes test results.

The result is an era in which the price for speaking up online—and, in especially virulent silo wars, the price of merely viewing certain content—can be very high. The danger of such information aggression has had a widespread chilling effect on public dialogue.

As an ultimate response, small groups of people who had been targeted began to join the "Off the Net" communities. Known collectively as "Off the Netters," these people had decided to back out of the public online world. While they made extensive use of cutting-edge technologies, such as renewable power and robotic medicine, they cut themselves off entirely from networked information systems: social media, the big five technology companies, smart homes, and the internet itself.[6] They established local banks, hospitals, grocery stores (an innovation that had not been seen since the Amazon Food Warehouse revolution of the early 2020s), all of which were entirely off-line. No data is collected on anyone in digital form except medical records, essential for effective diagnostics, and those are housed in air-gapped servers protected by high-level security. Several of these communities (which have now grown to contain more than 8 million residents in the United States and an equal number in Europe) began reaching out to

---

[6]    One irony of this development is that Off the Net communities at first had to reassemble construction firms that knew how to build a "dumb" home, without a high-speed nervous system of information pipes to connect and run every electronic system. Smart homes had become so ubiquitous that most construction companies had forgotten how to build anything else.

victims of massive cyberharassment campaigns, offering them a place of refuge where they can leave their corrupted public personas behind.

Part of the challenge in dealing with such attacks is that even today, a decade into the practice of cyberharassment, law enforcement authorities seldom give cyberharassment a high priority or have the technical skills to do much about it. To most local police, such an attack will typically seem like an abstract case for which they have no real expertise. National-level law enforcement, meanwhile—in addition to being overwhelmed these days with cases of extremists, radicals, militias, and other direct violent threats—typically has certain thresholds for being involved in a case. There are now so many national-level cyber threats that attacks on individuals generally go uninvestigated, unless the targets have the resources to hire a cyber detection and deterrence agency for themselves.

Such firms have become one of the fastest-growing components of the tech world. They represent a combination of antivirus software, private detective agency, home security company, and mafia protection racket. For a significant annual fee, tied to the "targetable ratio" of the potential customer (how likely they are to run afoul of some foreign government), these firms offer an insurance policy against cyberharassment. If and when it occurs, they will try to determine the source; send out notifications to friends, family, and coworkers; fix data corrupted in the attack; shut down fake sites and posts; and fight back, taking offensive action against any networks that seem to be responsible for the attack. Some of the rougher-edged firms even employ former special forces soldiers in a handful of countries to visit hackers and deliver the message with a personal touch.

This pattern of harassment also extends to organizations. North Korea set a modern precedent for such strategies with its attacks on Sony Pictures in 2014 and its parallel attack to undermine a British documentary about North Korean kidnapping. North Korea managed to scare away potential investors in the film.[7] Such strategies are commonplace today, and major U.S. and European media compa-

---

7    David E. Sanger, David D. Kirkpatrick, and Nicole Perlroth, "The World Once Laughed at North Korean Cyberpower. No More," *New York Times*, October 15, 2017.

nies generally refuse any project that they believe will offend any of the world's major cyberpowers. China has employed trolls and bots to crush any discussion online of unwelcome topics, including Tibet. These attacks have included direct harassment as well as the equivalent of denial-of-service attacks used to flood certain discussions.[8]

In a world of blurring boundaries between public and private actors, national governments do not have to undertake such campaigns of harassment directly. In many cases they can merely turn loose *script kiddies*: people willing to act as online proxies for the aggressive social manipulator. The larger echo chambers online have associated "militias" whose job it is to police countervailing opinions and launch counterattacks in response to any aggression against the silo of belief. Such retaliatory attacks have sometimes been empowered with innovative funding techniques. Hostile actors have crowdfunded the efforts, with Russian state agencies, for example, crowdsourcing "patriotic" Russians (and others around the world anxious to degrade U.S. power) to pay coders to attack U.S. targets.[9]

Another leading trend in these aggressive practices has been their growing precision through efforts to target specific foreign individuals marked as threats to the regimes. Many of these efforts take the form of classic cyberbullying, online harassment, and identity theft, including compromising targets' personal information, taking out loans or credit cards in their name, and sending threatening messages to home and work email accounts. But some campaigns have gone well beyond those prosaic approaches to many other forms of cyberharassment: creating false websites with allegedly compromising information; generating faked videos using high-grade digital mimicry programs that allegedly show the targets stealing, killing, or in intimate contexts; hacking official databases to corrupt the targets' tax or police records; sending critical emails to dozens of friends and colleagues; and hacking targets'

---

[8]   Segal, 2016, p. 215.

[9]   This strategy is already in evidence; see Hannes Grassegger and Mikael Krogerus, "Weaken from Within," *New Republic*, November 2, 2017.

social media pages to post offensive material supposedly in their name.[10] The attacks also combine real-world actions with cyberstrikes, such as planting drugs in a target's apartment and then notifying the police or having couriers deliver seemingly handwritten notes. But everything is done remotely. They even send crude and self-incriminating emails seemingly *from* the target, using spoofing techniques to conceal the origins of the messages.

## Information-Based Aggression and the Silo Future

The emergence of a more fragmented infosphere of dominant echo chambers has proved to be an enormous boon to information-based aggression.

One obvious technique has been to identify silos of especially extreme, grievance-fueled, and paranoid belief and amp the members up to violent levels of social discontent. There have been multiple examples already of local protests, some of which have turned violent, spurred by fabricated (or exaggerated) information pumped into these groups. These attacks have also been fueled by the acquisition of colossal databases of individualized data on Americans by foreign powers, in some cases directly stolen from social media platforms or marketing firms or painstakingly built from dozens of specific data thefts. It is said that there is a group of social scientists in Moscow with a more precisely tuned understanding of U.S. social dynamics than any political scientist in the United States, but this is only a rumor.

In the process, information aggressors are taking advantage of natural herd behaviors in large groups, which are even more consistent among echo chambers than among the population at large. Manipulators expertly target the influencers in specific social networks who dominate one silo or echo chamber and trigger cascades of discussion

---

10  Many of these examples are drawn from the case described in Brooke Jarvis, "Me Living Was How I Was Going to Beat Him," *Wired*, December 2017. It cites one statistic that by 2016 over 10 million Americans reported that they had been threatened with, or had experienced, the unauthorized sharing of explicit images online.

and belief—and, if they are lucky, fury and resentment—based on sometimes fabricated, sometimes simply exaggerated stories.

In the process, information aggressors are also seeking to exacerbate the siloization of U.S. society by spreading stories (sometimes real, sometimes not) that intensify mutual suspicions. Echo chambers around liberal scientific themes will get a steady stream of information about the evils of conservative scientists manning countervailing silos, and populist echo chambers will be bombarded with information about how daily events reflect the conspiratorial "deep state" in action; anyone speaking for one of a dozen alternative echo chambers should not be trusted. These trends were well under way in the infosphere, and they provided excellent raw material for manipulators to work with.

Campaigns of societal aggression are also turning the increasingly AI-driven, automated aspects of the information environment against democracies. One important tool now being used by hostile powers and groups is the corruption of the algorithms that targeted marketers use to access information bubbles.[11] In some cases, they will direct very partisan, hostile messages to the opposite side of the spectrum to cause anger and hostility. They will hack newspaper algorithms to push specific sets of stories onto people that either are favorable to the aggressor's point of view or simply cause anxiety.

This future is evolving rapidly and in ways clearly injurious to social and democratic stability. The degree of siloization of the U.S. public (and the publics of other advanced democracies) is mixed; some are much more deeply embedded in exclusive echo chambers than others, and the effect on shared perceptions is not uniform. But the general trend has been an acceleration and deepening of these developments and, in particular, the rise of increasing hostility and outright informational conflict among the silos. Where it is headed, and whether countertrends will emerge soon, remains unclear.

---

[11]  Danah Boyd, "Your Data Is Being Manipulated," *Data and Society, Points*, October 4, 2017.

# CHAPTER SEVEN

# Future 3: The Rise of the Algorithms (2026 Scenario)

## The General Future

In the decade leading up to 2026, vast amounts of personalized information about everyone have been integrated into huge databases across the IoT, social media, medicine, law, employment, and a dozen other fields. Increasingly, both public and private organizations are employing algorithmic decisionmaking to make sense of this flood of information. The process began with algorithms to determine internet search results and make suggestions to consumers based on their browsing and purchasing histories—the "if you liked that, you will love this" model. But now the use of algorithmic decisionmaking has exploded into a dozen different fields. Algorithms today decide, or at least make powerful initial recommendations for decisions, on the treatment of disease (and the point at which continued treatment is no longer justified), sentencing for criminals, hiring of employees, deployment of law enforcement units across cities, and much more. Those algorithms build on the essential foundation of an algorithmic era: the oceans of data available on citizens, or what might be called a *cloud of knowing*.

In so many ways, algorithmic decisionmaking has improved human life. It has offered unprecedented forecasting accuracy regarding a range of illnesses and medical conditions, allowing, in some cases, prompt treatment and cures. It has empowered targeted policing in some cities with measurable effects on crime rates. It has, in some specific instances, introduced a new degree of objectivity into sentencing, reducing the sentences faced by some new offenders for specific categories of crimes and producing what has been broadly viewed as enhanced justice in those areas. It has measurably improved the efficiency of thousands of businesses, including in their energy usage, which has contributed to the important goal of reducing carbon emissions.

But the rush to deploy such algorithms has taken place piecemeal, without much oversight or discussion of their social implications. And despite their favorable potential, they are vulnerable to social manipulation and indicative of a larger trend toward machine-driven decision-making with complex implications that are not well understood.

## The Cloud of Knowing

Over the last several years, progress in several information-related technologies, such as big data, the IoT, AI, and more, have accelerated and converged around one emerging reality: the intense, shared awareness of massive amounts of data about every individual human being in the developed world (and the more globally integrated elements of developing world populations as well). The total amount of data in these systems has continued to double roughly every two years,[1] generating requirements (and markets) for massive new cloud-based data hosting services, AI-driven search and manipulation functions, and other means of hosting and manipulating these mind-boggling amounts of information.

For years now, every person has been leaving a "digital exhaust"[2] of choices, preferences, habits, personal information, relationships, purchases, and much more. For a decade or more, every person's every move online has been tracked, cataloged, and assessed, in large part using tracking "cookies" sent to the user's browser by various sites. Peo-

---

[1]   International Data Cooperation, "Executive Summary: Data Growth, Business Opportunities, and the IT Imperatives," in *The Digital Universe of Opportunities: Rich Data and the Increasing Value of the Internet of Things*, Framingham, Mass., April 2014.

[2]   The term comes from Dale Neef, *Digital Exhaust*, Upper Saddle River, N.J.: Pearson FT Press, 2014. See also National Public Radio, "Big Data Revolution," *TED Radio Hour*, September 9, 2016.

ple's choices of movies, their web searches, their inputs to online dictionaries, and their tweets and social media comments have generated a fantastic amount of data. By 2016, Acxiom, Cambridge Analytica, and similar firms had collected between 1,000 and 5,000 individual pieces of information about every American.[3] With the advent of the IoT, that stream exploded and became increasingly interlinked. Billions of devices are now connected to shared data systems, and they are getting progressively smaller, with many smart sensors now smaller than the human eye can see. Some estimates suggest that the 500 billion IoT devices in place already account for nearly $3 trillion in world gross domestic product (GDP).[4]

Ubiquitous sensing and data collection now gathers information on a million distinct subjects, including how quickly people drink their milk, as sensed by their smart refrigerator; the quality of their personal waste, as assessed by their smart toilet; what they say as children, as recorded and archived by their smart toys;[5] how long they linger on stories about female U.S. novelists as opposed to male British film stars, as reported by their news subscriptions on their iPad; the precise measurements of their body as well as a hundred data points (many personality-related) that help virtual fashion assistants choose the right wardrobe for them;[6] and the ideas they express in their social media posts, as tracked, collated, and analyzed by AI-driven bots. Every day, terabytes of such data join the troves of personal information available on public and easily hackable databases, including the finest details of their medical, psychological, and educational histories, all now stored together to allow machine-learning analytics targeted at well-being, with their daily mood and location (and persistent location history) tracked by their new FitBit Emote or other mobile fitness-tracking

---

[3]   Pariser, 2011, pp. 6–7.

[4]   Global Agenda Council on the Future of Software and Society, 2015, p. 8.

[5]   Erik Silfversten, "A Smart Toy Could Have Personal Details for Life, Not Just for Christmas," *RAND Blog*, December 2017; Norwegian Consumer Council, *#Toyfail: An Analysis of Consumer and Privacy Issues in Three Internet-Connected Toys*, Oslo, December 2016.

[6]   Drew Harwell, "Companies Race to Gather a Newly Prized Currency: Our Body Measurements," *Washington Post*, January 16, 2018.

device. By 2021, almost 250 million such wearable devices were being sold every year.[7]

*The Cloud* (the term people are now using as a shorthand description of the mass of data hanging over their lives and crowding into every choice and opportunity) knows whether your children are on attention deficit/hyperactivity disorder (ADHD) medication, what their latest grades were, and the relationship between the two (and the relationship of each to a thousand other variables). It knows what their teachers think about them to a far greater degree than what their parents know. It knows who your friends are, knows about their habits and preferences, and knows how to use those data to predict your behavior, to a fine statistical probability. It knows the language you use when writing—favorite words and phrases, common grammatical errors, etc.—and what this says about your personality and preferences. It knows where you have driven your car, as gathered by GPS-enabled sensors (now standard in essentially every new vehicle sold in the United States) and communicated through the auto company, and, as a result, can make strong inferences about your behavior.[8] (Regular trips to the liquor store tell the system one thing; a sudden spate of stops at an urgent care center would tell it something else.) Through persistent surveillance and facial recognition, it knows what mood you are in and, in some cases, can approximate what you are thinking.

Increasingly, in fact, every item in society, whether financial, social, or political, is less important for what it is than for the data it gathers and transmits. Automobiles now have 200 to 300 times more lines of code than the original space shuttle.[9] A child's toy has the processing power of early supercomputers. Dolls, iPads, exercise equipment, diabetic sensors, and much more are most valuable for what they tell The Cloud—and those who seek to profit from it—about their users. Companies are selling the physical items as loss leaders

---

7    Patrick Tucker, "Strava's Just the Start: The US Military's Losing War Against Data Leakage," *Defense One*, January 31, 2018.

8    Peter Holley, "Big Brother on Wheels: Why Your Car Company May Know More About You Than Your Spouse," *Washington Post*, January 15, 2018.

9    The number in 2018 was 200 times greater (Holley, 2018).

to get customers into a permanent information relationship. And this information, coursing in unbelievably massive torrents through various information networks, is generally weakly protected and available to just about any enterprising hacker willing to dip a prospecting pan into the flowing streams of data.

Through about 2020, these trends continued to generate a debate about privacy. That term has now largely dropped from the public dialogue. The standing assumption—apart from a small but growing number of "Off the Netters," people forming high-tech but "data-free" communities in remote areas—is that everything you do, say, believe, or buy (if it is not consciously hidden from the array of sensors and bots surrounding us) is now captured into The Cloud. The goal is no longer to fight this reality but to navigate within it and make the best use of it possible.

There is no longer any such thing as a "private self" disconnected from The Cloud. There is only a collective self, a massive collection of data that exists as a virtual representation of our actual selves and drives a million AI-authored actions every day.[10] And this collection is increasingly orchestrated by a massive and interlinked spiderweb of algorithms.

The reality became unavoidable partly because of a continued trend of massive growth by the core tech companies of the emerging era: Alphabet (Google), Apple, Facebook, Amazon, and Microsoft.[11] Their growth was fueled by an accelerating cycle of profits, grabbing up innovating firms, research and development to generate new capabilities, and rising market share (and thus more profits). Any new firm or constellation of firms that sought to challenge them in any meaningful area, such as medical data, content provision, or smart home networks, has been crushed or bought. They became the inverse of what was expected from the high-tech era: large rather than small, with

[10]   On the growth of neural networks capable of data analysis, see Cade Metz, "Finally, Neural Networks That Actually Work," *Wired*, April 21, 2015.

[11]   China has a parallel set of firms—AliBaba, Baidu, Tencent, and others—but they have become largely walled off from the outside internet. Their reach beyond China is confined to secondary networks that are air-gapped from the core mainland networks and serve the ethnic Chinese diaspora throughout Asia.

central control rather than grassroots authority. The latest estimate is that these five companies control something like 85 percent of all the elements, such as databases, companies, and technologies, of the inter-linked big-data world.

## Interactive Data

Through about 2019–2020, this data remained a largely issue-specific collection of facts that could be purchased by marketers or politicians or used by websites to drive sales. Amazon used what people bought and looked at to predict future interest and push sales, Google continued to perfect its search engine algorithms for targeted marketing, and a drug company could buy data on people's medical histories to sell its product. But over the last two years, sparked by a surge in AI capabilities and tech company mergers, The Cloud has become much more interlinked and vastly smarter. It now anticipates, evaluates, and guesses with astonishing accuracy, at least about a certain category of individual and collective actions most subject to algorithmic prediction.

With a few keystrokes, one of the data engineers overseeing elements of The Cloud (though with the explosion of machine-learning–driven AI, the idea of "oversight" is becoming less and less meaningful) can get a highly accurate impression of many things about any individual: where they have been and where they are planning to go—and where they are likely to go; what they have bought; and, to a 70–80 percent probability, what they *will buy* over the coming month. The origins of this knowledge lie in the algorithms developed by such firms as Netflix, which have long been able to predict how well someone would like a given movie, within a roughly 10 percent margin of error.[12]

At the same time, The Cloud no longer waits on conscious human intervention to undertake such analysis or make such choices. It is home to millions of purpose-built algorithms that anticipate human behavior with growing accuracy, in many cases applied and continually refined by more than a billion AI-driven bots that constantly assess the data

---

12  Pariser, 2011, p. 8.

and then take actions to advance preprogrammed goals. With the IoT and other networked aspects of a broadly unified cloud, the messages, ads, tracing functions, and other contact points of this process follow users from device to device, site to site, and place to place. The Cloud observes and responds to actions without anyone being involved. In many important respects, it is a driverless network. "The algorithms that orchestrate our ads are starting to orchestrate our lives," Pariser wrote in 2011.[13] Today, in 2026, the effect is ubiquitous.

And The Cloud increasingly operates in real time. Long gone are the days when someone's digital exhaust was laboriously gathered into databases that could be weeks or even months old. Now, people interact with a dozen instantaneous information-gathering sensors: watches, implants, built-in cameras and microphones, social media platforms, and more.[14] Radio-frequency identification (RFID) devices have been implanted in just about all meaningful items you purchase, allowing them to be tracked when they pass within range of any RFID sensor—of which there are now billions spread throughout the country. Even your *possessions* are generating digital exhaust.[15] The result is a constantly updated sense of behavior and preferences that produces messages (such as ads) and is then iterated based on the reactions to those messages.

As a result, interactive platforms and systems have had to become far more responsive and nimbler. By 2019, basic personalized ad systems had arrived in stores, consisting of video banners and speakers that would offer specific products and discounts to specific individuals as they walked by, sometimes broadcast on their AR headsets (or generated as AR cartoons in the images captured by their smartphones). At first, though, they were single, inflexible messages. Within 18 months, that gave way to an agile, responsive engagement: The system would throw out an ad, gauge the emotional and biophysical response, see if

---

[13] Pariser, 2011, p. 9.

[14] By 2021, a third of Americans had accepted tiny implants in their forearms designed to convey health data to medical professionals, but which also offered marketers second-by-second readings of emotional reactions to advertisements and products.

[15] Pariser, 2011, p. 198.

the person was slowing to look or think, and then adapt the message.[16] It could lower the price, toss in one of a number of "nudges" (grounded in behavioral economics insights) judged to be effective with this individual, offer a message from a virtual avatar of a famous person, or more. The Cloud had empowered the world to interact with people on a constant basis in a highly personalized way.

Part of the problem, though—the significance of which few anticipated early on—is that even the designers of the algorithms often do not quite know why they spit out the results they do. This was clear enough at the beginning: Google coders, authors of some of the most sophisticated search algorithms on the planet, could build the equation and watch the data come in, but, at a certain point, there were so many variables involved that they could no longer follow the causal links to the outputs. They simply could not explain why their algorithmic machines generated the results they did. This mystery was less important when, for example, they could not explain the precise results of an internet search. In 2026, with algorithms generating conclusive social choices on everything from health care decisions to mortgage approvals and criminal sentences, people are starting to object to the standard-issue answer that "the numbers don't lie." Nobody knows, frankly, whether they are lying or not. All anyone knows are the high-level associational patterns that seem to prove the algorithms are working. But no one can know for sure whether any specific case—such as an output that recommends heart surgery instead of medication or a ten-year sentence instead of five—is an outlier.

One surprising source of data has come from the explosion of chatbots over the last decade. One of the first to gain widespread use and reaction was Microsoft's Tay, which served as a powerful warning of the risks of interactive machine learning. Trolls decided to corrupt the system and flooded it with comments in the voice of Nazi sympathizers, and Tay, "learning" from its interactions, began to repeat back those comments to many unsuspecting users. Subsequent efforts have become much more reliable and realistic: A Chinese version (Xiaoice, also from Microsoft) quickly followed, and by 2016 was producing

---

16  Silhavy et al., 2017, p. 377.

remarkably well-received dialogues, prompting some users to declare their love for the bot.[17] Generating powerful connective tissue between human beings and chatbots was easier than many had assumed.

Over the last two years on Facebook, through tailor-made phone apps or just online, chatbots have become the 2020s equivalent of the app craze of a decade ago. Thousands have emerged, each with a slightly different focus and all grounded in AI engines of varying sophistication. Many are counselors, programmed with hordes of clinical psychologists' wisdom. Some are trainers: Set up your EVM-enabled phone to watch you play basketball (or work out or ride a bike), and then discuss the results with your AI coach, which has evaluated the video for tendencies and problems. Some are religious advisors or life coaches. Some are educational and act as experts in any of a thousand subjects. Some are just friends, available in any race, gender, ethnicity, religion, personality, age, or any other variation you might want. (There are a wide variety of artificial romantic partners, for those so inclined.) Some are historical figures and others are avatars of present-day celebrities, athletes, or politicians.

Early versions of the chatbots were strictly textual: enter a message, get an AI-driven reply. Often, they were just good for a lark, to laugh at some of the silly responses the first-generation AI engines dreamed up. Very quickly, however, thanks to iterated improvement and machine learning, developers had generated avatars and then highly realistic embodiments of human forms that "say" the responses dictated by the AI engine. Now there is a huge range of chatbots, including a few old text ones, many audio ones, and an increasing number of high-fidelity video versions, which are so lifelike that, when encountered through Skype or another online portal, most users simply refuse to believe that they are not interacting with an actual person.

---

[17] See Hannah Devlin, "Human-Robot Interactions Take Step Forward with 'Emotional' Chatbot," *The Guardian*, May 5, 2017; Liz Tracy, "In Contrast to Tay, Microsoft's Chinese Chatbot, Xiaolce, Is Actually Pleasant," *Inverse*, March 26, 2016; and Taylor Soper, "Why People in China Love Microsoft's Xiaoice Virtual Companion, and What It Says About Artificial Intelligence," *GeekWire*, November 25, 2015.

## The Cloud Knows Where You Have Been—and What You Think

What users often do not realize, even though the dense user agreements make it clear, is that everything they say or do when engaging a chatbot is being recorded, processed, and evaluated for use by other elements of the IoT and The Cloud. Their opinions, thoughts, reactions to ideas raised by the chatbot, offhand comments, and even what they might be doing (doodling, knitting, multitasking with a phone, etc.) while talking to the bot are recorded. Selling "engagement time" on chatbots is now a huge market. A company might buy 30 seconds on a cooking education bot you use, direct it to suggest to you a particular product, sense your reaction, modify and iterate, and then track your later purchases to see if you buy it.

In some locations, The Cloud has come to include an ongoing record of recent events, which some have taken to calling a "digital past." A combination of closed-circuit television (CCTV) cameras, private security cameras that have agreed to be linked into The Cloud, and a web of constantly circling drones maintain an ongoing video portrait of a given city, generating a form of persistent surveillance. When a crime happens, police can go back to the digital record for that moment and then work backward, discovering the route of the criminals before the crime, or forward, tracing their movements.[18] Law enforcement departments across the country, partly funded by generous donations from law-and-order–focused wealthy philanthropists, are building a shared database of photos of everyone they arrest, which can be used in concert with pervasive facial recognition (PFR) to locate suspects.[19]

That backward-looking capability has been linked to real-time surveillance in the form of PFR systems. In most urban areas today, people who do not intentionally evade detection will be constantly scanned by high-resolution facial recognition technologies capable of

---

[18]   Such a system has already been used to track insurgents in Iraq and has been deployed on a trial basis in Dayton, Ohio. See "Eye in the Sky," *Radiolab*, June 18, 2015.

[19]   Pariser, 2011, pp. 194–195.

over 90 percent accuracy with less than a second of exposure time. Scanners can assign digital "ankle bracelets" to suspected individuals, and the system will track their movements on a constant basis.[20] Police in most major cities are now equipped with sunglasses with cameras that conduct a constant facial recognition search of passing citizens, looking for hits on suspected criminals.[21] When the system hits on a wanted individual, automatic signals are sent to tracker drones, which race to the location to detain the individual until police can arrive. In some cities, when habitual jaywalkers are sensed approaching an intersection, their phone beeps with a texted warning; people using public bathrooms who grab large amounts of toilet paper or paper towels get a similar note.

These broad-based surveillance systems have been joined by EVM technologies, which can sense the tiniest details in scenes captured by the cameras. These details can include everything from the twitches of a person's eye muscles, to changes in blood flow through veins sensed through the skin, to the tiniest shifts in solid objects.[22] People who seem to be trying to evade the recognition system—with distractions, such as sunglasses, hats, and beards—are routinely stopped for identity checks. Where such persistent surveillance is in place, no one can be confident that he or she can move around without being sensed. But the surveillance is often billed as helpful: Our iPads and Kindle readers now sense our reactions to every idea in every book we read.[23]

---

[20]  For a description of the technologies being developed as of 2018 by the Chinese firm SenseTime, see Osnos, 2018. The jaywalking and toilet paper examples that follow are drawn from this account.

[21]  Zheping Huang, "Chinese Police Are Wearing Sunglasses That Can Recognize Faces," *Defense One*, February 9, 2018.

[22]  Wu et al., 2012.

[23]  Suggested in Yuval Noah Harari, "Big Data, Google, and the End of Free Will," *Financial Times*, August 26, 2016.

## Ruled by Algorithm: Surrendering to the POPE

The system's Orwellian implications have been softened by reports of dozens of helpful and even lifesaving applications. Lost children have been recovered in minutes. Abducted children have been rescued: Parents can set a range warning on their children, so that if the system detects them moving more than a mile from home or school without prearrangement by the family, police are dispatched. Suicides have been prevented. Oncoming strokes have been diagnosed by EVM cameras and AI engines, with ambulances sent to arrive just *before* the stroke occurred. In more prosaic ways, stores can detect the preferences of passing customers to offer discounts, and marketers can promote products with surgical precision.

In the smart home of 2026, someone walking around in a bad mood is likely to be approached by his PFR- and EVM-guided, AI-driven virtual concierge (the vastly smarter and more human descendants of Siri, Alexa, and other crude, first-generation interactive systems).[24] "You seem to be bummed today, Jeremy," it might say, then:

> How about I order your favorite Chinese dish? I can have it here in 23 minutes, and there's still a Duvel beer left in the back of the fridge. The money you set aside for food this week still has $50 left, plenty for the order. Or I can suggest eight approved recipes you could put together with the food you have in the house, and we can walk through them together while I play some nice jazz in the kitchen.

The Cloud would be constantly gathering the results of millions of such interactions, parsing the resulting data for relationships and hints to iterate its performance.

In the same very fine-tuned and intuitive way a spouse might become attuned to his or her partner's facial expressions, able to read mood and preferences in ways that go well beyond verbal communication, The Cloud can perform a reasonable facsimile of such attunement.

---

24  A brief description of several emerging "digital counselors" is Signe Brewster, "I Spent a Week Living with Chatbots—Did All That Self-Help Help?" *Wired*, January 4, 2018.

The critical implication—already much in evidence a decade ago but now increasingly ubiquitous—is the fact that algorithms now make thousands of social decisions previously left to human judgment.

Today, when a teenager is arrested for the first time on a minor charge, it is an algorithm—not a judge—that will decide his or her punishment. When someone arrives at an emergency room, sensors will gather thousands of pieces of data, marry them to the individual's medical record on file, and then algorithms will direct the hospital staff on treatment. Algorithms, combined with AI-driven, VR interactive chatbots, have replaced therapists in many cases of lower-level therapeutic treatment. They are deciding how much of a city's welfare budget to spend on what programs and where to place foster children. They are determining the answers to mortgage applications and increasingly *predicting* who, at ages 22–25, will be financially responsible at ages 40–50 and therefore should be granted access to special financial programs.[25]

Equipped with this burgeoning range of capabilities, the activities of The Cloud have come to reflect a basic idea known as the "principle of passive election," or POPE.[26] If the AI programs can provide an accurate sense of what you are likely to do, need, or think regarding various issues,[27] why go through the trouble of making such a decision through conscious effort? ("Just do what the POPE says," people say.) The simplest example is shopping: The grocery store as we once knew it has become a thing of the past, replaced with vast warehouses

---

[25]  On the general trend and its risks, see Danah Boyd, "Beyond the Rhetoric of Algorithmic Solutionism," *Data and Society: Points*, January 11, 2018.

[26]  This concept emerged in part from the writings on behavioral economics and the analysis of how best to "nudge" people to make "more-accurate" decisions. Scholars writing in this field cataloged human "irrationalities"—consciously choosing to earn less interest than they might, for example—and sought to "correct" these anomalies with hints or implicit influence. A prominent example was in altering the default options on certain elective choices—saving for retirement, for example. This principle of determining objectively more efficient outcomes and presuming human choice to match them has now become generalized and superempowered by The Cloud.

[27]  Scott Magids, Alan Zorfas, and Daniel Leemon, "The New Science of Customer Emotions," *Harvard Business Review*, November 2015.

run by Amazon. Big data showed that most people's weekly food purchases were 73 percent standard, so why waste the time of driving to a 19th-century grocery store and going through the same annoying process every week? Smart refrigerators and preference algorithms, which generate experimental purchases on the same "if you liked that, you will love this" principle of Amazon's website, make people's choices for them. Consumers can always override the system, but few do, and surveys suggest that 90 percent of customers are satisfied with the decisions The Cloud makes for them.

Around 2016, the scholar Yuval Noah Harari began calling this mindset "Dataism." "Given enough biometric data and computing power," he explained, "this all-encompassing system could understand humans much better than we understand ourselves. Once that happens, humans will lose their authority, and humanist practices such as democratic elections will become as obsolete as rain dances and flint knives."[28] This loss of authority has now essentially occurred, with a combination of sensors capable of gathering millions of discrete biochemical, neurological, behavioral, and attitudinal data points on a second-by-second basis and translating them into algorithmically based preferences. The Dataists can rightly argue that on most choices, the system does, as Harari worried, "understand my feelings much better than I can," and therefore makes objectively more-accurate decisions.[29] As long as a decade ago, for example, it was established that algorithms could make better judgments about people's personalities, based on their digital exhaust, than humans could.[30]

The POPE has been extended to other categories of purchases, such as clothing, cars, and even houses. The Cloud often knows what you want better than you do, in that it is a more objective evaluator of preferences than your own bias-fueled decision engine. The principle was long established in online dating sites, which have now become

---

28   Harari, 2016.

29   Harari, 2016.

30   Wu Youyou, Michael Kosinski, and David Stilwell, "Computer-Based Personality Judgments Are More Accurate Than Those Made by Humans," *Proceedings of the National Academy of Sciences*, Vol. 112, No. 4, 2015.

radically more accurate and effective. Almost no one would hazard connecting with a possible mate against their advice: The numbers just do not add up. Match.com now boasts a 37 percent "eventually marry" figure for its "high-confidence" matches; data suggest that only 2 percent of people who manually chose their dating partners end up in an extended relationship.

The scholar Alex Pentland called one version of the resulting science "social physics": a "quantitative social science that describes reliable, mathematical connections between information and idea flow on the one hand and people's behavior on the other." The ambitions of the new science, as Pentland phrased them, were immodest: "Let us imagine," he hypothesized, "the ability to place an imaging chamber around an entire community and then to record and display every facet and dimension of behavior, communication, and social interaction among its members."[31] He had in mind using data-driven forecasts of human social behavior to design more–energy-efficient communities, smoother transportation flows, more-stable financial markets, and more-effective medical interventions.

All of this has come to pass in 2026, even very nearly the degree of data collection envisioned in his "imaging chamber" future. But his anticipated applications have emerged as part of something much bigger: the application of social physics to a growing number of human activities.

The principle extends to areas well beyond economic choices. The Cloud, expressed in the form of the POPE, instructs school principals on which kids to pair with which teachers. It, not the coach or offensive coordinator, comes into the National Football League (NFL) quarterback's earpiece to suggest the next play. Based on emotional reactions, it tells radio stations what songs to play next. It tells police forces where to deploy their beat cops to get the best crime-prevention results. In a first hint of the "predictive policing" described in such science-fiction films as *Minority Report*, The Cloud can identify a small number of people who have a greater-than-95-percent chance of committing a major crime in the next week. Such people are now routinely picked up

---

[31] Pentland, 2014, pp. 4, 9.

and warned, though society has not yet agreed to any actual punishments for precrime intentions.[32]

Innovative scholars and programmers are now beginning to toy with extending the POPE into politics. For the most part, the political institutions of the developed world have continued to operate as they were in the pre-Cloud days. (People increasingly refer to primitive, time-consuming, and inefficient deliberative judgment on probabilistic issues as "BTC [Before The Cloud] Junk.") Politicians employ all manner of sophisticated AI-driven advertising techniques, but the essential structures and processes of legislatures and executives have remained unchanged. The biggest difference has been in what decisions are being made: One effect of an intelligent, data- and AI-driven cloud has been to narrow dramatically the space for politics. The Cloud has rendered a hundred social issues as technical probability challenges, including education, law enforcement, poverty reduction, and energy security. In so many areas, the POPE has replaced conscious, dialogue-driven public choice as the way society applies resources and makes judgments. And because the results are good—and measurable—people are generally fine with this outcome.

Now there are proposals to essentially trade out the remaining openly political decisions for the POPE. The Cloud can know, to a high degree of probability, what people's choices, behaviors, thoughts, expressed ideas, and implied beliefs suggest they will want in a social system. And it can build algorithms to create the optimal satisfaction of the highest number of such preferences. It has the potential to become, in effect, an AI-driven automated version of the rationalization of interests that the Founding Fathers believed would happen through clash and compromise. All of that rationalization can happen inside an equation, without the costs, distractions, tensions, and sometimes outright conflict of an open political process. It presents the same choice, in the end, as when buying groceries: If The Cloud knows what

---

[32]  In less-open countries, such as Russia and China, the situation is very different. The governments are rumored to have set their threshold for warnings at a 60 percent likelihood of committing crimes, and they arrest and imprison anyone with a likelihood over 90 percent. Those thresholds are for traditional crimes; for political disloyalty, the thresholds are much lower.

people will end up preferring, why not empower it to take the actions necessary to fulfill that preference?

## Vulnerabilities and Risks

There have been glitches and there are risks, to be sure. Any large data network is hackable, and profit-driven hackers have used every possible angle to siphon resources off The Cloud. They steal FaceCoins and AlphaCash; reroute driverless electric trucks full of groceries to black market distribution points; and grab personal data and use it, as they have for decades, to fuel identity theft. An especially significant trend has been the use of supercharged ransomware attacks to lock down major pieces of the interlinked Cloud (typically things tied into the IoT), forcing either individual users or major corporations to pay massive amounts to unlock the information.

By and large, though, the system has proved more resilient than many feared. This resilience has been a product of two things. First, the very denseness and interconnectedness of the network turn out to make it less vulnerable. There are very few single points of failure and many backup systems and capabilities. Second, the most powerful AI advances are proprietary to the big five firms, and they are deployed to protect the stability of The Cloud. They anticipate, sense, and hunt down various efforts to undermine or steal from it. The result is nothing like perfect but has been largely good enough.

Another risk or popular vulnerability of The Cloud has been the sense that it increasingly reflects a series of constraints on individual freedom. Citizens of advanced democracies have increasingly begun to see aspects of this algorithmic reality as sinister, slightly muted versions of China's infamous "social credit score": a cruelly simplified number that reflects a person's reliability in economic and political terms.[33] Even in the United States, access to key social goods, including loans and jobs, as well as the best schools, doctors, and hospitals, is deter-

---

[33] For a description of how the social credit score is working, see Mara Hvistendahl, "Inside China's Vast New Experiment in Social Ranking," *Wired*, December 14, 2017.

mined by numeric representations of people's lifelong behavior, stored in databases whose operations are typically blocked to public scrutiny. People are denied homes, employment, and admission to college for reasons they do not understand. The public outcry against this trend is growing and reflects a major vulnerability of this algorithmic decisionmaking reality.

This trend reflects larger challenges with The Cloud's relationship to the populations it serves. One such challenge is the symbiosis between the system and its criminals and saboteurs. A few extreme neo-anarchist hackers style themselves as modern-day Unabombers, believing that the entire Cloud-based system is wicked and must be brought down. Mostly, however, the smarter hackers know that their success *depends on* functioning networks. They are self-conscious about their basic goal: to skim enough off the top to enrich themselves without threatening the basic integrity of The Cloud.

There have been hundreds of documented cases in which a new piece of profit-seeking malware began metastasizing through The Cloud in unexpected and dangerous ways, and then cybersecurity firms received mysterious instructions about how to best disable the worms. The relationship between security officials and hackers has taken on some of the characteristics of U.S.-Soviet relations in the late Cold War: hostile but governed by a dense network of formal and informal rules and norms and stabilized by some degree of personal relationships (even if often virtual to protect real identities) and a significant degree of mutual respect.

Still, a growing number of people, concerned about the fundamental absence of any shred of privacy, have taken to employing online avatars as their Cloud-based personae, while leaving many aspects of their real selves secret. These avatars have come to be known as "Echoes." Such an avatar reflects certain characteristics of the real person, in order not to generate a massive flow of totally useless ads, offers, and information, but is distinct in key ways: thus, an "echo" of the real person. The dark web is full of sites that sell fully fleshed-out Echoes embedded in primary databases and complete with personal information (e.g., birth certificates, tax returns, and school transcripts); long-term records of browsing and purchases; a fictitious address and whole residence history; family histories added to ancestry websites; and even fabricated appearances—faces generated with image-generation software and hacked into facial recognition databases to make it appear as if this invented "person" had been walking around various cities.

By far the biggest risk, however, is that such technologies, resulting in the automation of choice, have created a faceless hive mind that divides Americans into favored and disfavored groups across a wide range of issues. The technology is boosting inequality because it can only look at how past performance ought to guide future outcomes. It cannot account for the accidental, the change of trajectory, or the potential for change, nor can it account for outliers that do not match established patterns. The result has been to harden social divisions in a world of automated choice, in which it has seemingly become even more difficult to escape one's accumulated reputation.

## Information Aggression in an Algorithmic Future

The primary means of information-based aggression in this future has been the direct manipulation of the digitized decision levers of society. This emerging reality allows a far more sinister, indirect form of aggression than simple disinformation or cyberattack: Rather than interventions designed to use malware to corrupt systems, attackers are increasingly hoping to hack the algorithms governing much of human life. The goal is to make tiny tweaks, which would not be noticed for weeks or months, that skew outcomes in damaging ways and throw sand into the gears of the operation, exacerbating social frustrations and affecting attitudes.

Recent years have seen a cascade of "tuning the algo" attacks in sectors such as health care, human resources, internet searches, justice, and social media platforms.[34] It is believed that thousands of such modifications have taken place, though so far information security firms

---

[34] Hackers who specialize in such attacks have become known as "tuners." There are sites on the dark web specifically devoted to this practice, where tuners share techniques, vulnerabilities of algorithmic systems, and success stories.

have proven only several dozen, including a change to the programming of a hiring algorithm that sought to exclude several minority candidates from consideration; a tweak to the code of a cancer-screening algorithm that produced thousands of false-positive diagnoses; changes to an algorithm used to predict recidivism among first-time offenders, which began recommending long sentences to those with a high potential for reform and much shorter sentences for those likely to commit new crimes.

These campaigns have been undertaken by state and nonstate actors alike. Indeed, because of concerns about attribution, it is very uncommon for agencies directly affiliated with nation states to attack other states directly with such techniques. There is simply no need to do so: States now have at their disposal a tremendous array of nonstate militias, hacker collectives, patriotic cyber teams, profit-seeking cyber privateers, and crowdsourcing and similar techniques to inspire private actors without directing them. Most manipulation of algorithms that has been discovered traces back to such private actors; a handful have been arrested but most go unpunished. These opportunities have offered a way for powers hostile to the United States to knit together a global network of social manipulators, tens of thousands of people around the world dedicated to constraining U.S. power and who receive training, inspiration, and sometimes direction from quasi-state entities.

One result of this wave of attacks has been to depress public confidence in algorithmic decisionmaking as a rule. Because so many of these systems have been hacked, the accuracy of most others has been brought into question. Such lack of faith is exacerbated by the "black box" character of so many algorithms: In cases where decisionmaking processes have been developed through deep learning, the program itself has evolved the underlying relationships, and the programmers do not even know why it comes to some of its conclusions. In other cases, the workings of even well-understood algorithms are held as proprietary trade secrets, fueling conspiracy theories about their actual terms. It has not taken much outside hostile manipulation to spark a generalized loss of confidence in these programs.

The result of this range of attacks has been to further compromise social trust, specifically in the nature of decisionmaking that has become so characteristic of advanced democracies. For years, citizens have seen more and more of their lives taken over by algorithms; now, they are increasingly certain that these programs are regularly compromised and manipulated by hostile actors, whether domestic or foreign. Given the nature of the infosphere in this reality, these trends are having devastating effects on the level of social and institutional trust and causing rising grievances against the essential characteristics of postmodern advanced democracy.

# CHAPTER EIGHT

# The Emerging Risk of Virtual Societal Warfare

The three futures described in the preceding chapters point to one overarching truth about the emerging infosphere and the associated risk of information-based aggression: Many current trends are producing unprecedented vulnerabilities in the information environment of advanced democracies. This is the summary implication to be drawn from the combined implications of accelerating trends in the infosphere, the lessons of social science about attitudes and trust, and the potential of a range of fast-developing technologies that relate to information manipulation. Advanced democracies are increasingly dependent on a foundation of databases and information processing, much of it automated, for their daily activities and the fate and well-being of their citizens. But in ways well beyond traditional scenarios of cyberattack against physical targets, hostile actors, whether state or nonstate, will have growing opportunities to disrupt and corrupt these information foundations in coming years.

Free societies are, at their core, "information-processing mechanisms."[1] Their economic markets and political processes rely on the effective, secure handling and evaluation of various forms of information. Social trust, as we have seen, depends on accurate perceptions of other people and social institutions. The nature of these processing systems, however, is changing along with the infosphere. Although free societies have long been information-processing mechanisms in a broad and conceptual sense, they are increasingly becoming so in quite

---

[1] Braden R. Allenby, "The Age of Weaponized Narrative, or, Where Have You Gone, Walter Cronkite?" *Issues in Science and Technology*, Vol. 33, No. 4, Summer 2017, p. 68.

literal, often automated, and sometimes entirely mysterious ways. The character of the emerging infosphere is challenging enough to social trust and stability even before hostile actors reach into the gears to disturb the operation of these mechanisms.

Other major powers clearly view the manipulation of the information environment as a leading strategy for national competition. A 2011 statement of Russian cyber doctrine, to take just one example, calls for efforts to attack "information systems, processes, and resources" but also to undermine the adversary's "political, economic, and social system" and generate "massive brainwashing of the population for destabilizing the society and the state."[2] Gradually expanding techniques of aggression against the information foundations of democracies could be viewed as a major competitive advantage.

Beyond direct intervention in the societies of competitors for the purpose of disruption, illiberal regimes increasingly reach beyond their borders to influence, coerce, and intimidate populations worldwide, including claimed citizens, cultural fellows, or simply anyone who becomes of interest as either a friend or adversary. Critics of Russia, China, Iran, and other countries now face routine physical harassment and, in many cases, abduction and disappearance anywhere in the world.[3] The capability to reach into other societies through their infosphere offers an unprecedented ability for illiberal states to universalize their tactics of surveillance and intimidation in unprecedented ways.

Although this study has focused on informational mechanisms of coercion and manipulation, such attacks on a country's infosphere could be increasingly combined with more-physical or more-kinetic techniques that nonetheless stop short of what would be considered outright aggression. An obvious example is traditional clandestine targeting of specific individuals, such as regime opponents—as in the alleged Russian use of chemical and biological weapons in Europe in recent years. Other examples may soon include the use of autonomous

---

2    Quoted in Segal, 2016, p. 112.

3    See Osnos, 2018.

systems the size of insects (or eventually even smaller) in direct, drone-based attacks highly targeted to individuals or locations.[4]

## A New Form of Conflict: Virtual Societal Warfare

As we indicated in Chapter One, our research quickly suggested the need for a more encompassing and suggestive term for the emerging reality than *hostile social manipulation*. What is emerging is more encompassing than that term. States and nonstate actors increasingly possess the ability to reach into other societies and cause significant disruption short of major warfare or even any kinetic actions at all, as such actions would, for example, satisfy the definitions of armed conflict in the Charter of the United Nations. And yet the potential activities go well beyond the narrow confines of propaganda, targeted marketing, or other persuasive aspects of social manipulation.

We propose the term *virtual societal warfare* to capture the emerging reality. This warfare involves the use of largely nonkinetic, information-based aggression to attack the social stability of rival nations. It is *virtual* because, for the most part, these strategies do not employ direct physical violence or destruction. (This concept, there-fore, excludes both direct military attack as well as large-scale cyber-attacks designed to wreak havoc on a nation's physical infrastructure and cause actual damage.) It is *societal* because both the targets and the participants in such campaigns stretch across society, and because the goal is to undermine the efficient functioning, levels of trust, and ultimately the very stability of the target society. And it is *warfare* because, in its potentially more elaborate forms, it represents an activ-ity designed to achieve supremacy over rival nations, not merely to gain relative advantage in an ongoing competition but to gain decisive vic-tory in ways that leave the target nation subject to the attacker's will.

As the preceding chapters have suggested, virtual societal warfare can take many forms in the context of the character of the emerging

---

[4] Evans, 2015.

infosphere. It can involve any combination of the following techniques, among others:

- deploying classic propaganda, influence, and disinformation operations through multiple channels, including social media, though given what we know from social science research about attitude and attitude change, these operations are likely to take the form of targeting subsections of the population to intensify divisions and polarization rather than attempting to shift or create new beliefs wholesale in a population
- generating massive amounts of highly plausible fabricated video and audio material to reduce the confidence in shared reality
- discrediting key mediating institutions that are capable of distinguishing between true and false information
- corrupting or manipulating the databases on which major components of the economy increasingly rely
- manipulating or degrading systems of algorithmic decisionmaking, both to impair day-to-day government and corporate operations and to intensify loss of faith in institutions as well as social grievances and polarization
- hijacking VR and AR systems to create disruption or mental anguish or to strengthen certain narratives
- inserting commands into chatbot-style interactive systems to generate inefficiencies and, in some cases, personal frustration and anxiety.

In fully comprehensive virtual societal warfare, these informational components could be joined by other tools and techniques. These could include direct political warfare and clandestine operations designed to produce active fifth columns in a target country, perhaps drawn from the diaspora or ethnically connected community of the state using the above techniques. They could include the use of more-kinetic cyberattacks, including targeted assassinations of opponents or individuals of great importance to the adversary through microscopic drones or personalized biological weapons and many other forms of attack.

Virtual societal warfare is likely to have many essential characteristics, which together reflect the essential nature and character of this new form of warfare. A full understanding of these will only emerge over time, but this analysis points to an initial set of characteristics that can help to define and comprehend this emerging challenge. They are described in the following sections.

*National security will increasingly rely on a resilient infosphere and, even more fundamentally, on a strong social topography.* The elements of a resilient infosphere are not well understood, but they likely include classic forms of information security as well as strong mediating institutions and a population strongly inoculated against the techniques of social manipulation. The United States and many other advanced democracies have made some strides in information security but are nowhere close to real resilience. No significant efforts have been made to create a population and information environment resilient against efforts to shape and build destructive narratives. Increasingly, there may be a need for sources of information response alongside information security for some forms of information attack: Who will someone go to, for example, when they have become convinced that their therapeutic chatbot has been hijacked?

Pentland's notion of "social physics"—the relationships among elements of individual behavior and social capital and the way they relate to one another—offers one of the best conceptualizations of the terrain of virtual societal warfare. The scholar and practitioner of information science Tim Hwang has explained the issue as a challenge in assessing and managing the *social topography* of a nation and its contours and vulnerabilities.[5] Understanding this topography by mapping its strengths, weaknesses, emerging danger areas, and sources of resilience is likely to become an increasing preoccupation of democracies. But we have no sense of even where to begin or which office or agency in such a society should be responsible for the task.

*The barrier between public and private endeavors and responsibilities is blurring; national security will rely on the cooperation of private*

---

[5]   Tim Hwang, *Maneuver and Manipulation: On the Military Strategy of Online Information Warfare*, Carlisle Barracks, Pa.: Strategic Studies Institute, 2019.

*actors as much as public investments.* As noted in previous chapters, the technologies and techniques of this form of conflict are increasingly available to a wide range of actors. That will become even more true as AI allows for the automated deployment of propaganda and interactive bots. Private power in this realm matches and, in some cases, exceeds public power.

As a result, responses to this challenge are also increasingly dependent on the role of the private sector. "More and more of America's public conversation is happening in privately owned spaces, where no one knows who is doing what to influence whom."[6] Public and private institutions will need to cooperate in deep and ongoing ways to preserve the security of advanced democracies.

The result, Benjamin Wittes and Gabriella Blum suggest in their compelling analysis of the changing nature of conflict, is a gradual "migration in law, practice, and custom of important security functions—surveillance, analysis, interception, and even protection of the coastline—from government to private actors." This is happening "because of an underlying shift in actual control over the architecture through which attacks and other security threats take place and through which vulnerability to attacks expresses itself. It used to be that to attack America, one had to land troops on her shores or fly airplanes over her territories." Now, by contrast, "one can attack America—or any country—in a variety of ways while interacting only with architecture owned and operated by private parties of various sorts."[7]

These developments will weaken the traditional role of the state as the provider of territorial security. This role is its most fundamental obligation, but one that it will increasingly be unable to fulfill in a world of virtual societal aggression in which the channels of belligerence cannot be defended by armies but must be defended by corporations, social media platforms, and major news outlets. These developments are especially problematic for open societies, which have traditionally

---

6   Henry Farrell, "American Democracy Is an Easy Target," *Foreign Policy*, January 17, 2018.

7   Benjamin Wittes and Gabriella Blum, *The Future of Violence: Robots and Germs, Hackers and Drones*, New York: Basic Books, 2015, pp. 79–80.

erected a strong barrier between the public and the private, and could offer advantages to governments that blend such elements of society, such as China.

*Conflict will increasingly be waged between and among networks.* Wittes and Blum have described one implication of trends related to virtual societal warfare as a "many to many" pattern of security interactions. Every nation, company, group, and individual can threaten any other, they write. "We are thus in a moment unlike any other in the history of the world, one in which distance does not protect you and in which you are at once a figure of great power and great vulnerability."[8]

The result is war of networks against networks. "States will increasingly fight future wars using a multitude of partner organizations."[9] This pattern is emerging, for example, in the complex, international network of hackers, activists, and informal propagandists being employed by Russia as part of its information campaigns and in China's use of Chinese citizens and ethnic Chinese abroad to further its control over key narratives. State actors are likely to develop such networks to avoid attribution and also strengthen their virtual societal warfare capabilities against retaliation: It will be much more difficult to understand, maintain an accurate portrait of, and hit back against a shadowy global network.

Already today, another implication of this networked model of conflict is becoming apparent: the rise of what has been called a "privateering" approach to key security functions. "Privateers funded their own operations and made money by keeping the 'prizes' they seized," Wittes and Blum explain. "Precisely because of this decentralization, privateering became a tool for mustering private capital, private energy, and private risk in the service of public military objectives." This model is emerging not only in the use of private information security firms to sustain the health of a nation's information networks, but in the model of hackers using ransomware and other techniques to profit from their

---

[8]  Wittes and Blum, 2015, p. 120.

[9]  Wittes and Blum, 2015, p. 120.

activities. One accompanying risk of such a model is of vigilantism in the name of national security.[10]

In the process of such decentralization, government monopoly on security function is giving way to "a distributed defensive function." This idea

> cuts against centuries of developed understanding of how societies most effectively organize themselves against external and internal threats. They do not generally do it by diffusing power through a multiplicity of actors—much less a multiplicity of private actors, accountable to an even greater multiplicity of shareholders (including foreign shareholders).[11]

Private actors become inextricably linked with the security functions of government. This model looks less like national security than public health and safety, "which routinely involves distributing obligations to a diverse array of actors who do not think of themselves as in the business of health and safety."[12] Makers of cars, candy, and alcohol are regulated and incentivized to take actions that add up to public health and safety; more and more, social media platforms, traditional media outlets, entertainment companies, internet providers, universities, and other institutions will have to be incentivized to create a robust infosphere and social topography.

This distributed network model is likely to complicate efforts to control and regulate this new form of conflict. The existence of the growing ability of individuals, many of whom operate as private and independent actors, to do harm will make it far more difficult to enforce norms.

These are only three initial suggestions of the sorts of principles that will govern conflict in the virtual societal realm. More research is urgently required to understand this realm more fully and to begin to

---

[10]　Wittes and Blum, 2015, pp. 84, 87.

[11]　Wittes and Blum, 2015, p. 83.

[12]　Wittes and Blum, 2015, pp. 81, 83–84.

understand the sorts of responses that will protect democratic societies against its worst effects.

## Dealing with the Threat of Virtual Societal Aggression

This analysis focused on the future of hostile social manipulation and, in the process, has made the case to take seriously the broader risk of virtual societal aggression. This phase of work was not designed to develop a detailed agenda of policy recommendations and has not done so. However, it does point in a handful of obvious directions for the broad categories of response that advanced democracies, including and particularly the United States, must begin to assess to deal with the dangers outlined here.

The challenge of virtual societal warfare is a much bigger social problem than merely the activities of foreign actors. Preexisting social problems are being amplified rather than new ones being generated from whole cloth. The degree of polarization and social tension in the United States provides avenues for others to have influence they could not have without it. But those massive, foundational social issues cannot be resolved by policies aimed merely at their symptom, which is the manipulation and disruption of countries' infospheres. The foundational causes must be addressed, which constitutes a much tougher—and often more controversial—task.

Democracies undertaking such a task will need to decide what success looks like in virtual societal warfare. Success cannot be defined by the absence of falsehoods in the public debate or near-perfect public awareness: Such things have never existed, and democracies function perfectly well without them. It cannot be the absence of any form of hacking of the emerging technologies of AI, VR, or AR. The difficult questions now are how much destabilization democratic infospheres can take and where the lines must be drawn. These will inevitably be qualitative judgments. Broadly speaking, the goal is likely to be some sort of equilibrium in which influences on individuals are balanced and techniques of identifying and mitigating disinformation are effective.

One insight that must inform any policy response is that we simply do not know very much right now, including about the causal dynamics behind this larger challenge, the ways it might unfold, or the responses likely to make the biggest difference. Although the problem is urgent, it may still pay to go slow in formulating responses. We should not assume we have it figured out or know the right actions to take.

As just one example, the active regulation of fabricated or inaccurate reports as a route to protecting the resilience of infospheres carries many dangers, as well as practical problems. History suggests one obvious risk: Once established, the ability to regulate facts will be abused, employed by whomever is in power at the time to discourage inconvenient truths. Such activities might be strongly supported by a significant chunk of the electorate: Recent polls suggest, for example, that many Americans surveyed responded that they would approve of shutting down news outlets that broadcast "biased or inaccurate" reports.[13]

It is not clear, of course, who would make such judgments: While some reports are outright fabrications, what is biased or inaccurate in a broader sense is often in the eye of the beholder. Newspapers often rely on anonymous sources, and thus would be unable to prove that a given report was valid. By that standard, an enforcement body might well have refused the *Washington Post* the right to publish its Watergate stories; according to the White House, they were fabrications. Much of what the Russian broadcast network RT was doing before the 2016 election, for example, was only highlighting stories that appeared on the Breitbart News Network or other alt-right U.S. news organizations.

Efforts to obstruct the publication of demonstrably "fake" news also miss much of the point of disinformation. Propagandists understand the dangers of being caught in outright fabrications and often can avoid them easily enough. Skilled disinformation specialists gather together a blizzard of suspicious facts and half-truths into a larger narrative that may be misleading, but it is not always built on factually

---

13  Flemming Rose and Jacob Mchangama, "History Proves How Dangerous It Is to Have the Government Regulate Fake News," *Washington Post*, October 3, 2017.

incorrect assertions. The ultimate challenge is the difficulty of distinguishing between legitimate and "illegitimate" speech.

These issues, and the growing threat posed by virtual societal warfare, demand that we have a new dialogue about the nature and limits of free speech. In fact, we are already having it, whether we want to admit it or not: When platforms, such as Facebook or Twitter, agree that certain forms of racist or harassing posts must come down, there is clearly an implicit standard of balance rather than an absolutist stance that all speech must be allowed. But the slopes here are very slippery. What about right-wing nationalist viewpoints: Should they be allowed? If so, why not hateful, violence-promoting extremist messages? Resolving these questions will demand some of the most careful and nuanced discussions yet attempted about the character and limits of free speech.

## Designing a Response: An Initial Agenda

As such long-term discussions are under way, there are several steps that the United States and other democracies could take to shore up their resilience against these threats. A major challenge is determining how to organize the response to such threats within the U.S. government. There is no obvious home for "infosphere security." The question of institutional structures is beyond the scope of this analysis but must be addressed alongside the substantive reforms that can help mitigate these risks. Some of these reforms are outlined in the following sections.

### Invest in Research and Understanding

A consistent theme in many of our conversations and analyses for this study has been the limits of our awareness, including about the true character of the evolving infosphere, its likely directions, key causal dynamics in that process, how populations react to various forms of social manipulation, and what the most effective answers might be. What are the main hallmarks of a resilient infosphere and robust social topography? What metrics can we use to assess whether we are attaining those goals?

Democratic governments, social media companies, and other companies and foundations deeply engaged in the role of information in advanced societies should redouble their investment in conceptualizing, funding, promoting, and assisting with such research, even when their findings may be uncomfortable for a specific approach to governance or business model.

In the process, researchers are likely to need better access to many databases, algorithms, and other essential mechanisms of information storage and flow now kept secret. We largely have in mind proprietary models employed by the social media platforms that dominate key elements of the infosphere. It is understandable that companies have a vested interest in maintaining control of such information. But with the proper controls, such as nondisclosure agreements, they could "open their books" to researchers sufficiently to gain a better understanding of the sources of threat and risk.

### Begin Building Forms of Inoculation and Resilience Against the Worst Forms of Information-Based Social Manipulation

Campaigns should not limit themselves to countering outside claims after they occur but should also take steps in advance to create resilience against such claims and campaigns. Forewarning may be more effective than post hoc treatment of established narratives.[14] One study examined the means for inoculating the public against misinformation about climate change. It found that credible scientific consensus messages lose their efficacy when they are undermined by misinformation. But when the consensus is presented as a form of inoculation, it can remain resilient against subsequent misinformation.[15]

Efforts in the direction of societal inoculation can involve public and media training to increase the resilience of populations—or, as one source suggests, "systematically rebuild analytical skills across the American population and invest in the media to ensure that it is

---

[14]   Paul and Matthews, 2016, pp. 9–10.

[15]   Sander van der Linden, Anthony Leiserowitz, Seth Rosenthal, and Edward Maibach, "Inoculating the Public Against Misinformation About Climate Change," *Global Challenges*, Vol. 1, No. 2, 2017.

driven by truth, not clicks."[16] The Ukrainian and Finnish governments have experimented with programs in critical thinking and information consumption with some success; global democracies can share best practices as their experiments unfold. The effectiveness of large-scale public training remains open to doubt, but there are hopeful anecdotal examples—such as IREX's "Learn to Discern" program—that have achieved measurable improvements in the target population's ability to distinguish disinformation.[17]

In pursuing this goal, democratic governments can begin to inspire, fund, and support a range of private organizations that can play the role of the "white blood cells" of a democratic infosphere. This line of defense would represent trial and error attempts to respond to social manipulation campaigns, with citizen social scientists conducting hundreds of experiments and working off the results to hone ideas. One lesson of efforts to combat radical messages online is that governments in general, and the U.S. government in particular, have little credibility in such campaigns. The effort must be centered around more-credible independent actors online. The United States, therefore, needs its own "influencers campaign," designed to empower and support influential actors in social media to generate counter-disinformation messaging.[18]

Some of this campaign can be devoted to monitoring and assessment: Disinformation flows follow different patterns than accurate information. It will be quickly and massively hyped by a relatively few sites, whereas typical valid news follows a more gradual viral pattern. It is therefore possible to develop markers for such campaigns, detect disinformation, and potentially counter it early in its lifespan. Attribution research is improving; the way Facebook was able to trace Russian bots has to be turned into a general capability and deployed more broadly.

Other distributed efforts can be devoted to fact-checking or to providing a "rapid response team" to fight disinformation on a

---

[16] Nina Jankowicz, "The Only Way to Defend Against Russia's Information War," *New York Times*, September 25, 2017.

[17] For information on this program, see IREX, *Learn to Discern (L2D)—Media Literacy Training*, undated.

[18] Helmus and Bodine-Baron, 2017, pp. 2–3.

moment-to-moment basis. Such distributed efforts can focus on tagging stories based on the credibility of the source, as well as other qualities that give the reader an instant sense of the validity of the claim. This categorization will not always work: In particular, with certain self-defined echo chambers, such credibility reports may not make a difference and could even be counterproductive. For most consumers of information, however, they could help to give a sense of whether a report can be trusted.

### Take Seriously the Leading Role Played by Social Media Today, and the Precedent-Setting Character of Many of the Information Control Debates Playing Out in That Realm

Governments should increasingly look to actions that can incentivize social media platforms to solve the problems themselves to the greatest degree possible. In the process, governments should identify four to five things that the platforms can do over the next two to three years to make a dent in the problem.

Many social media companies are beginning to move in this direction, though perhaps more slowly than the risks warrant. Facebook is adding a button on news feed links that will connect to the Wikipedia site for the organization that published or posted that news story. The idea is to give users an ability to quickly get a sense of the credibility of the source.[19] Facebook has also established a set of outside fact checking organizations to identify articles that might be misinformation. It considered revisions to the algorithm that would have systematically downgraded articles hitting certain tripwires for sensing fabricated information—but then backed off when tests showed that it would disproportionately hit conservative sites. It then experimented with both user-driven and algorithmic responses (using keywords and phrases to identify them), eventually settling on the latter because it

---

19   Josh Constine, "Facebook Tries Fighting Fake News with Publisher Info Button on Links," *TechCrunch*, October 5, 2017.

performed better in practice and because concerns had been expressed about the political bias of human curators of news.[20]

## Make Investments Designed to Erect New, Broadly Trusted Informational Mediating Institutions That Can Help Americans Make Sense of Events

Governments (as well as private foundations and activists) can also prompt trial-and-error work among information companies, such as internet browsers (especially those willing to take the lead in new approaches), to experiment with revised algorithms, new browser extensions, and rating and ranking different sites and sources to see what works. The goal would be to send signals that would contribute to the overall inoculation effect being sought by government policy. A major source of the challenges today is the decline of any respected and trusted intermediary sources that the public can rely on to get a sense of whether what they are seeing is accurate. Apart from basic fact-checking organizations, experimenting with different varieties of revised intermediary institutions could help mitigate the effect of virtual societal aggression.

One example of such thinking would be to investigate the role of influencers in social media networks to better understand how they work and how the government (or philanthropic or analytical organizations) could empower them or build new ones to shape the flow of information. One finding of recent research is that influential hubs in social networks have a disproportionate responsibility for what information gets to what people. To the extent that such influencers could be persuaded to become sources of accuracy rather than disinformation, they could become a new sort of mediating information institution for the networked age.

---

[20]  Josh Constine, "Facebook Chose to Fight Fake News with AI, Not Just User Reports," *TechCrunch*, November 14, 2016.

## Begin Working Toward International Norms Constraining the Use of Virtual Societal Aggression

The biggest risk of virtual societal warfare may be that it represents an insidious, gradual degradation of the territorial integrity norm that has largely prevailed since 1945 and helped to keep the peace among countries. To the extent that nations begin attacking one another in virtual but highly damaging ways, the prevailing consensus on territorial nonaggression could collapse, leading eventually to large-scale armed adventurism. As with other forms of aggression, deterrence can contribute strongly to defense, but so can international norms that help tie the status and prestige of countries to their respect for fundamental principles.

Most leading participants in potential virtual conflicts are not in a position to agree to such formal norms at the moment. Partly this is true because of rising competitive mistrust among the United States, China, and Russia, and even (in the arena of information security) the European Union's lack of faith in U.S. approaches to these issues. Partly it is true because we simply do not yet know enough about these challenges to spell out effective rules of the road. The United States can, however, take at least two initial steps: (1) make clear its interest in such norms and (2) begin funding and actively participating in scholarly discussions on what such a normative architecture might look like.

## Better Understand the Workings and Vulnerabilities of Emerging Technologies, Especially AI-Driven Information Channels, Virtual and Augmented Reality, and Algorithmic Decisionmaking

If the United States and other democracies are not careful, advances in the private application of these technologies will race ahead of policy and even understanding, creating intense vulnerabilities for democratic societies. The dangers of virtual societal warfare and the specific emerging dependence of democratic societies and advanced economies on such information applications point to the need for research on their potential implications and steps democracies can take to protect themselves.

These categories represent only a broad sketch of the sorts of response likely to be required for democracies to armor themselves against the potential threat of virtual societal warfare, at least in terms of its informational aspects. These emerging forms of aggression represent a significant danger to advanced democracies, a national security threat that has not been seen before. Especially in the nuclear age, and in an era when a general global consensus has prevailed against outright territorial aggression, large-scale invasions have become mostly a thing of the past.

But while armies can be deterred, gradual, low-level hostile manipulation of the infosphere and larger social topography of nations may be the new frontier of aggression. The futures outlined in Chapters Five, Six, and Seven suggest strongly that emerging technologies and techniques mean that the *potential* for virtual societal warfare is almost certainly emerging. The only question today is whether democracies will band together to control and defend themselves against this threat. The categories summarized in this last chapter represent part of an initial agenda to do both.

# References

Adamic, Lada, and Natalie Glance, "The Political Blogosphere and the 2004 U.S. Election: Divided They Blog," paper presented at the Second Annual Workshop on the Weblogging Ecosystem, Chiba, Japan: Association for Computing Machinery, 2005.

Adler, Simon, "Breaking News," *Radiolab*, July 27, 2017. As of January 23, 2019: http://www.radiolab.org/story/breaking-news/

Adobe Inc., "#VoCo. Adobe MAX 2016 (Sneak Peeks)," November 4, 2016. As of January 23, 2019: https://www.youtube.com/watch?v=I3l4XLZ59iw

Aharanov, Alex, "What Is the Future of Augmented and Virtual Reality?" *Jabil Blog*, March 27, 2018. As of March 5, 2019: https://www.jabil.com/insights/blog-main/future-of-augmented-and-virtual-reality-technology.html

Ahluwalia, Rohini, "Examination of Psychological Processes Underlying Resistance to Persuasion," *Journal of Consumer Research*, Vol. 27, No. 2, 2000, pp. 217–232.

Allen, Greg and Taniel Chan, *Artificial Intelligence and National Security*, Cambridge, Mass.: Belfer Center for Science and International Affairs, Harvard Kennedy School, July 2017.

Allenby, Braden R., "The Age of Weaponized Narrative, or, Where Have You Gone, Walter Cronkite?" *Issues in Science and Technology*, Vol. 33, No. 4, Summer 2017.

Allport, Gordon, "Attitudes," in Carl Murchison, ed., *A Handbook of Social Psychology*, Worcester, Mass.: Clark University Press, 1935.

Anand, Bharat N., "The U.S. Media's Problems Are Much Bigger than Fake News and Filter Bubbles," *Harvard Business Review*, January 5, 2017. As of January 20, 2019: https://hbr.org/2017/01/the-u-s-medias-problems-are-much-bigger-than-fake-news-and-filter-bubbles

Andrasik, Andrew J., *Hacking Humans: The Evolving Paradigm with Virtual Reality*, SANS Institute, Information Security Reading Room, November 2017. As of January 22, 2019:
https://www.sans.org/reading-room/whitepapers/testing/
hacking-humans-evolving-paradigm-virtual-reality-38180

Arquilla, John, and David Ronfeldt, *The Emergence of Noopolitik: Toward an American Information Strategy*, Santa Monica, Calif.: RAND Corporation, MR-1033-OSD, 1999. As of March 1, 2019:
https://www.rand.org/pubs/monograph_reports/MR1033.html

Arsene, Codrin, "IoT Ideas That Will Soon Revolutionize Our World in 8 Ways," *Y Media Labs*, November 24, 2016. As of January 22, 2019:
https://ymedialabs.com/internet-of-things-ideas/

Auletta, Ken, "How the Math Men Overthrew the Mad Men," *New Yorker*, May 21, 2018. As of January 20, 2019:
https://www.newyorker.com/news/annals-of-communications/
how-the-math-men-overthrew-the-mad-men

Bakshy, Eytan, Jake M. Hofman, Winter A. Mason, and Duncan J. Watts, "Everyone's an Influencer: Quantifying Influence on Twitter," *Fourth ACM International Conference on Web Search and Data Mining, Conference Proceedings*, Hong Kong: Association for Computing Machinery, 2011, pp. 65–74.

Bakshy, Eytan, Solomon Messing, and Lada Adamic, "Exposure to Ideologically Diverse News and Opinion on Facebook," *Science*, Vol. 348, No. 6239, 2015, pp. 1130–1132.

Barabási, Albert-László, *Linked: How Everything Is Connected to Everything Else and What It Means for Business, Science, and Everyday Life*, New York: Basic Books, 2014.

Bennett, W. Lance, and Shanto Iyengar, "A New Era of Minimal Effects? The Changing Foundations of Political Communication," *Journal of Communication*, Vol. 58, No. 4, 2008, pp. 707–731.

Berger, Jonah, *Contagious: Why Things Catch On*, New York: Simon and Schuster, 2013.

Bialik, Kristen, and Katerina Eva Matsa, "Key Trends in Social and Digital News Media," *Pew Research Center*, October 4, 2017. As of January 20, 2019:
http://www.pewresearch.org/fact-tank/2017/10/04/
key-trends-in-social-and-digital-news-media/

Biocca, Frank, "Viewers' Mental Models of Political Messages: Toward a Theory of the Semantic Processing of Television," in Frank Biocca, ed., *Television and Political Advertising*, Vol. I: *Psychological Processes*, Hillsdale, N.J.: Lawrence Erlbaum Associates, 1991.

Bjørnskov, Christian, and Stefan Voigt, "Constitutional Verbosity and Social Trust," *Public Choice*, Vol. 161, No. 1/2, 2014, pp. 91–112.

"Blockchain and the Internet of Things: The IoT Blockchain Opportunity and Challenge," *i-SCOOP*, September 2016 (updated February 2018). As of January 22, 2019:
https://www.i-scoop.eu/blockchain-distributed-ledger-technology/blockchain-iot/

Bond, Robert M., Christopher J. Fariss, Jason J. Jones, Adam D. I. Kramer, Cameron Marlow, Jaime E. Settle, and James H. Fowler, "A 61-Million-Person Experiment in Social Influence and Political Mobilization," *Nature*, Vol. 489, 2012, pp. 295–298.

Boxell, Levi, Matthew Gentzkow, and Jesse M. Shapiro, "Greater Internet Use Is Not Associated with Faster Growth in Political Polarization Among U.S. Demographic Groups," *Proceedings of the National Academy of Sciences*, Vol. 114, No. 40, October 2017a, pp. 10612–10617.

———, "Is Media Driving Americans Apart?" *New York Times*, December 6, 2017b. As of January 24, 2019:
https://www.nytimes.com/2017/12/06/opinion/
is-media-driving-americans-apart.html

Boyd, Clark, "The Past, Present and Future of Speech Recognition Technology," *The Startup*, January 10, 2018. As of January 22, 2019:
https://medium.com/swlh/
the-past-present-and-future-of-speech-recognition-technology-cf13c179aaf

Boyd, Danah, "Your Data Is Being Manipulated," *Data and Society: Points*, October 4, 2017. As of January 23, 2019:
https://points.datasociety.net/your-data-is-being-manipulated-a7e31a83577b

———, "Beyond the Rhetoric of Algorithmic Solutionism," *Data and Society: Points*, January 11, 2018. As of January 23, 2019:
https://points.datasociety.net/
beyond-the-rhetoric-of-algorithmic-solutionism-8e0f9cdada53

Brennan, Jason, "Trump Won Because Voters Are Ignorant, Literally," *Foreign Policy*, November 10, 2016. As of January 24, 2019:
https://foreignpolicy.com/2016/11/10/
the-dance-of-the-dunces-trump-clinton-election-republican-democrat/

Brewster, Signe, "I Spent a Week Living with Chatbots—Did All That Self-Help Help?" *Wired*, January 4, 2018.

Brown, Ian, "Imagining a Cyber Surprise: How Might China Use Stolen OPM Records to Target Trust?" *War on the Rocks*, May 22, 2018. As of January 20, 2019:
https://warontherocks.com/2018/05/imagining-a-cyber-surprise-how-might-china-use-stolen-opm-records-to-target-trust/

Bulger, Monica, and Patrick Davison, *The Promises, Challenges, and Futures of Media Literacy*, New York: Data and Society Research Institute, February 2018. As of January 20, 2019:
https://datasociety.net/pubs/oh/DataAndSociety_Media_Literacy_2018.pdf

Cai, Haoye, Chunyan Bai, Yu-Wing Tai, and Chi-Keung Tang, "Deep Video Generation, Prediction and Completion of Human Action Sequences," *European Conference on Computer Vision 2018, Conference Proceedings*, Munich, Germany, September 2018. As of March 4, 2019:
https://arxiv.org/pdf/1711.08682.pdf

Campbell, Troy, and Justin Friesen, "Why People 'Fly from Facts,'" *Scientific American*, March 3, 2015. As of January 20, 2019:
https://www.scientificamerican.com/article/why-people-fly-from-facts/

Cardenal, Juan Pablo, Jacek Kucharczyk, Grigorij Mesežnikov, and Gabriela Pleschová, *Sharp Power: Rising Authoritarian Influence*, Washington, D.C.: National Endowment for Democracy, December 2017.

Carey, John M., Brendan Nyhan, Benjamin Valentino, and Mingnan Liu, "An Inflated View of the Facts? How Preferences and Predispositions Shape Conspiracy Beliefs About the Deflategate Scandal," *Research and Politics*, Vol. 3, No. 3, July–September 2016, pp. 1–9.

Casey, Michael J., and Paul Vigna, "In Blockchain We Trust," *MIT Technology Review*, April 9, 2018.

Castells, Manuel, *The Rise of the Network Society*, New York: Wiley-Blackwell, 2009.

Chan, Man-pui Sally, Christopher R. Jones, Kathleen Hall Jamieson, and Dolores Albarracín, "Debunking: A Meta-Analysis of the Psychological Efficacy of Messages Countering Misinformation," *Psychological Science*, Vol. 28, No. 11, 2017, pp. 1531–1546.

Cheng, Justin, Lada Adamic, P. Alex Dow, Jon Michael Kleinberg, and Jure Leskovec, "Can Cascades Be Predicted?" *Twenty-Third International World Wide Web Conference, Conference Proceedings*, Seoul: Association for Computing Machinery, 2014, pp. 925–936.

Chessen, Matt, "Understanding the Psychology Behind Computational Propaganda," in Shawn Powers and Markos Kounalakis, eds., *Can Public Diplomacy Survive the Internet?* Washington, D.C.: U.S. Advisory Commission on Public Diplomacy, 2017a, pp. 19–24.

———, *The MADCOM Future*, Washington, D.C.: Atlantic Council, 2017b.

Cialdini, Robert, *Pre-Suasion: A Revolutionary Way to Influence and Persuade*, New York: Simon and Schuster, 2016.

Clarke, Richard A., *Cyber War: The Next Threat to National Security and What to Do About It*, New York: Ecco, 2010.

Cobb, Michael D., Brendan Nyhan, and Jason Reifler, "Beliefs Don't Always Persevere: How Political Figures Are Punished When Positive Information About Them Is Discredited," *Political Psychology,* Vol. 34, No. 3, June 2013, pp. 307–326.

Constine, Josh, "Facebook Chose to Fight Fake News with AI, Not Just User Reports," *TechCrunch,* November 14, 2016.

———, "Facebook Tries Fighting Fake News with Publisher Info Button on Links," *TechCrunch,* October 5, 2017.

Cook, John, Ullrich K. H. Ecker, and Stephan Lewandowsky, "Misinformation and How to Correct It," in Robert Scott and Stephan Kosslyn, eds., *Emerging Trends in the Social and Behavioral Sciences,* New York: John Wiley and Sons, 2015.

———, "Neutralizing Misinformation Through Inoculation: Exposing Misleading Argumentation Techniques Reduces Their Influence," *PLOS One,* Vol. 12, No. 5, 2017, pp. 1–21.

Cummings, M. L., Heather M. Roff, Kenneth Cukier, Jacob Parakilas, and Hannah Bryce, *Artificial Intelligence and International Affairs: Disruption Anticipated,* London: Chatham House, 2018.

Cutsinger, Paul, "Mark Cuban: Voice, Ambient Computing Are the Future. Developers Should Get in Now," *Amazon Alexa Blog,* March 25, 2019. As of April 19, 2019:
https://developer.amazon.com/blogs/alexa/post/0902e3c5-9649-47e5-b705-984666b85125/mark-cuban-voice-ambient-computing-are-the-future-and-why-developers-should-get-in-now

DeMers, Jayson, "7 New Technologies Shaping Online Marketing for the Better (We Hope)," *Forbes,* August 15, 2016. As of January 22, 2019:
https://www.forbes.com/sites/jaysondemers/2016/08/15/7-new-technologies-shaping-online-marketing-for-the-better-we-hope/#4d8173761fd6

Devlin, Hannah, "Human-Robot Interactions Take Step Forward with 'Emotional' Chatbot," *The Guardian,* May 5, 2017. As of January 23, 2019:
https://www.theguardian.com/technology/2017/may/05/human-robot-interactions-take-step-forward-with-emotional-chatting-machine-chatbot

Diaz, Jesus, "The Weird, Wild Future of CGI," *Fast Company,* October 19, 2017. As of January 23, 2019:
https://www.fastcodesign.com/90147151/what-lies-beyond-the-uncanny-valley

Druckman, James, "On the Limits of Framing Effects: Who Can Frame?" *Journal of Politics,* Vol. 63, No. 4, 2001, pp. 1041–1066.

Duggan, Maeve, and Aaron Smith, "The Political Environment on Social Media," *Pew Research Center,* October 25, 2016.

Eagly, Alice H., and Shelly Chaiken, "An Attribution Analysis of the Effect of Communicator Characteristics on Opinion Change: The Case of Communicator Attractiveness," *Journal of Personality and Social Psychology*, Vol. 32, No. 1, 1975, pp. 136–144.

Edwards, George C., III, *On Deaf Ears: The Limits of the Bully Pulpit*, New Haven, Conn.: Yale University Press, 2006.

Edwards, Kari, and Edward E. Smith, "A Disconfirmation Bias in the Evaluation of Arguments," *Journal of Personality and Social Psychology*, Vol. 71, No. 1, 1996, pp. 5–24.

Engber, Daniel, "LOL Something Matters," *Slate*, January 3, 2018.

Epley, Nicholas, and Thomas Gilovich, "The Mechanics of Motivated Reasoning," *Journal of Economic Perspectives*, Vol. 30, No. 3, 2016, pp. 133–140.

Evans, Gareth, "Robotic Insects Add Whole New Meaning to 'Fly-on-the-Wall' Surveillance," *Army Technology*, March 16, 2015. As of January 23, 2019: https://www.army-technology.com/features/featurerobotic-insects-add-whole-new-meaning-to-fly-on-the-wall-surveillance-4531866/

"Eye in the Sky," *Radiolab*, June 18, 2015. As of January 23, 2019: http://www.radiolab.org/story/eye-sky/

"Fake News: You Ain't Seen Nothing Yet," *The Economist*, July 1, 2017. As of January 22, 2019: https://www.economist.com/news/science-and-technology/21724370-generating-convincing-audio-and-video-fake-events-fake-news-you-aint-seen

Farrell, Henry, "American Democracy Is an Easy Target," *Foreign Policy*, January 17, 2018. As of January 23, 2019: http://foreignpolicy.com/2018/01/17/american-democracy-was-asking-for-it/

Fazio, Lisa K., Nadia M. Brashier, B. Keith Payne, and Elizabeth J. Marsh, "Knowledge Does Not Protect Against Illusory Truth," *Journal of Experimental Psychology*, Vol. 144, No. 5, 2015, pp. 993–1002.

Ferran, Lee, "Beware the Coming Crisis of 'Deep Fake News,'" *RealClearLife*, July 27, 2018. As of January 23, 2019: http://www.realclearlife.com/technology/liars-dividend-beware-the-coming-crisis-of-deep-fake-news/#1

Flaxman, Seth, Sharad Goel, and Justin M. Rao, "Filter Bubbles, Echo Chambers, and Online News Consumption," *Public Opinion Quarterly*, Volume 80, No. S1, 2016, pp. 298–320.

Fleming, Jennifer, "Media Literacy, News Literacy, or News Appreciation? A Case Study of the News Literacy Program at Stony Brook University," *Journalism and Mass Communication Educator*, Vol. 69, No. 2, 2014, pp. 146–165.

Fletcher, Richard, Alessio Cornia, Lucas Graves, and Rasmus Kleis Neilsen, *Measuring the Reach of "Fake News" and Online Disinformation in Europe*, Oxford, United Kingdom: Reuters Institute for the Study of Journalism, University of Oxford, February 2018.

Flynn, D. J., Brendan Nyhan, and Jason Reifler, "The Nature and Origins of Misperceptions: Understanding False and Unsupported Beliefs About Politics," *Political Psychology*, Vol. 38, Supp. 1, 2017, pp. 127–150.

Fukuyama, Francis, *Trust: The Social Virtues and the Creation of Prosperity*, New York: Free Press, 1995.

Gal, David, and Derek D. Rucker, "When in Doubt, Shout! Paradoxical Influences of Doubt on Proselytizing," *Psychological Science*, Vol. 21, No. 11, 2010, pp. 1701–1707.

Gallup, *In Depth: Topics A to Z: Confidence in Institutions*, 2018. As of January 24, 2019:
https://news.gallup.com/poll/1597/confidence-institutions.aspx

Gans, John A., Jr., "Governing Fantasyland," *Survival*, Vol. 60, No. 3, June-July 2018, pp. 195–202.

Garrett, R. Kelly, "Echo Chambers Online?: Politically Motivated Selective Exposure Among Internet News Users," *Journal of Computer-Mediated Communication*, Vol. 14, No. 2, 2009a, pp. 265–285.

———, "Politically Motivated Reinforcement Seeking: Reframing the Selective Exposure Debate," *Journal of Communication*, Vol. 59, No. 4, 2009b, pp. 676–699.

Garrett, R. Kelly, Dustin Carnahan, and Emily K. Lynch, "A Turn Toward Avoidance? Selective Exposure to Online Political Information, 2004–2008," *Political Behavior*, Vol. 35, No. 1, 2013, pp. 113–134.

Garrett, R. Kelly, and Paul Resnick, "Resisting Political Fragmentation on the Internet," *Daedalus*, Vol. 140, No. 4, Fall 2011, pp. 108–120.

Gentzkow, Matthew, and Jesse M. Shapiro, "Ideological Segregation Online and Offline," *Quarterly Journal of Economics*, Vol. 126, No. 4, 2011, pp. 1799–1839.

Gholipour, Bahar, "New AI Tech Can Mimic Any Voice," *Scientific American*, May 2, 2017. As of January 23, 2019:
https://www.scientificamerican.com/article/new-ai-tech-can-mimic-any-voice/

Giddens, Anthony, *The Consequences of Modernity*, Cambridge, United Kingdom: Polity, 1990.

Glanville, Jennifer L., Matthew A. Andersson, and Pamela Paxton, "Do Social Connections Create Trust? An Examination Using New Longitudinal Data," *Social Forces*, Vol. 92, No. 2, 2013, pp. 545–562.

Glanville, Jennifer L., and Pamela Paxton, "How Do We Learn to Trust? A Confirmatory Tetrad Analysis of the Sources of Generalized Trust," *Social Psychology Quarterly*, Vol. 70, No. 3, 2007, pp. 230–242.

Global Agenda Council on the Future of Software and Society, *Deep Shift: Technology Tipping Points and Social Impact*, Cologny, Switzerland: World Economic Forum, 2015.

Gorman, Jack, and Sara Gorman, *Denying to the Grave: Why We Ignore the Facts That Will Save Us*, New York: Oxford University Press, 2016.

Grassegger, Hannes, and Mikael Krogerus, "Weaken from Within," *New Republic*, November 2, 2017.

Grieco, Elizabeth, "More Americans Are Turning to Multiple Social Media Sites for News," *Pew Research Center*, November 2, 2017. As of January 20, 2019: http://www.pewresearch.org/fact-tank/2017/11/02/more-americans-are-turning-to-multiple-social-media-sites-for-news/

Grigonis, Hillary, "A.I. Creates Some of the Most Realistic Computer-Generated Images of People Yet," *Digital Trends*, October 30, 2017. As of January 23, 2019: https://www.digitaltrends.com/computing/nvidia-research-computer-generated-images/

Guess, Andrew M., *Media Choice and Moderation: Evidence from Online Tracking Data*, job market paper, New York: New York University, September 6, 2016. As of November 15, 2017: https://www.scribd.com/document/323356298/Media-Choice-and-Moderation-Evidence-from-Online-Tracking-Data

Guyer, Joshua J., and Leandre R. Fabrigar, "Attitudes and Behavior," in James Wright, ed., *International Encyclopedia of the Social & Behavioral Sciences*, Vol. II, 2nd ed., New York: Elsevier, 2015.

Haidt, Jonathan, "Moral Psychology for the Twenty-First Century," *Journal of Moral Education*, Vol. 42, No. 3, 2013, pp. 281–297.

Harari, Yuval Noah, "Big Data, Google, and the End of Free Will," *Financial Times*, August 26, 2016. As of January 23, 2019: https://www.ft.com/content/50bb4830-6a4c-11e6-ae5b-a7cc5dd5a28c

Harwell, Drew, "Companies Race to Gather a Newly Prized Currency: Our Body Measurements," *Washington Post*, January 16, 2018. As of January 23, 2019: https://www.washingtonpost.com/business/economy/companies-race-to-gather-a-newly-prized-currency-our-body-measurements/2018/01/16/5af28d98-f6e8-11e7-beb6-c8d48830c54d_story.html

Heaven, Douglas, "Dr. Bot Will See You Now," *MIT Technology Review*, November/December 2018.

Heffernan, Virginia, "Twilight of the Hackers," *Wired*, February 2018.

Helmus, Todd C., and Elizabeth Bodine-Baron, "Empowering ISIS Opponents on Twitter," Santa Monica, Calif.: RAND Corporation, PE-227-RC, 2017. As of March 4, 2019:
https://www.rand.org/pubs/perspectives/PE227.html

Heritage Foundation, "Deep Fakes: A Looming Challenge for Privacy, Democracy, and National Security," panel discussion, Washington, D.C., July 19, 2018. As of January 23, 2019:
https://www.heritage.org/homeland-security/event/
deep-fakes-looming-challenge-privacy-democracy-and-national-security

Higginbotham, Stacey, "IBM Is Bringing in Watson to Conquer the Internet of Things," *Fortune*, December 15, 2015. As of January 20, 2019:
http://fortune.com/2015/12/15/ibm-watson-iot/

Holley, Peter, "Big Brother on Wheels: Why Your Car Company May Know More About You Than Your Spouse," *Washington Post*, January 15, 2018. As of January 23, 2019:
https://www.washingtonpost.com/news/innovations/wp/2018/01/15/big-brother-on-wheels-why-your-car-company-may-know-more-about-you-than-your-spouse/

Horowitz, Michael C., "Artificial Intelligence, International Competition, and the Balance of Power," *Texas National Security Review*, Vol. 1, No. 3, May 2018, pp. 36–57.

Hosanagar, Kartik, and Vivian Jair, "We Need Transparency in Algorithms, but Too Much Can Backfire," *Harvard Business Review*, July 25, 2018.

Huang, Jian, Henriëtte Maassen van den Brink, and Wim Groot, "College Education and Social Trust: An Evidence-Based Study on the Causal Mechanisms," *Social Indicators Research*, Vol. 104, No. 2, 2011, pp. 287–310.

Huang, Zheping, "Chinese Police Are Wearing Sunglasses That Can Recognize Faces," *Defense One*, February 9, 2018.

Hvistendahl, Mara, "Inside China's Vast New Experiment in Social Ranking," *Wired*, December 14, 2017.

Hwang, Tim, *Maneuver and Manipulation: On the Military Strategy of Online Information Warfare*, Carlisle Barracks, Pa.: Strategic Studies Institute, 2019.

"Imitating People's Speech Patterns Precisely Could Bring Trouble," *The Economist*, April 20, 2017. As of January 23, 2019:
https://www.economist.com/news/science-and-technology/21721128-you-took-words-right-out-my-mouth-imitating-peoples-speech-patterns

Inglehart, Ronald, and Pippa Norris, *Trump, Brexit, and the Rise of Populism: Economic Have-Nots and Cultural Backlash*, faculty research working paper, Cambridge, Mass.: Harvard Kennedy School, RWP16-026, August 2016.

International Data Cooperation, "Executive Summary: Data Growth, Business Opportunities, and the IT Imperatives," in *The Digital Universe of Opportunities: Rich Data and the Increasing Value of the Internet of Things*, Framingham, Mass., April 2014.

IREX, *Learn to Discern (L2D)—Media Literacy Training*, undated. As of January 23, 2019:
https://www.irex.org/project/learn-discern-l2d-media-literacy-training

Isenberg, Daniel J., "Group Polarization: A Critical Review and Meta-Analysis," *Journal of Personality and Social Psychology*, Vol. 50, No. 6, 1986, pp. 1141–1151.

Ismail, Kaya, "AI vs. Algorithms: What's the Difference?" *CMS Wire*, October 26, 2018. As of January 20, 2019:
https://www.cmswire.com/information-management/ai-vs-algorithms-whats-the-difference/

Iyengar, Shanto, Guarav Sood, and Yphtach Lelkes, "Affect, Not Ideology: A Social Identity Perspective on Polarization," *Public Opinion Quarterly*, Vol. 76, No. 3, 2012, pp. 405–431.

J. Walter Thompson Intelligence, *Speak Easy*, New York, June 2017. As of January 22, 2019:
https://www.jwtintelligence.com/trend-reports/speak-easy-global-edition/

Jain, Shailendra Pratap, and Steven S. Posavac, "Prepurchase Attribute Verifiability, Source Credibility, and Persuasion," *Journal of Consumer Psychology*, Vol. 11, No. 3, 2001, pp. 169–180.

Jankowicz, Nina, "The Only Way to Defend Against Russia's Information War," *New York Times*, September 25, 2017. As of January 23, 2019:
https://www.nytimes.com/2017/09/25/opinion/the-only-way-to-defend-against-russias-information-war.html

Jarvis, Brooke, "Me Living Was How I Was Going to Beat Him," *Wired*, December 2017.

Joseph, Regina, "A Peek into the Future: A Stealth Revolution by Influence's New Masters," in Weston Aviles and Sarah Canna, eds., *White Paper on Influence in an Age of Rising Connectedness*, Washington, D.C.: U.S. Department of Defense, August 2017.

Jowett, Garth S., and Victoria O'Donnell, *Propaganda and Persuasion*, 3rd ed., Thousand Oaks, Calif.: SAGE Publications, 1999.

Judis, John B., *The Populist Explosion*, New York: Columbia Global Reports, 2016.

Kaplan, Jonas T., Sarah I. Gimbel, and Sam Harris, "Neural Correlates of Maintaining One's Political Beliefs in the Face of Counterevidence," *Scientific Reports*, Vol. 6, Article 39589, 2016.

Karras, Tero, Timo Aila, Samuli Laine, and Jaakko Lehtinen, "Progressive Growing of GANs for Improved Quality, Stability, and Variation," *Sixth International Conference on Learning Representations, Conference Proceedings*, Vancouver, Canada, 2018.

Kavanagh, Jennifer, and Michael D. Rich, *Truth Decay: An Initial Exploration of the Diminishing Role of Facts and Analysis in American Public Life*, Santa Monica, Calif.: RAND Corporation, RR-2314-RC, 2018. As of March 4, 2019: https://www.rand.org/pubs/research_reports/RR2314.html

Kelman, Herbert C., "Attitudes Are Alive and Well and Gainfully Employed in the Sphere of Action," *American Psychologist*, Vol. 29, No. 5, 1974, pp. 310–324.

Kilovaty, Ido, "Doxfare: Politically Motivated Leaks and the Future of the Norm on Non-Intervention in the Era of Weaponized Information," *Harvard National Security Journal*, Vol. 9, No. 1, 2018, pp. 146–179.

Knack, Stephen, and Philip Keefer, "Does Social Capital Have an Economic Payoff? A Cross-Country Investigation," *Quarterly Journal of Economics*, Vol. 112, No. 4, 1997, pp. 1251–1288.

Knight, Will, "The Dark Secret at the Heart of AI," *MIT Technology Review*, April 11, 2017. As of January 22, 2019: https://www.technologyreview.com/s/604087/the-dark-secret-at-the-heart-of-ai/

———, "The US Military Is Funding an Effort to Catch Deepfakes and Other AI Trickery," *MIT Technology Review*, May 23, 2018a.

———, "This AI Program Could Beat You in an Argument—But It Doesn't Know What It's Saying," *MIT Technology Review*, June 19, 2018b. As of January 22, 2019: https://www.technologyreview.com/s/611487/this-ai-program-could-beat-you-in-an-argumentbut-it-doesnt-know-what-its-saying/

———, "Hordes of Research Robots Could Be Hijacked for Fun and Sabotage," *MIT Technology Review*, July 24, 2018c.

———, "The Defense Department Has Produced the First Tools for Catching Deep Fakes," *MIT Technology Review*, August 7, 2018d.

———, "These Incredibly Realistic Fake Faces Show How Algorithms Can Now Mess with Us," *MIT Technology Review*, December 14, 2018e.

Kolbert, Elizabeth, "Why Facts Don't Change Our Minds," *New Yorker*, February 27, 2017. As of January 20, 2019: https://www.newyorker.com/magazine/2017/02/27/why-facts-dont-change-our-minds

Kozinets, Robert, "How Social Media Fires People's Passions—and Builds Extremist Divisions," *The Conversation,* November 13, 2017. As of January 20, 2019:
http://theconversation.com/
how-social-media-fires-peoples-passions-and-builds-extremist-divisions-86909

Kravetz, Lee Daniel, *Strange Contagion*, New York: HarperCollins, 2017.

Kunda, Ziva, "The Case for Motivated Reasoning," *Psychological Bulletin*, Vol. 108, No. 3, November 1990, pp. 480–498.

Lakoff, George, "Mapping the Brain's Metaphor Circuitry: Metaphorical Thought in Everyday Reason," *Frontiers in Human Neuroscience*, Vol. 8, Article 958, 2014.

Langston, Jennifer, "Lip-Syncing Obama: New Tools Turn Audio Clips into Realistic Video," *UW News*, July 11, 2017. As of January 23, 2019:
http://www.washington.edu/news/2017/07/11/
lip-syncing-obama-new-tools-turn-audio-clips-into-realistic-video/

Lau, Richard R., David J. Andersen, Tessa M. Ditonto, Mona S. Kleinberg, and David P. Redlawsk, "Effect of Media Environment Diversity and Advertising Tone on Information Search, Selective Exposure, and Affective Polarization," *Political Behavior*, Vol. 39, No. 1, 2017, pp. 231–255.

Lazarsfeld, Paul, Bernard Berelson, and Hazel Gaudet, *The People's Choice: How the Voter Makes Up His Mind in a Presidential Campaign*, New York: Duell, Sloan, and Pearce, 1948.

Lelkes, Yphtach, Guarav Sood, and Shanto Iyengar, "The Hostile Audience: The Effect of Access to Broadband Internet on Partisan Affect," *American Journal of Political Science*, Vol. 61, No. 1, 2017, pp. 5–20.

Letki, Natalia, "Investigating the Roots of Civic Morality: Trust, Social Capital, and Institutional Performance," *Political Behavior*, Vol. 28, No. 4, 2006, pp. 305–325.

"Let's Get Experimental: Behind the Adobe MAX Sneaks," *Adobe Blog*, November 4, 2016. As of January 22, 2019:
https://theblog.adobe.com/lets-get-experimental-behind-the-adobe-max-sneaks/

Leviathan, Yaniv, "Google Duplex: An AI System for Accomplishing Real-World Tasks Over the Phone," *Google AI Blog*, May 8, 2018. As of January 22, 2019:
https://ai.googleblog.com/2018/05/duplex-ai-system-for-natural-conversation.html

Lewandowsky, Stephan, Ullrich K. H. Ecker, and John Cook, "Beyond Misinformation: Understanding and Coping with the 'Post-Truth' Era," *Journal of Applied Research in Memory and Cognition*, Vol. 6, No. 4, December 2017, pp. 353–369.

Lewandowsky, Stephan, Ullrich K. H. Ecker, Colleen M. Seifert, Norbert Schwarz, and John Cook, "Misinformation and Its Correction: Continued Influence and Successful Debiasing," *Psychological Science in the Public Interest,* Vol. 13, No. 3, 2012, pp. 106–131.

Li, Yitong, Martin Renqiang Min, Dinghan Shen, David Carlson, and Lawrence Carin, "Video Generation from Text," *Thirty-Second AAAI Conference on Artificial Intelligence, Conference Proceedings,* New Orleans, La.: Association for the Advancement of Artificial Intelligence, February 2018.

Lin, Herbert, and Jackie Kerr, *On Cyber-Enabled Information/Influence Warfare and Manipulation,* working paper, Stanford, Calif.: Stanford Center for International Security and Cooperation, August 13, 2017. As of April 19, 2019: https://cisac.fsi.stanford.edu/publication/ cyber-enabled-informationinfluence-warfare-and-manipulation

Lord, Charles G., Lee D. Ross, and Mark R. Lepper, "Biased Assimilation and Attitude Polarization: The Effects of Prior Theories on Subsequently Considered Evidence," *Journal of Personality and Social Psychology,* Vol. 37, No. 11, 1979, pp. 2098–2109.

Lyrebird, "With Great Innovation Comes Great Responsibility," undated. As of December 12, 2017: https://lyrebird.ai/ethics

Magids, Scott, Alan Zorfas, and Daniel Leemon, "The New Science of Customer Emotions," *Harvard Business Review,* November 2015. As of January 23, 2019: https://hbr.org/2015/11/the-new-science-of-customer-emotions

Maio, Gregory R., and Geoffrey Haddock, *The Psychology of Attitudes and Attitude Change,* Thousand Oaks, Calif.: SAGE Publications, 2009.

Manjoo, Farhad, "Tech's 'Frightful 5' Will Dominate Digital Life for Foreseeable Future," *New York Times,* January 20, 2016. As of January 20, 2019: https://www.nytimes.com/2016/01/21/technology/techs-frightful-5-will-dominate-digital-life-for-foreseeable-future.html

Martin, Gregory J., and Ali Yurukoglu, "Bias in Cable News: Persuasion and Polarization," *American Economic Review,* Vol. 107, No. 9, 2017, pp. 2565–2599.

Matsa, Katarina Eva, and Elisa Shearer, "News Use Across Social Media Platforms 2018," *Pew Research Center,* September 10, 2018. As of January 20, 2019: http://www.journalism.org/2018/09/10/ news-use-across-social-media-platforms-2018/

Mazarr, Michael J., "The Pessimism Syndrome," *Washington Quarterly,* Vol. 21, No. 3, 1998, pp. 93–108.

Mercier, Hugo, and Dan Sperber, *The Enigma of Reason,* Cambridge, Mass.: Harvard University Press, 2017.

Metz, Cade, "Finally, Neural Networks That Actually Work," *Wired*, April 21, 2015.

Metz, Cade, and Keith Collins, "How an A.I. 'Cat-and-Mouse Game' Generates Believable Fake Photos," *New York Times*, January 2, 2018. As of January 23, 2019:
https://www.nytimes.com/interactive/2018/01/02/technology/
ai-generated-photos.html

Meyer, Jared, "The Ignorant Voter," *Forbes*, June 27, 2016. As of January 24, 2019:
https://www.forbes.com/sites/jaredmeyer/2016/06/27/
american-voters-are-ignorant-but-not-stupid/#3d425e67ff17

Mitzen, Jennifer, "Ontological Security in World Politics: State Identity and the Security Dilemma," *European Journal of International Relations*, Vol. 12, No. 3, 2006, pp. 341–370.

Moore, James W., "What Is the Sense of Agency and Why Does It Matter?" *Frontiers in Psychology*, Vol. 7, Article 1272, August 2016.

Müller, Jan-Werner, *What Is Populism?* Philadelphia, Pa.: University of Pennsylvania Press, 2016.

Munro, Geoffrey D., and Peter H. Ditto, "Biased Assimilation, Attitude Polarization, and Affect in Reactions to Stereotype-Relevant Scientific Information," *Personality and Social Psychology Bulletin*, Vol. 23, No. 6, 1997, pp. 636–653.

Mutz, Diana C., and Paul S. Martin, "Facilitating Communication Across Lines of Political Difference: The Role of Mass Media," *American Political Science Review*, Vol. 95, No. 1, 2001, pp. 97–114.

Nagle, Angela, *Kill All Normies: Online Culture Wars from 4chan and Tumblr to Trump and the Alt-Right*, Winchester, United Kingdom: Zero Books, 2017.

National Public Radio, "Trust and Consequences," *TED Radio Hour*, May 15, 2015. As of January 23, 2019:
https://www.npr.org/programs/ted-radio-hour/406238794/trust-and-consequences

———, "Big Data Revolution," *TED Radio Hour*, September 9, 2016. As of January 23, 2019:
https://www.npr.org/programs/ted-radio-hour/492296605/big-data-revolution

———, "How 5 Tech Giants Have Become More Like Governments Than Companies," *Fresh Air*, October 26, 2017. As of January 20, 2019:
https://www.npr.org/2017/10/26/560136311/
how-5-tech-giants-have-become-more-like-governments-than-companies

Neef, Dale, *Digital Exhaust*, Upper Saddle River, N.J.: Pearson FT Press, 2014.

Newman, Eryn J., Mevagh Sanson, Emily K. Miller, Adele Quigley-McBride, Jeffrey L. Foster, Daniel M. Bernstein, and Maryanne Garry, "People with Easier to Pronounce Names Promote Truthiness of Claims," *PLOS One*, Vol. 9, No. 2, 2014.

Ng, Alfred, "VR Systems Oculus Rift, HTC Vive May Be Vulnerable to Hacks," *CNET*, April 17, 2018.

Nicas, Jack, "How YouTube Drives People to the Internet's Darkest Corners," *Wall Street Journal*, February 7, 2018. As of January 24, 2019:
https://www.wsj.com/articles/
how-youtube-drives-viewers-to-the-internets-darkest-corners-1518020478

Nichols, Tom, "Our Graduates Are Rubes," *Chronicle of Higher Education*, January 15, 2017a.

———, "How America Lost Faith in Expertise," *Foreign Affairs*, March–April 2017b. As of January 23, 2019:
https://www.foreignaffairs.com/articles/united-states/2017-02-13/
how-america-lost-faith-expertise

Nie, Norman H., Darwin W. Miller III, Saar Golde, Daniel M. Butler, and Kenneth Winneg, "The World Wide Web and the U.S. Political News Market," *American Journal of Political Science*, Vol. 54, No. 2, 2010, pp. 428–439.

Nietzsche, Friedrich, *On Truth and Untruth: Selected Writings*, trans. and ed. Taylor Carman, New York: Harper Perennial, 2010.

Norwegian Consumer Council, *#Toyfail: An Analysis of Consumer and Privacy Issues in Three Internet-Connected Toys*, Oslo, December 2016. As of March 1, 2019:
https://www.forbrukerradet.no/siste-nytt/connected-toys-violate-consumer-laws/

Nyhan, Brendan, and Jason Reifler, "When Corrections Fail: The Persistence of Political Misperceptions," *Political Behavior*, Vol. 32, No. 2, 2010, pp. 303–330.

———, *Misinformation and Fact-Checking: Research Findings from Social Science*, Washington, D.C.: New America, February 2012.

———, "Displacing Misinformation About Events: An Experimental Test of Causal Corrections," *Journal of Experimental Political Science*, Vol. 2, No. 1, 2015a, pp. 81–93.

———, "Does Correcting Myths About the Flu Vaccine Work? An Experimental Evaluation of the Effects of Corrective Information," *Vaccine*, Vol. 33, No. 3, 2015b, pp. 459–464.

———, "The Effect of Fact-Checking on Elites: A Field Experiment on U.S. State Legislators," *American Journal of Political Science*, Vol. 59, No. 3, 2015c, pp. 628–640.

————, "The Roles of Information Deficits and Identity Threat in the Prevalence of Misperceptions," *Journal of Elections, Public Opinion and Parties*, 2018, pp. 1–23.

O'Neil, Cathy, *Weapons of Math Destruction: How Big Data Increases Inequality and Threatens Democracy*, New York: Broadway Books, 2016.

Osnos, Evan, "Making China Great Again," *New Yorker*, January 8, 2018.

Pardes, Arielle, "What My Personal Chat Bot Is Teaching Me About AI's Future," *Wired*, November 12, 2017. As of January 22, 2019:
https://www.wired.com/story/
what-my-personal-chat-bot-replika-is-teaching-me-about-artificial-intelligence/

Pariser, Eli, *The Filter Bubble: What the Internet Is Hiding from You*, New York: Penguin Press, 2011.

Pasquale, Frank, *The Black Box Society: The Secret Algorithms That Control Money and Information*, Cambridge, Mass.: Harvard University Press, 2015.

Paul, Christopher, and Miriam Matthews, "The Russian 'Firehose of Falsehood' Propaganda Model: Why It Might Work and Options to Counter It," Santa Monica, Calif.: RAND Corporation, PE-198-OSD, 2016. As of March 4, 2019:
https://www.rand.org/pubs/perspectives/PE198.html

Pentland, Alex, *Social Physics: How Good Ideas Spread—The Lessons from a New Science*, New York: Penguin Press, 2014.

Perez, Sarah, "Voice-Enabled Smart Speakers to Reach 55% of U.S. Households by 2022, Says Report," *TechCrunch*, November 8, 2017.

Persily, Nathaniel, "Can Democracy Survive the Internet?" *Journal of Democracy*, Vol. 28, No. 2, April 2017.

Petty, Richard E., Russell H. Fazio, and Pablo Briñol, eds., *Attitudes: Insights from the New Implicit Measures*, New York: Psychology Press, 2008.

Pew Research Center, *Public Knowledge of Current Affairs Little Changed by News and Information Revolutions*, Washington, D.C., April 15, 2007.

Phillips, Whitney, *This Is Why We Can't Have Nice Things: Mapping the Relationship Between Online Trolling and Mainstream Culture*, Cambridge, Mass.: MIT Press, 2015.

Pierce, David, "Enjoy Your New Virtual Office," *Wired*, February 2018.

Pollard, Neal A., Adam Segal, and Matthew G. Devost, "Trust War: Dangerous Trends in Cyber Conflict," *War on the Rocks*, January 16, 2018. As of January 23, 2019:
https://warontherocks.com/2018/01/trust-war-dangerous-trends-cyber-conflict/

Pratkanis, Anthony R., and Elliot Aronson, *Age of Propaganda: The Everyday Use and Abuse of Persuasion*, New York: Henry Holt and Company, 2001.

Price, Rob, "AI and CGI Will Transform Information Warfare, Boost Hoaxes, and Escalate Revenge Porn," *Business Insider*, August 12, 2017. As of January 23, 2019: http://www.businessinsider.com/ cgi-ai-fake-video-audio-news-hoaxes-information-warfare-revenge-porn-2017-8

Putnam, Robert, *Bowling Alone: The Collapse and Revival of American Community*, New York: Simon and Schuster, 2001.

Rabin-Havt, Ari, *Lies, Incorporated: The World of Post-Truth Politics*, New York: Anchor Books, 2016.

Radinsky, Kira, "Your Algorithms Are Not Safe from Hackers," *Harvard Business Review*, January 5, 2016. As of January 22, 2019: https://hbr.org/2016/01/your-algorithms-are-not-safe-from-hackers

Redlawsk, David P., "Hot Cognition or Cool Consideration? Testing the Effects of Motivated Reasoning on Political Decision Making," *Journal of Politics*, Vol. 64, No. 4, 2002, pp. 1021–1044.

Redlawsk, David P., Andrew J. W. Civettini, and Karen M. Emmerson, "The Affective Tipping Point: Do Motivated Reasoners Ever 'Get It'?" *Political Psychology*, Vol. 31, No. 4, 2010, pp. 563–593.

Richardson, John H., "AI Chatbots Try to Schedule Meetings—Without Enraging Us," *Wired*, May 24, 2018. As of January 22, 2019: https://www.wired.com/story/xai-meeting-ai-chatbot/

Robbins, Blaine G., "Institutional Quality and Generalized Trust: A Nonrecursive Causal Model," *Social Indicators Research*, Vol. 107, No. 2, 2012, pp. 235–258.

Roberts, Graham, "Augmented Reality: How We'll Bring the News into Your Home," *New York Times*, February 1, 2018. As of January 24, 2019: https://www.nytimes.com/interactive/2018/02/01/sports/olympics/ nyt-ar-augmented-reality-ul.html

Rodriguez, Ashley, "In Five Years, VR Could Be as Big in the US as Netflix," *Quartz*, June 6, 2018. As of January 22, 2019: https://qz.com/1298512/ vr-could-be-as-big-in-the-us-as-netflix-in-five-years-study-shows/

Romano, Andrew, "How Ignorant Are Americans?" *Newsweek*, March 20, 2011.

Roose, Kevin, "Here Come the Fake Videos, Too," *New York Times*, March 4, 2018. As of January 23, 2019: https://www.nytimes.com/2018/03/04/technology/fake-videos-deepfakes.html

Rose, Flemming, and Jacob Mchangama, "History Proves How Dangerous It Is to Have the Government Regulate Fake News," *Washington Post*, October 3, 2017. As of January 23, 2019: https://www.washingtonpost.com/news/theworldpost/wp/2017/10/03/ history-proves-how-dangerous-it-is-to-have-the-government-regulate-fake-news/

Ross, Alec, *The Industries of the Future*, New York: Simon and Schuster, 2016.

Ross, Lee D., Mark R. Lepper, Fritz Strack, and Julia Steinmetz, "Social Explanation and Social Expectation: Effects of Real and Hypothetical Explanations on Subjective Likelihood," *Journal of Personality and Social Psychology*, Vol. 35, No. 11, 1977, pp. 817–829.

Rothman, Joshua, "Afterimage," *New Yorker*, November 12, 2018.

Rothstein, Bo, and Eric M. Uslaner, "All for All: Equality, Corruption, and Social Trust," *World Politics*, Vol. 58, No. 1, 2005, pp. 41–72.

Rubin, Peter, "You'll Go to Work in Virtual Reality," *Wired*, June 2018, p. 61.

Sabelman, Eric E., and Roger Lam, "The Real-Life Dangers of Augmented Reality," *IEEE Spectrum*, June 23, 2015. As of January 22, 2019:
https://spectrum.ieee.org/consumer-electronics/portable-devices/
the-reallife-dangers-of-augmented-reality

Sanger, David E., David D. Kirkpatrick, and Nicole Perlroth, "The World Once Laughed at North Korean Cyberpower. No More," *New York Times*, October 15, 2017. As of January 23, 2019:
https://www.nytimes.com/2017/10/15/world/asia/
north-korea-hacking-cyber-sony.html

Scharre, Paul, and Michael C. Horowitz, *Artificial Intelligence: What Every Policymaker Needs to Know*, Washington, D.C.: Center for a New American Security, June 2018.

Schiff, Stacy, "The Interactive Truth," *New York Times*, June 15, 2005. As of January 23, 2019:
https://www.nytimes.com/2005/06/15/opinion/the-interactive-truth.html

Schneier, Bruce, *Click Here to Kill Everybody: Security and Survival in a Hyper-Connected World*, New York: W. W. Norton, 2018.

Segal, Adam, *The Hacked World Order: How Nations Fight, Trade, Maneuver, and Manipulate in the Digital Age*, New York: PublicAffairs, 2016.

Selk, Avi, "This Audio Clip of a Robot as Trump May Prelude a Future of Fake Human Voices," *Washington Post*, May 3, 2017. As of January 22, 2019:
https://www.washingtonpost.com/news/innovations/wp/2017/05/03/
this-audio-clip-of-trump-as-a-robot-may-prelude-a-future-of-fake-human-voices/

Sen, Conor, "The 'Big Five' Could Destroy the Tech Ecosystem," *Bloomberg*, November 15, 2017. As of January 20, 2019:
https://www.bloomberg.com/view/articles/2017-11-15/
the-big-five-could-destroy-the-tech-ecosystem

Shaikh, Faizan, "Introductory Guide to Generative Adversarial Networks (GANs) and Their Promise!" *Analytics Vidhya*, June 15, 2017. As of January 23, 2019: https://www.analyticsvidhya.com/blog/2017/06/ introductory-generative-adversarial-networks-gans/

Shearer, Elisa, and Jeffrey Gottfried, "News Use Across Social Media Platforms 2017," *Pew Research Center*, September 7, 2017. As of January 20, 2019: http://www.journalism.org/2017/09/07/ news-use-across-social-media-platforms-2017/

Sherman, Justin, and Deb Crawford, "Securing America's Connected Infrastructure Can't Wait," *War on the Rocks*, December 4, 2018. As of January 22, 2019: https://warontherocks.com/2018/12/ securing-americas-connected-infrastructure-cant-wait/

Shields, David, *Reality Hunger: A Manifesto*, New York: Knopf, 2010.

Sides, John, and Jack Citrin, *How Large the Huddled Masses? The Causes and Consequences of Public Misperceptions About Immigrant Populations*, paper presented at the 65th Annual National Conference of the Midwest Political Science Association, Chicago, 2007.

Silfversten, Erik, "A Smart Toy Could Have Personal Details for Life, Not Just for Christmas," *RAND Blog*, December 2017. As of March 5, 2019: https://www.rand.org/blog/2017/12/a-smart-toy-could-have-personal-details-for-life-not.html

Silhavy, Radek, Roman Senkerik, Zuzana Kominkova Oplatkova, Zdenka Prokopova, and Petr Silhavy, eds., *Artificial Intelligence Trends in Intelligent Systems: Proceedings of the 6th Computer Science On-Line Conference 2017 (CSOC2017)*, Vol. I, Cham, Switzerland: Springer International Publishing, 2017.

Skurnik, Ian, Carolyn Yoon, Denise C. Park, and Norbert Schwarz, "How Warnings About False Claims Become Recommendations," *Journal of Consumer Research*, Vol. 31, No. 4, 2005, pp. 713–724.

Sloman, Steven, and Philip Fernbach, *The Knowledge Illusion*: *Why We Never Think Alone*, New York: Riverhead Books, 2017.

Smiley, Lauren, "Something to Watch Over Me," *Wired*, January 2018.

Soper, Taylor, "Why People in China Love Microsoft's Xiaoice Virtual Companion, and What It Says About Artificial Intelligence," *GeekWire*, November 25, 2015. As of January 23, 2019: https://www.geekwire.com/2015/ people-china-love-microsofts-xiaoice-virtual-companion-says-artificial-intelligence/

Specter, Michael, *Denialism: How Irrational Thinking Hinders Scientific Progress, Harms the Planet, and Threatens Our Lives*, New York: Penguin Press, 2009.

Stafford, Tom, "Psychology: Why Bad News Dominates the Headlines," *BBC*, July 29, 2014. As of January 20, 2019: http://www.bbc.com/future/story/20140728-why-is-all-the-news-bad

Stone, Peter, Rodney Brooks, Erik Brynjolfsson, Ryan Calo, Oren Etzioni, Greg Hager, Julia Hirschberg, Shivaram Kalyanakrishnan, Ece Kamar, Sarit Kraus, Kevin Leyton-Brown, David Parkes, William Press, AnnaLee Saxenian, Julie Shah, Milind Tambe, and Astro Teller, *Artificial Intelligence and Life in 2030: One Hundred Year Study on Artificial Intelligence*, Stanford, Calif.: Stanford University, September 2016.

Strange, Adario, "Face-Tracking Software Lets You Make Anyone Say Anything in Real Time," *Mashable*, March 20, 2016. As of January 23, 2019: http://mashable.com/2016/03/20/face-tracking-software/#U3o58PfqH8ql

Stubbersfield, Joseph M., Jamshid J. Tehrani, and Emma G. Flynn, "Serial Killers, Spiders and Cybersex: Social and Survival Information Bias in the Transmission of Urban Legends," *British Journal of Psychology*, Vol. 106, No. 2, 2015, pp. 288–307.

Suh, Chan S., Paul Y. Chang, and Yisook Lim, "Spill-Up and Spill-Over of Trust: An Extended Test of Cultural and Institutional Theories of Trust in South Korea," *Sociological Forum*, Vol. 27, No. 2, 2012, pp. 504–526.

Sunstein, Cass R., *#Republic: Divided Democracy in the Age of Social Media*, Princeton, N.J.: Princeton University Press, 2017.

Swift, Art, "Americans' Trust in Mass Media Sinks to New Low," *Gallup*, September 14, 2016.

Taber, Charles S., and Milton Lodge, "Motivated Skepticism in the Evaluation of Political Beliefs," *American Journal of Political Science*, Vol. 50, No. 3, 2006, pp. 755–769.

Tan, Chenhao, Vlad Niculae, Cristian Danescu-Niculescu-Mizil, and Lilian Lee, "Winning Arguments: Interaction Dynamics and Persuasion Strategies in Good-Faith Online Discussions," *25th International World Wide Web Conference, Conference Proceedings*, Montreal, Canada: International World Wide Web Conferences Steering Committee, April 2016, pp. 613–624.

Taub, Amanda, "The Real Story About Fake News Is Partisanship," *New York Times*, January 11, 2017. As of January 23, 2019: https://www.nytimes.com/2017/01/11/upshot/the-real-story-about-fake-news-is-partisanship.html

Thies, Jutus, Michael Zollhöfer, Marc Stamminger, Christian Theobalt, and Matthias Nießner, "Face2Face: Real-Time Face Capture and Reenactment of RGB Videos," *IEEE Conference on Computer Vision and Pattern Recognition, Conference Proceedings*, Las Vegas, Nev.: Institute of Electrical and Electronics Engineers, 2016.

Thompson, Nicholas, and Fred Vogelstein, "Facebook's Two Years of Hell," *Wired*, March 2018.

Thorson, Emily, "Belief Echoes: The Persistent Effects of Corrected Misinformation," *Political Communication*, Vol. 33, No. 3, 2016, pp. 460–480.

Thussu, D. K., *News as Entertainment: The Rise of Global Infotainment*, London: SAGE Publications, 2007.

Tiku, Nitasha, "We'll Share Our Emotional State as Willingly as We Share Our Photos," *Wired*, June 2018.

Tormala, Zakary L., and Richard E. Petty, "What Doesn't Kill Me Makes Me Stronger: The Effects of Resisting Persuasion on Attitude Certainty," *Journal of Personal and Social Psychology*, Vol. 83, No. 6, 2002.

———, "Source Credibility and Attitude Certainty: A Metacognitive Analysis of Resistance to Persuasion," *Journal of Consumer Psychology*, Vol. 14, No. 4, 2004, pp. 427–442.

Tracy, Liz, "In Contrast to Tay, Microsoft's Chinese Chatbot, Xiaolce, Is Actually Pleasant," *Inverse*, March 26, 2016. As of January 23, 2019: https://www.inverse.com/article/13387-microsoft-chinese-chatbot

Tucker, Patrick, "Strava's Just the Start: The US Military's Losing War Against Data Leakage," *Defense One*, January 31, 2018.

U.S. Department of Defense, *Joint Publication 1-02: Department of Defense Dictionary of Military and Associated Terms*, Washington, D.C., November 2010.

Ullah, Haroon K., *Digital World War: Islamists, Extremists, and the Fight for Cyber Supremacy*, New Haven, Conn.: Yale University Press, 2017.

United States Code, Title 47, Section 230, Protection for Private Blocking and Screening of Offensive Material, January 3, 2012.

Uslaner, Eric M., "Where You Stand Depends upon Where Your Grandparents Sat: The Inheritability of Generalized Trust," *Public Opinion Quarterly*, Vol. 72, No. 4, 2008, pp. 725–740.

van den Oord, Aäron, Tom Walters, and Trevor Strohman, "WaveNet Launches in the Google Assistant," *DeepMind Blog*, October 4, 2017. As of January 23, 2019: https://deepmind.com/blog/wavenet-launches-google-assistant/

van der Linden, Sander, Anthony Leiserowitz, Seth Rosenthal, and Edward Maibach, "Inoculating the Public Against Misinformation About Climate Change," *Global Challenges*, Vol. 1, No. 2, 2017.

Vanian, Jonathan, "Facebook, Twitter Take New Steps to Combat Fake News and Manipulation," *Fortune*, January 20, 2018. As of January 24, 2019: http://fortune.com/2018/01/19/facebook-twitter-news-feed-russia-ads/

Verghese, Abraham, "How Tech Can Turn Doctors into Clerical Workers," *New York Times Magazine*, May 16, 2018.

Vettehen, P. H., and M. Kleemans, "Proving the Obvious? What Sensationalism Contributes to the Time Spent on News Video," *Electronic News*, Vol. 12, No. 2, 2018, pp. 113–127.

Vincent, James, "Artificial Intelligence Is Going to Make It Easier Than Ever to Fake Images and Video," *The Verge*, December 20, 2016. As of January 23, 2019: https://www.theverge.com/2016/12/20/14022958/ ai-image-manipulation-creation-fakes-audio-video

VivoText, homepage, undated. As of March 6, 2019: https://www.vivotext.com/

Vlahos, James, "Fighting Words," *Wired*, March 2018.

Vosoughi, Soroush, Deb Roy, and Sinan Aral, "The Spread of True and False News Online," *Science*, Vol. 359, No. 6380, 2018, pp. 1146–1151.

Waltzman, Rand, "The Weaponization of Information: The Need for Cognitive Security," testimony presented before the Senate Armed Services Committee, Subcommittee on Cybersecurity, Santa Monica, Calif.: RAND Corporation, CT-473, April 27, 2017. As of March 5, 2019: https://www.rand.org/pubs/testimonies/CT473.html

Weaver, Kimberlee, Stephen M. Garcia, Norbert Schwarz, and Dale T. Miller, "Inferring the Popularity of an Opinion from Its Familiarity: A Repetitive Voice Can Sound Like a Chorus," *Journal of Personality and Social Psychology*, Vol. 92, No. 5, 2007, pp. 821–833.

West, Darrell M., "Will Robots and AI Take Your Job? The Economic and Political Consequences of Automation," *Brookings Institution*, April 18, 2018. As of January 22, 2019: https://www.brookings.edu/blog/techtank/2018/04/18/will-robots-and-ai-take-your-job-the-economic-and-political-consequences-of-automation/

Wharton, Bruce, "Remarks on 'Public Diplomacy in a Post-Truth Society,'" in Shawn Powers and Markos Kounalakis, eds., *Can Public Diplomacy Survive the Internet?* Washington, D.C.: U.S. Advisory Commission on Public Diplomacy, 2017, pp. 7–11.

Whitson, Jennifer, and Adam Galinsky, "Lacking Control Increases Illusory Pattern Perception," *Science*, Vol. 322, No. 5898, 2008, pp. 115–117.

Witte, Kim, "Putting the Fear Back into Fear Appeals: The Extended Parallel Process Model," *Communication Monographs*, Vol. 59, No. 4, 1992, pp. 329–349.

Witte, Kim, and Mike Allen, "A Meta-Analysis of Fear Appeals: Implications for Effective Public Health Campaigns," *Health Education and Behavior*, Vol. 27, No. 5, 2000, pp. 591–615.

Wittes, Benjamin, and Gabriella Blum, *The Future of Violence: Robots and Germs, Hackers and Drones*, New York: Basic Books, 2015.

Wu, Hao-Yu, Michael Rubinstein, Eugene Shih, John Guttag, Frédo Durand, and William Freeman, "Eulerian Video Magnification for Revealing Subtle Changes in the World," *ACM Transactions on Graphics*, Vol. 31, No. 4, 2012, pp. 1–8.

Wu, Tim, *The Attention Merchants: The Epic Scramble to Get Inside Our Heads*, New York: Vintage Books, 2016.

Yam, CY, "Emotion Detection and Recognition from Text Using Deep Learning," *Microsoft Developer Blog*, November 29, 2015. As of January 22, 2019:
https://www.microsoft.com/developerblog/2015/11/29/
emotion-detection-and-recognition-from-text-using-deep-learning/

Yearsley, Liesl, "We Need to Talk About the Power of AI to Manipulate Humans," *MIT Technology Review*, June 5, 2017. As of January 22, 2019:
https://www.technologyreview.com/s/608036/
we-need-to-talk-about-the-power-of-ai-to-manipulate-humans/

You, Jong-sung, "Social Trust: Fairness Matters More Than Homogeneity," *Political Psychology*, Vol. 33, No. 5, 2012, pp. 701–721.

Youyou, Wu, Michael Kosinski, and David Stilwell, "Computer-Based Personality Judgments Are More Accurate Than Those Made by Humans," *Proceedings of the National Academy of Sciences*, Vol. 112, No. 4, 2015, pp. 1036–1040.

Zhang, Han, Tao Xu, Hongsheng Li, Shaoting Zhang, Xiaogang Wang, Xiaolei Huang, and Dimitris Metaxas, "StackGAN: Text to Photo-Realistic Image Synthesis with Stacked Generative Adversarial Networks," *IEEE International Conference on Computer Vision, Conference Proceedings*, Venice, Italy: Institute of Electrical and Electronics Engineers, October 2017.

Zmerli, Sonja, and Ken Newton, "Social Trust and Attitudes Toward Democracy," *Public Opinion Quarterly*, Vol. 72, No. 4, 2008, pp. 706–724.